Marketing
Financial Services

The Institutional Investor Series in Finance

Marketing Financial Services

EDITED BY

David B. Zenoff

Ballinger Publishing Company

Cambridge, Massachusetts
A Subsidiary of Harper & Row, Publishers, Inc.

Copyright © 1989 by David B. Zenoff. All rights reserved.
No part of this publication may be reproduced, stored in a retrieval system, or transmitted in any form or by any means, electronic, mechanical, photocopy, recording, or otherwise, without the prior written consent of the publisher.

International Standard Book Number: 0-88730-298-X

Library of Congress Catalog Card Number: 8834948

Printed in the United States of America

Library of Congress Cataloging-in-Publication Data

Marketing financial services.
  (The Institutional investor series in finance)
  Includes index.
  Bibliography: p.
  1. Financial services industry. I. Zenoff, David B. II. Series.
HG173.M3525   1989   332.1′068′8   88-34948
ISBN 0-88730-298-X

To Patricia A. Dougherty, whose sensitivity, diligence, initiative, integrity, energy, and friendship stabilize a frenetic executive lifestyle; create bonds across the miles; get the job done with perfection; and add a touch of color and comfort to otherwise routine communiques. In a world that relies increasingly on impersonal information technology to bring together remote participants, Pat is a reminder of the positive power and potential of a very human executive secretary.

Contents

Contributing Authors

Richard J. Borda, Vice Chairman, National Life Insurance Company

Kathryn Britney, Vice President, Chase Manhattan Bank

Charlotte A. Chamberlain, Executive Vice President and Director of Strategic Planning, Glendale Federal S&L Association

Michael Coles, Former Chairman, Goldman Sachs & Co.

J. Hallam Dawson, Chairman, IDI Associates

Philip A. Dover, Associate Professor of Business Administration and Director of the International M.B.A. Program, Babson College

Bradford K. Gallagher, President, Fidelity Investments Institutional Services Company

John W. Heilshorn, Principal, Avenir Group Inc.

Richard P. Kotz, Executive Vice President, Bond Investors Guaranty

James C. Lam, Vice President and Manager of the Strategic Risk Management Group, Glendale Federal S&L Association

Bruce M. Lloyd, Senior Vice President, Far West Savings & Loan

Richard W. Nelson, Vice President and Chief Economist, Federal Home Loan Bank of San Francisco

Andreas R. Prindl, Managing Director, Nomura Bank International plc

James S. Riepe, President, T. Rowe Price

Roger V. Smith, President and CEO, Silicon Valley Bank

Marshall C. Tyndall, Executive Vice President, Texas Commerce Bancshares, Inc.

Thomas J. Wacker, President, Royal Trust International Limited

Anthony J. Walton, Executive Vice President and General Manager, Westpac Banking Corporation

David B. Zenoff, President, David B. Zenoff & Associates, Inc.

List of Figures

Chapter 12

Chapter 13

Chapter 14

Chapter 17

List of Tables

Chapter 4

Chapter 6

Chapter 12

Chapter 13

Chapter 14

Chapter 17

Introduction:
Perspectives on Financial Services Marketing

David B. Zenoff

This book is a collection of original contributions by practitioners and others close to the financial services industry. It provides a managerial perspective on the ways in which a cross section of competitors in the industry view their marketplace and meet its marketing challenges. All of the contributors are successful senior officers of financial services firms or consultants to the industry. They represent commercial banks, investment banks, savings and loans, mutual funds, insurance companies, trust companies, fund management companies, consulting firms, and academia. Some of the firms represented are huge, well-established international competitors, others are principally regional in scope, and still others are start-ups. These firms are located throughout the United States and in London, Toronto, and Sydney. In some instances, the marketing challenges and the firms' responses took place a few years ago; these chapters therefore present the outcomes and the lessons learned. Other chapters describe contemporary situations, managerial thinking, and approaches, the results of which have yet to be seen.

Throughout the book, the contributors discuss how today's financial services marketplace is viewed, how firms are struggling to define opportunities while minimizing their risks, how marketing strategies and tactics are developed and which approaches are the most competitive in this dynamic marketplace.

The book has been developed to serve the needs of a broad range of professional readers who share an interest in the marketing of financial services. General managers and functional managers of financial services firms will find insights into how an array of key marketing decisions and programs as well as market assessments are made, and how the marketing function and a marketing "philosophy" operate. Strategies of firms in the industry and consultants serving the industry will discover many ways of viewing the marketplace, determining what constitutes an opportunity, and what is required to implement marketing strategy. Industry outsiders such as consultants, academia, and regulators will read the book for its comprehensive overview of the evolving financial services industry. These readers will learn how it is managed and what are likely to be the relevant strengths and weaknesses of various types of activities within the industry.

To put in perspective the marketing issues faced by the contributors, the reader will need an understanding of the recent charges that have rocked financial services. What new marketing challenges have been brought about by these changes? What are the special requirements of marketing services? And what are the key issues faced by those who attempt to promote financial services in today's competitive marketplace?

The Financial Service Industry: An Overview

Basically, all aspects of the worldwide financial services industry are undergoing extraordinary change. These dramatic changes intensify and blur the lines of competition, change the nature and scope of opportunities and threats, and warrant new patterns of management thinking and response. The principal forces of change are: (1) deregulation, (2) information technology, (3) globalization of markets, (4) huge and rapidly growing financial transactions and volumes, (5) environmental volatility and risk, and (6) increased customer sophistication.

Deregulation   The deregulation of financial markets has proceeded at a quickening, significant, and uneven pace across the industry and geography. At the national level, deregulation has had a variety of effects. It has tended to reduce structural barriers to competition in domestic financial markets by abolishing interest rate ceilings on deposits and lending by financial intermediaries. One related result has been that U.S. banks currently operate with a significantly lower level of demand deposits as a percentage of total liabilities. In 1950, demand deposits were 70 percent of the total, compared with only 25 percent in 1984.

Deregulation has opened markets to foreign competitors. For example, in 1984 Australia deregulated its financial markets and invited applications for wholly owned foreign merchant banks. In the following three years, the number of merchant banks increased from 87 to 160.

Closer to home, some U.S. banks were permitted to conduct business across state lines in the early 1980s. By 1983 there were fully 7,000 bank holding company offices outside their home states, 1,500 of them conducting full-service banking.

Deregulation has liberalized the franchises within which certain types of institutions can compete. In 1981, when U.S. banks were allowed to act as discount brokers, approximately 2,000 to 3,000 banks purchased or allied themselves with stockbrokers. In 1987, the Federal Reserve decided to permit three major New York money center banks to underwrite and deal in commercial paper, mortgage-backed securities, and municipal revenue bonds—three profitable securities markets that heretofore had been dominated by the big U.S. investment banks.

Deregulation has also abolished exchange controls and changed the bases for the fees that institutions charge. Several of these types of deregulation have affected Japanese banks that for years had enjoyed limited competition with each other and virtually none from foreign institutions, along with controlled interest rates that guaranteed profitable lending. Gradual deregulation in recent years has diluted profit margins. The return on assets of all Japanese banks fell from 0.75 percent in 1970 to only 0.25 percent in 1987. During the same period, Japanese banks' return on equity slid from 20 percent to about 10 percent.

Within markets and between them, the uneven spread of deregulation has conferred temporary competitive advantages on some fortunate financial institutions by enhancing their abilities to compete on more favorable terms and in broader markets. Less fortunate institutions have faced new, sometimes nontraditional, competitors without the freedom to compete at maximum strength.

Reflecting the uneven spread of deregulation among various nations is the increasing importance of foreign banks in various national markets. As shown in Table 1, some nations (notably Belgium and the United Kingdom[1]), have been open to foreign banks, while others (for example, Japan and Canada) have been considerably more protectionist.

Table 1. Foreign Banks' Assets in Selected Countries as a Percentage of Total Assets of All Banks Operating in Those Countries Selected Years 1960–1985.

Host Country	Years			
	1960	1970	1980	1985
Belgium	8.2	22.5	41.5	51.0
Canada	0	0	0	6.3
Japan	0	1.3	3.4	3.6
U.K.	6.7	37.5	55.6	62.6
U.S.	—	5.8	8.7	12.0

Information Technology More than ever before, financial services firms are relying on sophisticated and powerful information technology to communicate with customers and competitors, deliver financial services, simplify record keeping, process payments, design and deliver new products, and manage their businesses.

In the past quarter century, data processing has greatly enhanced financial institutions' penetration of new markets. These institutions have dramatically increased their new-product development and delivery and their administrative capacity to grow.

Data processing and communications costs have declined approximately 25 percent and 15 percent, respectively, per annum, diminishing institutions' transaction costs and stimulating trading activity. One important example is the dramatic reduction of transaction costs in the payment system—down approximately 90 percent in the past 20 years. By now, major financial institutions have computerized their accounting and transaction-processing functions. In a recent year, the U.S. commercial banking industry as a whole spent between $8 billion and $10 billion for computer processing, including hardware and software.

Institutions have also pared employment costs along the way. Automation-related expenses currently account for 11 to 15 percent of large banks' total non-interest expense.[2]

Low-cost, instantaneous communications and electronic funds transfer are a requisite for integrating international financial markets and 24-hour trading. Technology also permits monitoring of complex exposures, such as financial futures and options contracts used for low-cost hedging of various exposures. Optimal hedging strategies require complex processing of data from various markets around the globe. Speed is mandatory since trading opportunities can be short-lived.[3]

Processing speed facilitated by instantaneous telecommunications is also key in arranging syndicated and similar financings. For example, in just five business days in 1987, the market provided the money to finance a $7.4 billion, 45 percent Standard Oil tender offer; 64 banks committed $15 billion to the financing.

In the retail financial services market, where electronic banking is now possible through the "bank-through-the-wall" (automatic teller machine), the "bank-in-the-store" (electronic funds transfer at point of sale), and home banking, the banks have had to rethink their marketing and distribution. They have relied heavily on the application of electronic technology. Credit card companies now offer rival payments systems, customers are willing to shop for the service that best meets their needs, and retailers themselves are offering more financial services.

Information technology is currently focused on building and protecting market position. The challenge is to integrate customer files so that a financial services firm can obtain a customer business profile for marketing purposes. With customer data presently stored in separate files, integration will be a major 1990s project for most institutions.

Globalization of Markets   The globalization of markets and the international involvement of firms and their customers have been influenced by the following factors: deregulation that opens doors to foreign competitors; information technology that permits instantaneous linkage of foreign markets and 24-hour trading; the growth of international business with accompanying needs for financial services around the world; and the appetites for expansion that has caused firms to look abroad.

There are numerous examples of the globalization of financial markets and the influence it exercises:

- *Eurobonds*. For example, in London's international capital markets, Eurobond market issues outstanding rose to $560 billion in 1986 from $225 billion in 1983.
- *Global equities*. New international equity issues and equity-linked debt totaled $36 billion in the first nine months of 1987, more than three times the total for 1985. Several investment banks have expanded their international equity capabilities enormously, notably Swiss Bank Corporation International, Baring Securities, Crédit Suisse First Boston, Morgan Stanley, Deutsche Bank, Merrill Lynch, and Goldman Sachs.[4]

- *Japanese foreign purchases.* In 1987, Japan, the world's largest creditor nation, had total net purchases of $10 billion in foreign stocks and $49 billion in foreign bonds.
- *International mutual funds.* The large and growing number of such funds enables investors to select among foreign stock and international bond portfolios. Through late 1987, approximately 70 such U.S.-registered funds existed, twice the number operating in 1984. Assets in these funds totaled $22 billion, four times greater than in 1984. Most prominent among them are Fidelity Overseas, T. Rowe Price International, Trustees Commingled International, Templeton World, Templeton Growth, New Perspective, and Pru-Bache Global.
- *Foreign exchange trading.* With daily trading volume of $50 billion in the United States, $90 billion in London, and $50 billion in Japan, many large banks prefer 24-hour trading by "passing the book" to branch offices as the sun moves west around the globe. Some banks, including Citibank, Chase Manhattan, and Harris Trust, maintain all-night staffs in their U.S. headquarters cities to monitor developments and execute trades for corporate clients. During the fourth quarter of 1987, the foreign exchange profits for the nine U.S. money center banks totaled $818.6 million, approximately one-third of the banks' after-tax income for the period.
- *Stock trading on the London market.* As a result of "Big Bang" in May 1986, there was a sizable increase in London stock trading business from other countries, as shown in Table 2.
- *International investors.* To service this growing and powerful group of investors, Morgan Stanley provides a World Index that tracks 2,000 stocks in the Far East, Europe, and Australia. To provide suitable bases for portfolio measurement, the Financial Times and others launched in 1987 the Financial Times-Actuaries World Indices, an index matrix that covers 23 countries. A notable example of an investor with global horizons is the British institution Scottish Amicable, a Glasgow-based life assurance company that has 1,000 securities from around the world in its 40 separate portfolios.

Table 2. Percentage of Stock Trading Done in London.

Country	October 1986	October 1987
Sweden	25	65
Netherlands	10	25
West Germany	7	25
France	8	20
Australia	10	17

Huge and rapidly growing financial transactions and volumes   In the 1980s there have been rapidly growing, extraordinarily large financial transactions, accelerated financial activity and funds movements, and sudden changes in financial market relationships. These changes stem from the normal growth in world commerce; the rapid globablization of financial markets; the extraordinary growth in sovereign indebtedness (principally the United States and developing countries such as Brazil, Mexico, and Argentina); the power of global information transfer; and innovation in financial instruments and financially oriented transactions.

The rapid growth and huge size of the financial transactions present unprecedented risks as well as new business opportunities for (1) national and international financial markets; (2) firms that provide financial services; (3) customers involved in these markets; (4) market regulators; and (5) suppliers of goods and services to all of the foregoing participants.

For example, Merrill Lynch, which is prepared to bet nearly $1 billion of its own money to make bridge loans to get deals going, earned more than $70 million in fees in 1987 when it led an investment group that acquired Borg-Warner Corporation.

Thus, far, the most conspicuous results of the rapid growth and magnitude of financial transactions and volumes have been: (1) the emergence of "superpowerful" and "supersuccessful" participants (for example, in 1961, Morgan Stanley had approximately 150 total staff; in 1987, it hired 1,400 persons and employed about 6,000); (2) dramatic shifts in competitors' strength and market share, (3) scaled-up norms and expectations for "how big is big" in designing deals and making plans, (4) almost daily headlines about stock and commodity market volatility, (5) renewed attempts by regulators to understand and ultimately influence financial market stability, (6) dilution and reappraisal of relevant business ethics, and (7) selective failures and large losses among financial market participants.

For example, during October 1987, total assets of U.S. stock mutual funds fell by $54.3 billion to $179.1 billion. In spring 1987, municipal bond investors had received severe jolts. In a market that regarded price moves of one-half point a day as big, bond prices went into a free fall of nearly 13 points (a decline in value of almost $130 on each $1,000 bond).

The rapid buildup to these magnitudes and the absolutely large scale mean that financial service institutions have had to struggle to develop management practices and systems to accommodate the funds flows, services all parties to the transactions, and contain the risk to themselves and to their customers.

A dramatic presentation of the broad scope and large scale of the financial services business was provided by Richard Braddock, a Citibank executive, in a 1985 speech, cited by *The Economist* (March 22, 1986). Referring to the United States, Mr. Braddock said:

> During the next *hour*, 14 million personal checks will be written by American consumers; 7,000 new bank accounts will be opened; nearly 6,000 consumer CDs (certificates of deposit) will be negotiated; 22,000 airline tickets will be purchases by bank, travel and entertainment cards; 45,000 insurance policies will be written; over 1,000 money-market fund and money-market deposit accounts will be opened; 12,000 securities transactions will occur in the United States; 260,000 ATM transactions will be completed; and two new ATMs will be added to the nearly 60,000 now in operation around the country.

An example of service institution risk is Goldman Sachs's loss of about $80 million as an underwriter of the British Government's 1987 sales of shares in British Petroleum. In February 1988, First Boston announced that it faced possible pretax losses of $10 million to $50 million because its former head mortgage trader had purchased a number of mortgage-backed securities that turned out to be less valuable than those the firm thought he had purchased. The incident marked the second time in two years First Boston faced a large loss on mortgage-related securities.

To a notable degree, many firms expanded rapidly without ensuring that they were adequately managed, producing a variety of unfavorable effects: new products behaved unpredictably in unusual market conditions; seasoned traders moved into managerial roles (which were new to them) and left trading to less experienced staff; new recruits could not be taught wisdom in a short time period; dramatic shifts in the market undermined hedges; and management information systems could not be developed as quickly as ambitious firms expanded.

An important example relates to back-office operations and settlement systems. From the mid-1950s until the early 1980s, there was growth in trading volumes but very little change in products. Recently, volumes have grown dramatically and the products and businesses of financial services firms have expanded. Back offices are scrambling to catch up; few have practical solutions and there are virtually no working models to copy. Hence, managements are forced to make systems upgrading and restructuring decisions without certainty about the steps and risks to take and the amount of money to spend.

Risk containment processes broke down or were inadequately designed under duress and conditions of rapid change. During the October 1987 crash, First Boston lost approximately $60 million and L.F. Rothschild, $44 million in risk arbitrage. Bear Stearns lost $96 million on arbitrage and options business. County NatWest lost $1.76 million when a low-paid trainee accountant was found to have engaged in trading options. In all, County NatWest's parent had to inject £80 million of new capital to cover losses and provisions incurred after the October 1987 crash.

Overhead expenses built up to unrecognized and sometimes uncontrolled rates when a firm's focus was on marketplace growth. One 1987 report assessed how financial service companies coped with the rapid increase in volumes and values:

> Shearson Lehman Brothers has come relatively late to the idea of managing risk with the aid of systems. "As a result of the merger (with Lehman) in 1984, our systems are not as developed or mature as most of our competitors," conceded a Shearson senior executive vice president in New York. "We tend to rely more on people and manual risk evaluation." But this, surprisingly, does not put the firm at too much of a disadvantage.
>
> "We called in Coopers and Lybrand to look at our competitors' systems as we did not want to reinvent the wheel. They came back and said there was very little out there to copy and nothing to buy. They established that there are very few true risk-management systems in the marketplace."
>
> A partner in Coopers' management consulting services agreed. "The way most bankers manage risk is so primitive, I don't know how they can sleep at night. People are still looking at systems in a very cavalier way. They may have got live front-end trading systems but back offices are most unsophisticated. And those few that do have sophisticated back offices cannot offer multi-currency or risk management services."[5]

The huge size and rapid growth rates of markets and participants are exemplified and dramatized in the following examples:

- Mortgage-backed securities, born in the 1970s and now accounting for most of the securitized credit outstanding, totaled approximately $600 billion at year-end 1986. This exceeded all the outstanding loans to the nation's businesses from commercial banks.

- General Motors Acceptance Corporation has originated more than $7 billion of securitized car loans in less than one year (1987).

- In the year after the London equity market liberalized (the "Big Bang"), trading volume quadrupled.

- The U.S. securities industry's earnings increased by 622 percent between 1976 and 1986, reaching $2.7 billion by the end of that period. Revenues were $50 billion in 1986.

- The 1987 daily volume of U.S. government securities transactions totaled $265 billion, which equals the total volume of all debt securities transactions 12 years earlier.

- In Japan, over-the-counter trading volume in government securities multiplied 15 times from 1980 to 1984, then grew four times from 1984 to 1985 alone.

- Nomura Securities of Japan has approximately $6 billion of equity capital and a market value of some $60 billion.

- The October 19, 1987 stock market crash decreased the value of stock portfolios in the United States by approximately $500 billion.

- The U.S. commercial paper market grew from about $180 billion in 1982 to $360 billion through September 1987.

- On "Black Monday 1987," the New York Stock Exchange handled 600 million shares, compared with an average daily volume of 45 million shares in 1980 and 109 million shares in 1985.

- Pension funds held nearly $500 billion, or 22 percent of all U.S. equities outstanding, in 1985, up from 14 percent in 1980.

- Between 1981 and 1986, Japan's net overseas holdings climbed from $11 billion to $180 billion; by contrast, the U.S. net overseas investment position declined from $141 billion to −$263 billion during the same period.

- Between 1983 and 1986, Japan's overseas portfolio investments expanded from $13 billion to $100 billion.

- U.S. pension funds purchased $80 billion in foreign stocks in 1986, up from $10 billion in 1977.

- U.S. trading in financial instruments has tripled in the five years from 1983 to 1987, reaching $400 billion per day.

- The number of employees of New York security, commodities, and brokerage houses and related services increased from 70,200 in 1977 to 90,000 in 1980; 121,000 in 1984; and 138,000 in 1986. Likewise, the number of registered securities representatives in the United States (approximately 40 percent of whom have only limited licenses that permit them to sell mutual funds and variable annuities or tax shelters) has grown from about 245,000 in 1982 to 455,000 in 1987.

- Between 1980 and 1986, U.S. mutual fund assets grew from $135 billion to $716 billion, managed by 1,800 mutual funds.

- From 1982 to 1986, U.S. portfolio investment in overseas equities grew sixfold to $60 billion.

- The Euronote/Eurocommercial paper market (outstandings) grew from $8 billion in 1984 to $30 billion in 1986 and $54 billion in 1987.
- Contracts traded on the London Traded Options Market increased fivefold between 1984 and 1986.
- One billion shares traded daily in 1987 on the Tokyo Stock Exchange. One-half of these trades were handled by the four largest Japanese brokers.
- Foreign exchange trading volume in the United States averaged $50 billion daily in 1986, compared with $18 billion in 1980.
- Non-U.S. securities held by 150 U.S. pension funds totaled $58 billion in mid-1987.
- Between the beginning of 1986 and the close of 1987, more than 60 closed-end funds were launched in the United States. They accounted for 60 percent of the $25 billion in assets held by all closed-end funds in late 1987. Only 12 new funds had been introduced in the five preceding years.
- In the October 19, 1987 U.S. stock market crash, five institutions sold the equivalent of $4.8 billion in stocks and stock index futures contracts, and one mutual fund group sold approximately $900 million in stocks.
- In the early 1980s, three million Britons owned publicly traded shares. By 1987, there were nine million shareholders in the United Kingdom.
- Americans currently hold more than 600 million credit cards.
- The volume of trading on the London Stock Exchange grew rapidly in the "Big Bang" era:

Average Daily Volume ($ millions)	Fiscal 1986	Fiscal 1987
Equities	$ 939	$3,258*
Bonds (British government)	$2,064	$5,900

*Includes intramarket deals.

- The U.S. government debt has grown from $383 billion in the mid-1970s to approximately $2,450 billion in early 1988.

Environmental Volatility and Risk These trends and forces in the world economy and world financial markets have created unprecedented volatility and risk for investors, creditors, and market-makers. Compared with earlier times, the values reached in the late 1980s are much greater, participants' stakes are enormous, and results are frequently very surprising, while conditions are continuously unstable and often disappointing.

For example, in the three-month period following the October 19, 1987 market crash, there was a 50-point decline in volume in the Standard & Poor's 100 stock index—the most actively traded options contract in the United States, which accounts for 60 percent of the Chicago Board Options Exchange trading volume.

The risks associated with the increasingly high degree of linkage between national and international financial markets is best illustrated by the "Black Monday" stock market crash in October 1987. Professional money managers and investors discovered that in a "global crunch there is nowhere to hide." The extent of concurrent collapses in various other stock markets is summarized in Table 3.

Table 3. Percentage Change in Each Stock Market Between August 25 and October 19, 1987.

Country	Percent Change (in Local Currency)
United States	−27.8
Japan	−19.8
U.K.	−27.2
Germany	−38.4
Canada	−28.4
France	−34.7
Switzerland	−30.5
Australia	−43.4
Italy	−18.7
The Netherlands	−33.6

Source: Morgan Stanley, *Morgan Stanley Index*, New York.

For financial institutions, broadly considered, there are five traditional types of risk associated with financial assets: (1) market or price risk—the market value of a financial instrument may decline over time; (2) credit risk—a counterparty to a financial transaction may fail to perform according to the terms and conditions of the contract; (3) market liquidity risk—a negotiable or assignable financial instrument cannot be sold quickly at close to full market value; (4) settlement risk—a financial institution may pay out funds before it can be certain it will receive proceeds from the counterparty; (5) country and transfer risk—a country may be unable or unwilling to fulfill international financial obligations.

For all financial market participants, greater volatility and risk have been powerful stimuli for financial innovation, with a resulting explosion in concepts, services, and relationships intended to identify exposures to risk and minimize or hedge these exposures. For customers, the result has been a much wider array of products and capabilities, with more flexibility, lower risk premiums, more opportunity to speculate as well as protect against uncertainty, and less likelihood of loss.

While financial service firms have offered more products to their customers, there have also been such operating changes as new emphases on internal risk management; forays into new, uncharted market areas; greater dependence on trading as a source of profits; and unexpectedly severe losses when risk management policies and management have been unheeded, exceeded, or incorrect. (For example, in 1987 Merrill Lynch lost $377 million by trading just one complex mortgage vehicle.)

Increased Customer Sophistication Over time, particularly since the worldwide 1970s experience with inflation, large and small customers of financial services have become better equipped to seek out, evaluate, and select financial services.

As customers have learned more about risk, return, and cost characteristics of financial instruments, transactions, and relationships, they have come to demand quality service from competing financial service vendors.

Large U.S. corporate borrowers have, on the average, reduced their overall borrowings. They have substantially increased their commercial paper borrowing (by 200 percent since 1983) and reduced the number of banks with which they have important relationships. These approaches are intended to reduce companies' costs of capital, increase their funding flexibility, and increase the productivity of the corporate treasurers' functions. Such actions have resulted in fewer business opportunities for traditional suppliers of credit and in new opportunities for financial service firms that are able to meet the new-look requirements.

Supporting the widespread development of customer "sophistication" has been the post-1960s explosion in formal education and training by universities, institutes, and rival vendors of financial services. There has also been a tremendous expansion in the market information and market evaluation provided in several media by commercial news and data services as well as competing financial services firms.

In these circumstances, the "winners" are those providers of financial services who correctly anticipate customers' values and requirements. These winners effectively sell both themselves and new concepts, and they develop ongoing relationships with customers. They provide superior value to customers by innovating continuously to meet the changing needs and threats of the market. The "losers" are those who fail in part or altogether to keep pace with dynamic and evolving customer preferences.

Consolidation of the Financial Services Industry

The myriad dynamic forces, pressures, and changes affecting the industry in recent year have led to new positive market gains and positioning for some firms, significant losses and even failures for others, and loss of autonomy for those that have been acquired.

U.S. "superregional" commercial banks have gained in strength, market position, and preparedness for the future. Their size, profitability, and market position growth—principally through strong management and regional mergers and acquisitions—have shifted the industry's profit and overall growth emphases from the large money center banks that have been burdened by their loans to less developed countries. From 1975 to 1985, the nation's 100 largest banks lifted their share of the industry's assets from 50 percent to 57.7 percent, but the asset share of the ten largest banks did not change. The number of money center banks now operating on a nationwide scale has decreased from 20 to about 10.

As examples of significant losses, one-quarter of the 3,200 savings and loans in the United States are currently in serious trouble or insolvent, losing at least $10 million daily.

Most financial services firms had to review carefully the economics of their businesses. They needed to revise their strategies and their management systems and practices, and to reconstitute their balance sheets to provide more cash and greater stability.

The big four U.K. clearing banks, for instance, are likely candidates for overhead reduction review. Together, they recently employed 362,000 staff worldwide, a larger combined work force than that of international banks two to three times their size.

Another example of restructuring can be found in First Boston, which was hit by heavy trading losses during 1987 and subsequently sold its 22 percent interest in its New York headquarters building.

Wall Street's profit margin squeeze has led to a "consolidation" in the investment banking-brokerage business. Pretax profit margins had been 12 percent from 1981 to 1983 and fell to less than nine percent through September (pre-crash) 1987. The industry's pretax return on equity was 38 percent in the early 1980s and only 23 percent in 1987. Concurrently, the industry's equity capital increased from $7 billion in 1981 to $26 billion in third quarter 1987.

Many U.S. and European investment banks have been reallocating resources, shifting from overly competitive lines of business to more promising business opportunities, and seeking to reduce overhead.

Firms have increased their capital bases. Several U.S investment banks did so during 1986 and 1987 through outside infusions of equity by large institutions. Paine Webber Group sold an 18 percent voting share to Yasuda Mutual Life Insurance Company (Japan's fifth largest life insurance company) for $300 million. American Express Shearson Lehman Brothers sold a 13 percent voting share to Nippon Life Insurance Company. Goldman Sachs sold 12.5 percent to Sumitomo Bank Ltd. for $500 million, and Salomon Brothers sold 12 percent to investor Warren Buffett's Berkshire Hathaway Company for $700 million.

Companies have been acquired by, have merged with, or have acquired other firms in pursuit of survival, capital, market franchises, or specialists. Among these companies were world reknowned names.

- In October 1987, Goldman Sachs & Co. abandoned its long-standing policy of exclusivity in serving as dealer for client commercial paper issuance. This policy change reflected the fact that the firm had been missing out on too much commercial paper business.
- In October 1987, Salomon Brothers announced a bold plan to revive its profit potential. Plan goals included the following: cut the work force by 800 to 5,700 as part of a $150 million reduction in overhead; refocus trading operations by pulling out of underwriting and trading municipal bonds, commercial paper, and short-term liabilities; and develop a more prudent balance between trading and investment banking.
- In December 1987, Kidder Peabody announced a $100 million annual cost-cutting program that included laying off 1,000 persons (14 percent of its work force), closing 10 percent of its branch offices, and reducing bonuses by 20 percent.
- In December 1987, Merrill Lynch announced a $200 million reduction in overall salary costs, including a reduction in wage scales for its retail brokerage sales force.
- Another example of "consolidation" by a commercial bank is Midland Bank of the United Kingdom. In mid-1987, Midland was the country's third largest

clearing bank. At that point it announced a "restructuring" package that was comprised of: (a) the sale of its Scottish and Irish operations (approximately 500 branches) because of slow growth experience and difficult competition; (b) a £916 million reserve for Third-World debt, in concert with other world-class banks; and (c) a £700 million rights issue to enhance its capital base. Geographically, the bank's strategy placed considerably greater emphasis on its origins in the English heartland.

■ An example of a financial firm positively positioning itself for the future is the early 1988 Hongkong and Shanghai Banking Corporation's £400 million investment in Midland Bank. Hongkong acquired a 14.9 percent equity stake in the U.K. institution—a stake that provides a long-sought "third strategic leg" in Europe to complement its Asian home base and ownership of U.S. Marine Midland Bank. For financially weak Midland Bank, the added capital permits a further £100 million reserve against Third-World loans and financing of its active domestic growth strategy.

■ Examples of acquisitions to provide capital to weakened firms while adding marketing strength to the acquirers are Shearson Lehman's 1988 purchase of E.F. Hutton Group, and Bear Stearns & Company's 1988 purchase of the New York Stock Exchange specialist operations Asiel & Company. The Bear Stearns acquisition added 12 stocks to the listings for which the firm acts as primary dealer. (Following the October 19, 1987 stock market crash, the New York Stock Exchange waived various restrictions on outside ownership of specialists, many of which firms had sustained heavy losses and required extra capital injections.)

Shearson Lehman's $1 billion merger with E.F. Hutton leaves the acquiring firm with a retail brokerage force exceeding 12,000, one of the nation's largest, and a greatly enhanced money-management operation. Hutton, on the other hand, had been suffering from inconsistent financial results and recent scandals.

■ Barclays Bank PLC's U.S. operation is an example of reallocating resources from underperforming units to more promising opportunities. The U.S. retail business has caused the profitability of the rest of the banking group to lag. As Barclays' 1988 international investment strategy is focused on building corporate business, the bank may sell or close 135 branches in New York and California.

Another example of industry "consolidation" is bank mergers. Whereas from 1976 to 1980 the total assets acquired in U.S. bank mergers was $35 billion, representing an average of 156 bank mergers annually for each year since 1982, the total assets acquired in bank mergers exceeded this sum; and, from 1981 to 1985, the number of bank mergers per year almost tripled to 441.[6]

Management Requirements of Financial Service Firms

Companies have had to dramatically adapt their business strategies, management practices, organization structures, and value systems to deal with the complexity, surprises, and novelty of the competitive arenas they have created in this new financial era.

Aside from marketing management, financial services firms need the following qualities and capabilities to achieve viability and success: global intelligence networks to identify immediate opportunities and threats as well as longer-term trends;

strong capital bases to financial growth and withstand unfavorable shocks; considerable flexibility and creativity in thinking about their businesses; ability to think ahead about their opportunities, threats, and resources and make strategic investments for future positioning in target markets; soundly formulated business visions to drive the firm's energies; realistic strategies for achieving and defending profitable bases; sound administrative practices and skills for implementing designated strategies; innovative spirit and capability; strong management information systems for reflecting and analyzing the firm's economics; risk management policies, skills, and sensitivities; hedging capabilities to minimize exposure to volatility, risk, and loss; and overall devotion to meeting customer requirements and values.

The Special Features of Services Marketing

A second appraoch to understanding contemporary financial services marketing is to recognize that marketing services differs somewhat from marketing "tangible" products. Financial services firms must be responsive to four principal differences:

1. Services are intangible for the consumer. Customers cannot try on services or taste, touch, or feel them as a means of predicting how the purchase of a given service will provide satisfaction. Goods producers sell things, service firms sell performance.[7] Services cannot be possessed; they can only be experienced, created, or participated in.[8]

2. Services depend on the collaboration of both the supplier and the consumer of the services. The customer must normally specify the service requirements, provide descriptive and evaluative feedback as the service is delivered, and provide ongoing and postservice feedback to ensure continuing satisfaction. Such collaboration requires (1) a willingness and capability by the consumer to be involved, and (2) the availability and skill of the supplier to help the consumer gain benefits. Effective communications and cooperation are needed to link both parties.

3. Services cannot always be repeated with uniform quality because of the high human content involved in their delivery. Thus, service quality will vary from time to time, place to place, and customer to customer.

4. In the service firms, the finished service is consumed as it is produced. There should be direct contact between production and the consumer. Usually, no inventories can be created to insulate production capacity from demand patterns. Marketing and operations functions have to be closely integrated or coordinated.[9]

Given these characteristics of services marketing, customers must use a different, more difficult process for evaluating service suppliers and their services than in assessing "tangible" products and their suppliers.

How do customers cope with these requirements? Basically, they attempt to anticipate what they would experience if they were to make the purchase. They seek tangible evidence and reassurances of satisfaction that would accrue to them during the process of delivery as well as the final outcome. Because consumers may experience considerable difficulty in recognizing and evaluating the outcome of a service, the delivery of the service, particularly the interaction between consumer and service deliveries, frequently dominates customer evaluation of the service.[10]

For would-be purchasers, reassurances can be gleaned from many sources: the length of time the supplier has been in business; the names of customers that a supplier has served successfully; the modes of dress and the professional manner of service representatives; the appearance of suppliers' offices; the titles and credentials of service representatives; the suppliers' general reputations, specific references, and referrals; and public recognition through seminars, publications, or professional competition.

In their marketing efforts, vendors of services need to provide presentations and reassurances for what will happen after the sale. They must reiterate regularly the promises made to gain the customer. These can be provided principally through advertising, along with appropriate behavior and appearance of vendor personnel, quality products, and attractive physical facilities.

Until financial service companies have differentiated their services, the public's primary perception is likely to be that of the individual firm as a whole. The firm's image can be thought of as a promise of the firm made tangible in the minds of customers.[11] For firms that advertise extensively to strengthen and reinforce their corporate image, customer recognition and response can be substantial. Figure 1 shows the results of a 1984 survey conducted by the *American Banker* (and cited in the American Express 1984 *Annual Report),* which measured the level of consumer familiarity with widely advertised U.S. financial services competitors.

Figure 1. Level of Consumer Familiarity with Widely Advertised Financial Services Firms.

Who Consumers Know (%)*

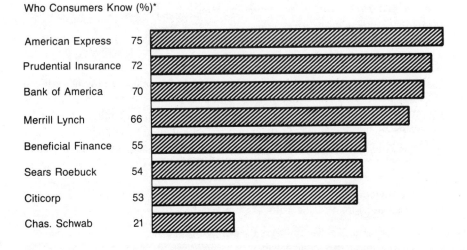

American Express	75
Prudential Insurance	72
Bank of America	70
Merrill Lynch	66
Beneficial Finance	55
Sears Roebuck	54
Citicorp	53
Chas. Schwab	21

Source: American Express 1984 *Annual Report.*

Key Issues and Practices in Contemporary Marketing of Financial Services

The trends and forces characterizing the contemporary financial services industry, along with the special qualities of services and associated requirements for their marketing, all warrant highly thoughtful, skilled, and committed approaches to the marketing of financial services. Seven key concepts constitute "cornerstones" for meeting marketing challenges today and in the years to come.

Customer Focus

This is the principal cornerstone for firms seeking to adapt their marketing to the rigors of the financial services marketplace. In the past, financial service institutions had sufficient market power to profitably offer a relatively stable and narrow line of services. Today's marketplace demands that a strong customer focus be incorporated into all aspects of (1) the marketing, management, and back-office operations that meet customer needs, (2) the pursuit of innovative possibilities, and (3) the effective delivery of services designed to satisfy customers' needs. Customer focus must become a dominant firmwide value, that represents a strategic orientation. This management priority must form the basis on which to measure, evaluate, and reward performance.

Consider, for example, Lloyd's Bank, one of the big four U.K. clearers. It requires all 54,000 members of its staff to take part in a one-day "Customer Trait" workshop designed to heighten awareness of the importance of customer service. In addition, the bank has begun a program of customer opinion surveys. Every month, 550 customers at each of Lloyd's 60 branches throughout the United Kingdom are asked to respond to questionnaires concerning the degree of their satisfaction with the bank's service.

Identifying Attractive Growth Opportunities

In the intensely competitive industry environment, high-quality telecommunications enable numerous competitors to learn simultaneously about world developments and conditions, while also learning relatively easily about each other's marketing programs and tactics. Business success depends largely on competitors' abilities to identify new opportunities for business development and realistically project the anticipated risk and return associated with each opportunity before deciding whether to pursue it.

Two financial companies that recently identified and seized new business opportunities are Financial Security Assurance (FSA) and American Express.

■ At Financial Security Assurance, the market opportunities were related to asset-backed financings (excluding the mortgaged-backed securities market), which totaled $5 billion in 1986 and are expected to exceed $100 billion by the early 1990s. FSA was formed in 1985 by several large insurance companies and banks to pioneer the corporate financial guarantee business: FSA's surety bond provides an AAA rating for such financings. With $300 million in equity, FSA is allowed an operating leverage of 100 to 1. In its first two years, the pioneering company guaranteed $3 billion worth of financings, from commercial paper to auto-backed securities, and was very profitable.

■ American Express provides an example of contemporary opportunity analysis in the highly competitive U.S. credit card market. Except for young people coming into the work force, most of the existing creditworthy base has been penetrated already, chiefly by the giant card companies. Thus, card marketers focus primarily on attempts to steal one another's market share. In this context, American Express recently began to offer its Optima card to present Amex customers with good credit records. Optima comes with a revolving credit line, an interest rate that is 1.8 times prime, and a modest annual fee. As such, Optima can be viewed as a smart offensive move that is designed to aggressively "skim the cream" of the bank card segment while defensively protecting the American Express card base against premium cards being offered now by the banks.

Differentiation

A tremendous premium is available to competitors who can achieve positive differentiation for their products in the minds of target customers in these times of intense industry competition, customer ability to choose among competing vendors, and relative ease of copying strategies and services.

Successful differentiation should: (1) be based on what the target customers value; (2) be perceived as providing superior value; (3) derive from combinations of "tangible" and "intangible" attributes of the vendor's products and services; and (4) be priced competitively. To meet these requirements, a firm must have an appropriate "state of mind" and determination. It must have a customer focus, combined with the commitment and skills to deliver to the customer through its product features, product line, delivery system, selling effort, and communications.

Barclays Bank provides a good example of successful differentiation. In the United Kingdom in 1987, there was keen competition among building societies, savings banks, the post office, and clearing banks for young customers entering the job market or universities. The premise was "catch 'em young." People tend to stay with the institution to which they first entrust their cash unless there is a real incentive or pressing need for a change. To differentiate itself from competitors by providing far more value to this target market, Barclays offered a package that provided a number of benefits:

■ free charge account banking regardless of balance, together with monthly statements;

■ the new Barclays Connect Visa card;

■ £15 cash, which is paid into the account of a student who can produce either a local education authority tuition fees award letter or a maintenance grant check;

■ up to £200 overdraft at a preferential interest rate that is 1 percent above the base interest rate;

■ advice and assistance from a specially trained young staff (called Student Business Officers);

■ special student insurance (arranged in conjunction with Provincial Insurance);

- a graduation loan scheme at a reduced interest rate (up to £1,000 depending on the graduate's having a firm job offer);
- a Barclaycard (for those over 18 who have satisfied a credit assessment; and
- other gifts such as advisory booklets ("Getting to College," "Student Banking," "Starting Work," "Getting a Job") and folders for conveniently storing financial documents.

Innovation

Given the multitude of industry competitors, the relative ease of copying competitive programs, and the ever-more-demanding customer, financial services firms must be able to innovate effectively to avoid competing only on price. Competitors' abilities to innovate are aimed largely at giving their customers a broader, more flexible range of approaches for raising funds and hedging interest and exchange rate exposure. These are key ingredients in meaningful differentiation and provision of value-added services for customers. But financial services firms should be cautioned that, in their rush to develop new products and services, they must guard against innovation that seeks differentiation for its own sake without giving customers benefits they value or can use.

For example, from 1985 to 1987, the U.S. commodity exchanges introduced very few new products that became successful. In 1987, the commodity exchanges launched 16 new contracts, but only one or two of them received customer interest. The most notable failure occurred in 1985, when the Chicago Board of Trade brought out a very heavily promoted National Association of Securities Dealers futures contract while the rival Chicago Mercantile Exchange launched a similar Standard & Poor's futures index of over-the-counter issues. Customer interest was lacking and both contracts died.

On the positive side, there are several successful examples:

1. As shown in Figure 2, there has been a growth in recent years of large, liquid swap markets in several currencies (plus related products such as "cape," "collars," and "floors").
2. In recent years, the Euromarkets have rapidly diversified the currencies used for new issues, shifting from the once dominant U.S. dollar to favor the yen, the Australian dollar, the deutsche mark, and the European Currency Unit (ECU). (U.S. dollar denominated issues accounted for 40 percent of all Euromarket issues in 1987.) The diversification of currency reflected the weakening U.S. dollar, increasing investor sophistication, and the liberalization of domestic financial markets (principally the yen markets).
3. In recent years, large companies have made increasing use of receivable-backed financing, wherein manufacturing companies such as Michelin Tire, Union Carbide, and Mattel reduce their financing costs by using their receivables to back new issues of commercial paper and preferred stock in the capital markets. In November 1987, Chrysler Financial sold $1 billion of certificates backed by automobile loans in the bond market, the largest-ever public financing by that entity. This AAA-rated offering carried an attractive cost to Chrysler Financial.

Figure 2. Swap Market Outstandings.

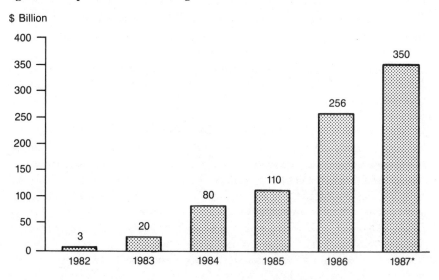

$ Billion

Ability to Operate Successfully in Unfamiliar Marketpaces

In the present competitive environment, financial services firms are propelled into considering and entering new market arenas, sometimes with new, untested services and approaches. Some of these forays are motivated by defensive needs to protect existing client relationships and market franchises. Others are undertaken for offensive reasons, to seize newly recognized opportunities or to diversify the firm's revenue or funding bases.

A prominent current example with both offensive and defensive motivations is the increasing orientation of commercial banks to investment banking, principally in search of fee/non-asset revenues, new business growth opportunities, and defenses against the loss of valued client relations to aggressive, able investment banks. In their quest to develop investment banking business, the commercial banks have encountered severe competition in the strongly entrenched, concentrated market power possessed by the leading houses. The top five U.S. investment banks account for more than 50 percent of all business. They dominate the highest-margin product sales, sell more products to any given client than do commercial banks, possess a considerably broader relevant product range, and have broader relevant market sales coverage than the banks do. At this writing, the top five U.S. investment banks controlled approximately 90 percent of the commercial paper market, 80 percent of the mortgage-backed securities underwriting market and 70 percent of the corporate debt market.

Commercial banking institutions have struggled hard to integrate investment banking into their operations because of the cultural and behavioral differences between commercial and investment bankers in terms of loyalty to their firms, personal aggressiveness, and relationship versus transactional approaches to customers. The commercial banks want to leverage their existing customer bases, but to achieve this, investment and commercial bankers must learn to work together in identifying opportunities, sales activities, and structuring of deals.

The complex issue of compensation becomes relevant. Historically, the two types of bankers have been paid in accord with substantially different criteria and at substantially different rates. These disparities are causing banks to reevaluate their performance goal setting, evaluation, and reward systems, teamwork-enhancing management practices, and organizational structures.

To meet these important challenges associated with "forays" into investment banking, commercial banks have undertaken various adaptations: (a) recruitment of investment bankers and traders to provide requisite skills and contracts; (b) retraining of commercial bankers for selected selling functions; (c) experimentation with new forms of organization structures to foster communication, teamwork, cross-selling, and cultural interchange; (d) acquisition of specialized investment banks/securities houses, and the like, with requisite client bases and operating capabilities;[12] (e) development of risk assessment and risk management capabilities relating to new products and new transactions; (f) experimentation with new pay-for-performance personnel programs; (g) attempted repositioning of the banks in target-market perceptions as having investment banking and trading capabilities and/or being full-fledged investment banks.

Banks and other financial services firms that seek to penetrate unknown markets need the following qualities and capabilities: market intelligence, ability to assess opportunities and risks in advance, strategic orientation and realism, decisive senior management, adroit risk identification and risk management, product innovation, new product management, communication with the marketplace, management information systems, and the ability to manage change and operate in new circumstances with uncertain outcomes.

Quality Service

Increasingly high-quality services are now available industry wide, due to the proliferation of competitors' offerings, the increased sophistication and demands of customers, and the enhanced general capabilities of financial services suppliers.

Hence, supplier offerings are almost always evaluated on the basis of service quality as well as price competitiveness. Service quality is frequently the most important ingredient that enables a competitor to distinguish itself and deliver superior value to targeted customers. Service quality usually encompasses the manner in which the service is performed as well as the outcome for the customer. Research suggests that the principal determinants of service quality will include the ten factors summarized in Table 4.

Delivery of high-quality service requires a clear and strong commitment by senior management and a carefully formulated program for implementation. The latter usually requires clearly defined service standards, training for employees involved in service delivery, design of procedures for providing service to customers, effective communication of the service commitment to meet employees

Table 4. Likely Determinants of Service Quality.

RELIABILITY involves consistency of performance and dependability. It means that the firm performs the service right the first time. It also means that the firm honors its promises. Specifically, it involves:
— accuracy in billing;
— keeping records correctly;
— performing the service at the designated time.

RESPONSIVENESS concerns the willingness or readiness of employees to provide service. It involves timeliness of service:
— mailing a transaction slip immediately;
— calling the customer back quickly;
— giving prompt service (e.g., setting up appointments quickly).

COMPETENCE means possession of the required skills and knowledge to perform the service. It involves:
— knowledge and skill of the contact personnel;
— knowledge and skill of operational support personnel;
— research capability of the organization, e.g., securities brokerage firm.

ACCESS involves approachability and ease of contact. It means:
— the service is easily accessible by telephone (lines are not busy and they don't put you on hold);
— waiting time to receive service (e.g., at a bank) is not extensive;
— convenient hours of operation;
— convenient location of service facility.

COURTESY involves politeness, respect, consideration. and friendliness of contact personnel (including receptionists, telephone operators, etc.). It includes:
— consideration for the consumer's property (e.g., no muddy shoes on the carpet);
— clean and neat appearance of public contact personnel.

COMMUNICATION means keeping customers informed in language they can understand and listening to them. It may mean that the company has to adjust its language for different consumers—increasing the level of sophistication with a well-educated customer and speaking simply and plainly with a novice. It involves:
— explaining the service itself;
— explaining how much the service will cost;
— explaining the trade-offs between service and cost;
— assuring the consumer that a problem will be handled.

CREDIBILITY involves trustworthiness, believability, honesty. It involves having the customer's best interests at heart. Contributing to credibility are:
— company name;
— company reputation;
— personal characteristics of the contact personnel;
— the degree of hard sell involved in interactions with the customer.

SECURITY is the freedom from danger, risk, or doubt. It involves:
— physical safety (Will I get mugged at the automatic teller machine?);
— financial security (Does the company know where my stock certificate is?);
— confidentiality (Are my dealings with the company private?).

Table 4. *Continued.*

UNDERSTANDING/KNOWING THE CUSTOMER involves making the effort to understand the customer's needs. It involves:
— learning the customer's specific requirements;
— providing individualized attention;
— recognizing the regular customer.

TANGIBLES include the physical evidence of the service:
— physical facilities;
— appearance of personnel;
— tools or equipment used to provide the service;
— physical representations of the service, such as a plastic credit card or a bank statement;
— other customers in the service facility.

Source: A. Parasuraman, V. Zeithaml, L. Berry, "A Conceptual Model of Service Quality and Its Implications for Future Research," *Journal of Marketing*, Fall 1985, p. 47. Reprinted by permission.

and customer expectations, and comprehensive monitoring of the quality that is actually delivered by management.

Research has shown that both employees and customers of service organizations experience positive outcomes when the organization operates with a customer service orientation. This orientation seems to result in superior service practices and procedures that are observable by customers and also seem to fit employee views of the appropriate style for dealing with customers.[13]

The following are examples of such elements of service quality:

■ Several years ago, the Chase Manhattan Bank launched a program to upgrade nonloan products, improve external communications and customer service, and make its back-office (production) operations more market-oriented. Chase's international business was a weak spot. In the highly visible "product" of international money transfer, communications were frustrated by differences of viewpoint between marketing (exemplified by the account relations manager in the field) and the back office in New York. Errors were frequent. A large backlog of inquiries about balances and transactions had built up and operations group morale was low.

The executive who was put in charge of the program ordered a study, which found that (1) headquarters accounted for operational errors in only about one-third of all the inquiries and that (2) the marketing people had little idea of the services that operations could offer the bank's customers. The executive traced the backlogged errors to their sources—frequently correspondent banks—and resolved these mistakes. To improve operations staff morale, he launched a campaign with the theme "We make it happen." He also formed a new customer mobile unit, consisting of the bank's most experienced international operations people. The unit visited Chase customers at their businesses to help resolve problems and smooth operations.

This executive brought the marketing and back-office people together to discuss ways to improve the flow of information. Perhaps most important, the bank revised reporting relationships so that operations units serving specific market segments reported to both the customer relationship manager and the head of operations, a move that improved financial coordination.[14]

- At Glendale Federal Savings in California, management realized that its best (i.e., its most affluent) retail customers are "time-bankrupt." As a result, Glendale heavily advertises its documentation service: a local branch will deliver loan applications or other documents to mortgage customers if they are too busy to come into the office.

Professionalism

As in most competitive industries, customers tend to expect and value professional standards and behavior from vendors of financial services.

"Professionalism" may seem a rather vague term, but financial service competitors as well as customers demand and take pride in it. In most areas of the financial service industry, professionalism seems to comprise knowledge of customers' requirements and behavior; ability to communicate in language acceptable to customers; familiarity with the financial service institution's capabilities; ability to meet customers' requirements through "financial engineering" that matches those requirements with the institution's capabilities; maintenance of high ethical and legal standards; and pertinent knowledge of the competitive and regulatory environment.

J.P. Morgan is an excellent example of professionalism in general institutional image and reputation as well as all the aforementioned marketing requirements for the financial services industry of the 1990s. Over time, the bank has developed a unique global reputation for: (1) quality in relationships with its blue-chip clients in the delivery of financial services, (2) knowledge of finance and its clients' businesses, and (3) integrity in its dealings with clients and competitors. Its financial strength and results have reflected the payoffs that can accrue because of such capability in the marketplace over the long run. More recently, Morgan appears to have aimed increasingly for investment banking business, with the prospect of less dependence on asset-based revenues and more reliance on the lucrative fees in corporate finance and profits in successful trading.

Gaining this market position has required innovative skills and reputation, a global stature and transaction capability, a strong capital base, strong relationships with target clients, an active selling program, and evidence of a long-term commitment to the business.

Morgan also had to differentiate itself from (1) other commercial banks that did not offer world-class investment banking services, (2) other commercial banks that offered increasingly capable investment banking services (e.g., Citibank and Bankers Trust), and (3) investment banks that offered traditional capabilities (e.g., Merrill Lynch and Goldman Sachs) but did not possess the large commercial banks' selective services or lending capabilities.

Morgan met these requirements strongly and effectively through an advertising program in the leading financial and business newspapers and magazines that are read in important world commercial centers. The series provided continuity in the Morgan image and theme while presenting various messages about the bank's intent, business philosophy, banking capabilities, global scope, capital strength, and professionalism. Three advertisements from the series are provided as examples in Figures 3, 4, and 5.

Today's environment for delivering financial services is dynamic and somewhat without historic precedent. Firms in the financial services industry are fully challenged by the opportunities and the threats associated with the rapidly evolving marketplace, and few role models exist among financial services firms to demonstrate how to effectively market highly competitive products. Nevertheless, there are compelling management principles and concepts that can guide executives in their choices. It is these principles and concepts, and how they are used by competitors in the financial services arena, that provide the focus of this book.

Notes

1. In the 1980s, there were more than one hundred foreign banks operating in London.
2. Salomon Brothers, "Technology in Banking—A Path to Competitive Advantage."
3. Morgan Guaranty Trust Company, *World Financial Markets*, December 1986, New York.
4. *Financial Times,* October 31, 1987.
5. Excerpted from Tony Shale, "Crisis in the Back Office," *Euromoney,* July 1987, pp. 58–66.
6. See R.P. Beatty, A.M. Santomero, M.L. Smirlock, "Bank Merger Premiums: Analysis and Evidence," *Monograph Series in Finance and Economics*, New York University, No. 1987-3.
7. L.L. Berry, "Big Idea in Services Marketing," *The Journal of Services Marketing* (Summer 1987), pp. 5–9.
8. As noted by G. Lynn Shostack, "Service Positioning Through Structural Change," *Journal of Marketing* (January 1987).
9. C. Lovelock, E. Langeard, J. Bateson, P. Eiglier, "Some Organizational Problems Facing Marketing in the Service Sector" (Working paper).
10. A. Parasuraman, "Customer-Oriented Corporate Cultures Are Crucial to Services Marketing Success," *The Journal of Services Marketing* (Summer 1987).
11. Thomas J. Vos, "Sharpening the Corporate Image for a Service Company," *The Journal of Business and Industrial Marketing*, Spring 1987, pp. 69–76.
12. For example, in December 1987, the Royal Bank of Canada, Canada's largest chartered bank, announced its intention to purchase 75 percent of Dominion Securities Inc., to broaden the range of its financial products in the Canadian securities business.
13. Benjamin Schneider, "The Service Organization: Climate Is Crucial," *Organization Dynamics*, AMACOM, 1980, pp. 52–65.
14. James L. Heskett, "Lessons in the Service Sector," *Harvard Business Review,* March–April 1987, pp. 118–126.

Figure 3. J.P. Morgan Advertisement.

"Some might say encouraging clients to become competitors is the height of folly. We feel otherwise."

There are times when helping clients meet a strategic need means helping them do what we used to do for them. For example, with J.P. Morgan's guidance a number of multinationals have set up their own in-house banks to achieve better treasury management. Now they arrange their own swaps, manage their own currency exposures, provide credit to their clients, finance major projects. Results: funding costs are reduced and credit ratings are often strengthened. At J.P. Morgan we welcome the fact that clients are dealing in the markets for themselves. The more professional our clients become, the more opportunities there are to interest them in new ideas.

Clients with in-house banking capabilities don't stop being Morgan clients; they just test our resources in different ways.

JPMorgan

Figure 4. J.P. Morgan Advertisement.

"J.P. Morgan is an international firm with a very important American business."

J.P. Morgan was an international firm long before the integration of world financial markets. Over the last century we have established a presence in major financial centers everywhere, building the global resources and experience multinational clients need. Today, whether we're raising capital in London or investing funds in Tokyo, trading currencies in Frankfurt or restructuring assets in New York, J.P. Morgan draws on in-depth company and industry research generated by our 120 analysts worldwide, and minute-by-minute data from Morgan market-makers in each financial center. Our clients know the advice we offer and the solutions we structure come from a global perspective no other firm can match.

For over 125 years J.P. Morgan has put its clients' interests first, in a context of absolute confidentiality and objectivity.

JPMorgan

Figure 5. J.P. Morgan Advertisement.

"Situations will always arise that can only be solved by bright people backed by uncompromised capital strength."

Large corporations have drastically reduced their reliance on traditional bank borrowing. But there will always be complex financings that need the brains and specialized experience only a firm like J.P. Morgan can supply. In addition to our ability and willingness to find the right solution, Morgan clients have access to another singular benefit: our role as principal backed by our financial strength. More than $8.2 billion in total capital allows Morgan to work closely with you, stay with you, and act only when it benefits you most in terms of risks and costs. We have the freedom not to compromise.

Which is the client and which the Morgan banker? It's hard to say, illustrating the kind of financial partnership we build.

JPMorgan

1

Perspectives on the Management of Commercial Banks*

David B. Zenoff

I. Introduction

Managing large banks has become more challenging recently because of the dramatic changes in bank regulation, technology, customers' requirements, financial markets, and competing financial institutions. In this chapter, we describe the management characteristics of large commercial banks, assess the challenges that confront their management, and review the associated marketing requirements and issues.

There are important exceptions to the generalizations that follow. However, most medium-size and large banks can be compared because of similarities in their business economics, value systems, marketplaces, product offerings, and governing regulations. Further, their frequent collaboration and consultation with one another, along with the movement of bank officers among various institutions over their careers, have facilitated "cross-pollinization" and emulation of banks' management style and strategy.

II. Legacies from Yesterday

Broadly, banks' roles have been to (1) take deposits, (2) lend money, (3) pool and transform risk, (4) direct the transfer of financial assets, and (5) provide financial advice and service to wholesale[1] and retail customers.

*This chapter is adapted from Chapter 1 in David B. Zenoff, *International Banking: Management and Strategies*, Euromoney (London) 1986.

Favorable regulatory circumstances, a sufficiently strong economic environment, and strong demand for banking services enabled many banks to perform these services and grow profitably without requiring particularly strong marketing, general management, or innovation.

Low-Cost Funding

Until a few years ago, one of the most favorable circumstances for banks was low-cost funding. This reflected government-regulated ceilings on the rate of interest that banks could pay their depositors, including *no* interest on demand deposits. And holding down the effective cost of banks' funds has been the sizable float that exists as funds pass through the banking system, providing banks with free funds.

Limited Competition

Concurrently, most banks operated with relatively limited competition. Market franchises were granted to banks by national and state governments empowered to award banking licenses for a designated geographic area; generally, banks could operate in only one state. Through such regulation, it was possible to *limit* the degree of outside competition[2] permitted in each home market as well as the number of institutions empowered to perform specific banking functions.

Another factor that has moderated the intensity of competition among banks is their *collaboration*: Banks are both competitors and collaborators. Banks have long worked jointly on various syndicated credits, as correspondents, on loan work-out problems, and selectively, in sponsoring electronic transaction systems for use by their retail customers. They maintain strong, often cordial, and usually respectful working relationships. In most respects, competition has been polite.

Aided by low-cost funds and limited competition, the banks' profitable growth also reflected the increasing demand for banking services that was fueled by growth in North America and world commerce; affluence among businesses and households; savings available for deposit; and demand for credit and payment statements to support consumption and investment by governments, households, and businesses. Moreover, in the United States, legislation provided that *all* financial transactions must be processed through commercial banks.

III. Market Insensitivity and Conservatism

Because of limited and polite competition as well as the growing demand for their services and credit facilities, most banks evolved without being particularly market sensitive. Often, they were *acceptors* of deposits and *rationers* of credit. With such asset and liability opportunities, avoiding large credit losses was a principal management consideration in ensuring attractive profitability. Without such losses, banks had generally attractive return-on-equity potential. Among bankers, this gave rise to a general philosophy of *conservatism* in extending credit, developing new products, entering new markets, delivering new services, and developing new ways of funding their institutions.

In the marketplace for both deposit- and revenue-building, an important feature of banking was the *loyalty* that developed between customers and their banks. Both parties generally perceive benefits from knowing each other, testing each other's competence and goodwill, and developing the sense of security that comes with goodwill and commitment. But over time, this testing process also raises barriers and increases the costs to both parties if they should desire to terminate or significantly alter the relationship.

In this setting, "no need to be first" was a maxim often pursued among bankers. Most banks believed that innovative risk-taking was unnecessary since it was relatively easy to copy one another's product developments, new delivery systems, new liability instruments, and so on. Such market information was disseminated quickly because bankers spoke to one another often about business, clients pressured banks to meet competitor's new offerings, many services and products had relatively low technological complexity and were unpatentable and banks advertised their advances. Regulatory constraints were a further damper on the innovative spirit since new products had to be designed to meet regulations and, often, required government approval.

These developments had the following results:

1. Bank products and services tended to become commodities over their life cycles. Initially, for an innovator, a market leader's price could be charged. Soon, with the appearance of *multiple* competitors offering similar products, price competitiveness became an important competitive tactic to protect or gain market share. Ultimately, many such bank products did not carry an explicit cost to customers.

2. Beyond duplicating one another's products, banks tended to follow one another more widely, into new market segments and geographic areas where permitted. Thus certain types of customers and markets became popular among banks. For example, there was cyclic market overcrowding in lending to commercial real estate developers, developing countries, multinational corporations, middle-market companies, and the energy industry. Today, the move is into investment banking. The inevitable result of this relatively undifferentiated competition has been the *overbanking* of customers and market segments.

IV. Vertical Integration

As banks grew in size, they serviced, by intent and circumstance, *large* numbers of customers (for example, every year Bank of America finances 250,000 California home buyers), entailing huge volumes of transactions.

The operations of many commercial banks were fully vertically integrated, producing a great part of the financial products they sold. Commercial banks performed the accounting and payments services they required to service demand deposits. They invested their funds in the commercial loans they originated and serviced. Except for certain correspondent banking services (interbanking lending, check-clearing and so on), many commercial banks did not purchase or sell significant amounts of services or assets from or to other institutions.

V. International Banking

International banking was an important element in banks' recent asset growth, particularly between 1970 and 1985. U.S. banks, which in 1960 included only eight with foreign branches, led most of the world in international expansion that was directed mainly toward industrialized countries. By 1975, 125 U.S. banks had one or more foreign branches. By 1980, approximately 151 U.S. banks owned 800 foreign branches and 113 foreign subsidiaries and had 244 foreign associates.

Although banks' precise objectives and strategies for international expansion differ somewhat, there have been three generally prevalent motives: (1) financing domestic customers' international trade, (2) financing domestic customers' foreign operations and providing them with money transfer and investment services, and (3) accessing international capital and money markets to supplement the banks' funding activities.

VI. Management Style and Management Practices

Despite regional, cultural, regulatory, and market differences, the management style of banks had several common characteristics.

Personnel Intensive

They developed highly personnel-intensive organizations believing that selling and distributing financial services and products required customer contact and relationship. When carried out professionally and systematically, personal contact in banking relationships has enabled some banks to differentiate themselves through customer-focused "relationship management." Notable examples are Morgan Guaranty and Bankers Trust Company with blue chip wholesale clients (corporations, financial institutions, and governments), Citibank with multinational corporations, and Wells Fargo and First Interstate of California with middle-market and smaller regional companies.

Bureaucratic Processes

To preserve control over credit allocation and retain a generally conservative approach, large banks developed a *bureaucratic* style of management. They had many levels of control, elaborate rules and well-defined boundaries, and limits for individual decisionmaking and initiative.

Slow moving and cautious, the banks valued ethical, polite, and nonconfrontational behavior when resolving organizational issues; were generally civic-minded; and sought to avoid lending and funding mistakes. As employers, they were generally paternalistic and provided secure employment.

Focus on Assets

Success among bank officers was equated principally with asset growth and prudent lending judgment. Thus most bankers focused on assets: extending credit, negotiating loan terms, seeking secure documentation and security. Not nearly as much attention was paid to liability management, for during most periods, the *availability* and *cost* of funds to banks were very attractive. Similarly, as banks earned good profits, management was unconcerned about the adequacy of the capital base on which it could build assets through leverage and reserves for loan losses.

Management Information

Given this backdrop and the overall attractiveness of banks' profitability over time, few institutions developed particularly meaningful cost accounting or management information systems. Most did not measure their profitability by customer market segment, or product or geographic unit. Most bank officers were not oriented to focus on the bottom line in decisionmaking and made few attempts to do so. Instead, bankers assumed profits would follow once good-quality assets were booked. Most bank performance was measured by asset growth. Officers who rose to senior positions were considered good bankers or "dealmakers" although they were not necessarily highly experienced or proven managers or leaders.

VII. Pressures and Circumstances for Change

In the past decade, many changes have caused banks to *reexamine* their values, management practices, business definitions, market strategies, and funding approaches. They have had to redefine the key success factors for overall long-term viability. The forces of change have affected state and regional banking markets at differing rates and for sometimes different reasons. But by the late 1980s, most medium-size and large banks have experienced similar effects.

Overall, in the mid-1980s, commercial banking appeared to be a *declining industry.* From 1975 to 1985, banks' share of all financial assets held by U.S. financial institutions fell from 38 to 31 percent. The large banks' share of credit extended to nonfinanical corporations dropped from 71 to 53 percent. Domestic bank deposits increased by 130 percent, and savings and loan industry deposits increased by 203 percent. Pension fund assets grew by 264 percent, mutual funds by 496 percent, and money market mutual funds by 5,508 percent. From 1981 to 1986, banks' return on assets declined from 0.75 to 0.64 percent, whereas return on equity dropped from 13.6 to 10.2 percent.[3]

Increased Competition

Competition in formerly "protected markets increased significantly. In recent years, new forms, sources, and types of competition have emerged, including out-of-state and foreign banks and nonbanks.

Nontraditional competitors (that is, nonbanks), aided by regulatory changes, technological developments, and changing customer preferences, have introduced new products, alternative delivery systems, better-focused niche strategies, lower-cost services, and higher yields that are more attractive to depositors.

With new, strong competition, many of the traditional geographic, market-segment, and industry-definition lines have been blurred. Stockbrokerage is now associated with commercial banking. Money market mutual funds have become huge because they offer market rates, convenience, and ready liquidity that attract household and small-business deposits. Credit cards have gained wide acceptance among customers and business establishments (for example, American Express has 17 million U.S. cardholders, and its card is accepted at 1,800,000 stores and establishments). Financial services are part of soft-goods retailing (for example, Sears Roebuck's credit card is held by approximately 19 million persons and is honored at 700,000 retail outlets). Industrial companies have become active in selected financial services. For example, General Motors Acceptance Corporation has become one of the nation's largest mortgage service firms. Ford Motor Company purchased U.S. Leasing International for $500 million in 1987. Savings and loans and other thrifts now offer a broad line of heretofore bank-dominated products and services to retail customers. Figure 1 shows a recent example of the latter.

Increasing numbers of banks have moved into one another's home markets as expanding nationwide banking and internationalism in world commerce have exerted reciprocity pressures on federal and state banking regulators.[4] In London, the major international capital market, 463 foreign banks were represented in 1987, including 46 from Japan, 64 from the United States, and 189 from Europe. In California, a state whose gross product ranks sixth among free-world industrialized nations, more than 190 Japanese-owned banking units compete. In the United States as a whole, by the early 1980s, there were more than 375 foreign banks with one or more affiliates, representing more than 55 countries. As of 1987, commercial lending by foreign banks accounted for 16 percent of the U.S. credit market, compared with 9 percent in the late 1970s. Also in 1987, the assets of Japanese banks operating in the United States exceeded $200 billion, their direct investment in U.S. banks totaled $2.2 billion, and they held 9 percent of U.S. commercial and industrial loans.

Consider these two recent examples of de facto interstate banking in the United States. Chase Manhattan Bank of New York has acquired and established in Florida a bank, trust company, international banking operation, home mortgage and personal finance offices, and a real estate financing operation. And since 1968, Banc One of Columbus, Ohio, has acquired 58 banks in Ohio, Indiana, Michigan, Kentucky, and Wisconsin.

The *regulatory changes* opening banks' home markets to competition have removed ceilings on rates that various financial institutions could pay on specified types of deposits. The resulting competition for depositors' funds has increased banks' requirements for skillful and creative liability management. As a result, most "cheap" core deposits were lost as new competition forced banks to pay "market rates."

For competitors, these regulatory changes have brought new challenges and opportunities as well as loss of market share. The costs and benefits have not been distributed equally among banks, due in part to differing business strategies, strengths and abilities to respond quickly, and the intensity and shape of new competition.

Figure 1. Advertisement for California Federal Bank.

It's a widely-held belief that when responding to customers, the faster the better.
Well, yes.
And no.
At California Federal, we believe the best way to make the right decisions for our customers is to know exactly when to move swiftly.

SPEED IS RELATIVE. ESPECIALLY IN COMMERCIAL BANKING.

And when to take time. Time to get a thorough understanding of your business, and customize financing to fit it perfectly.

All of which takes a commercial banking division structured to be lean. Experienced. And responsive.

One that doesn't get tangled up in red tape, or bogged down with layers of approval. One that doesn't let committees delay decision-making, or the inexperienced service clients.

California Federal's hand-picked bankers work at a pace that matches the pace of your business. Deadlines are met. Things get done.

From timely loan approvals to moving your money worldwide, that's how we work. And it's how we've built loan outstandings and commitments of over $1 billion in four short years.

Time is money.
We make sure neither is handled sluggishly.

CALIFORNIA FEDERAL
COMMERCIAL BANKING

Source: Ogilvy and Mather, Los Angeles, California. Reprinted by permission of California Federal Bank.

Capital adequacy is another area of government regulation of banks that has recently become more important. There is worldwide concern about the sizable bank exposure to troubled developing countries[5] and to "soft" domestic industry segments affected by the slow-growth world economy. The amount of U.S. commercial bank net charge-offs in the 1980s is more than *25 times* what it was in the late 1960s.[6] Central banks and bank supervisors have collaborated internationally in promulgating higher capital-to-asset standards for their large banks, raised banks' consciousness about capital adequacy, and mandated minimum tolerable levels for the amount of capital required to support a given level of risk assets.

Tables 1 and 2 show the recent increase in the capital base of U.S. banks.

The increased capital-adequacy requirements have constrained the banks' freedom to grow[7] and caused them to seek to increase their capital through new equity[8] and "quasi-equity" issues[9] (for example, perpetual bonds and multicurrency capital). These requirements have also spurred the banks' drive for noncredit, fee-based revenue sources instead of an "assets-only" growth strategy. Table 3 depicts this trend.

Banks have also added to their capital by retaining a higher share of current earnings, in some cases selling their undervalued real estate and business assets. (Between 1982 and 1986, nine U.S. money center banks increased their primary capital from $29 billion to $46.7 billion.) For example, in 1984, Security Pacific Corporation added all the proceeds from the sale of its Los Angeles headquarters to its reserves. In 1986, Bank of America sold its San Francisco headquarters. In the late 1987, Citibank sold most of its Manhattan property holdings, including two thirds of its Citicorp Center, for $670 million. The bank derived a $270 million after-tax gain to strengthen its balance sheet after an earlier $3 billion provision for loans to less developed countries. In early 1988, Standard Chartered Bank of the United Kingdom agreed to sell Union Bank, its California subsidiary for $750 million. The sale was part of a broader strategy of asset disposals to realize fresh capital resources to replenish its reserves, which were depleted by provisions for doubtful Third-World loans.

A related phenomenon of significant economic and strategic importance to most banks has been the recent creation of sizable loan loss reserves, with Citicorp leading in this practice during 1987. This practice will likely widen the competitive gap between strong and weaker banks in relation to their equity positions, return-on-assets profitability, and earnings momentum.[10]

Table 4 shows the equity-to-asset ratios of the 15 largest U.S. commercial banks as of mid-1987.

Availability of Improved Information Processing Technology

Technological improvements in computer hardware and software have strengthened the banks' delivery systems; information transmittal, storage, and retrieval; data processing; and capabilities to offer interactive financial transactions with customers. In general, these advances have facilitated the development of new and broader lines of products to meet customers' needs. The availability of technological improvements has pushed banks to make many critical choices and sizable capital

Table 1. Primary Capital, Percent of Gross
Assets, Small, Medium, and Large Insured
Commercial Banks.

Median Percent

Year	Under $1 Bn	Asset Size $1-$10 Bn	Over $10 Bn
1976	8.20	6.44	4.93
1977	8.15	6.33	4.80
1978	8.26	6.13	4.61
1979	8.47	6.13	4.50
1980	8.65	6.08	4.45
1981	8.64	6.20	4.83
1982	8.66	6.13	4.81
1983	8.60	6.27	5.07
1984	8.57	6.43	5.81
1985	8.67	6.64	6.40

Source: Call reports. Data excludes banks in operation
less than three years.

Table 2. Selected U.S. Bank Groups Average Equity to Average
Assets, 1981-1986.

Weighted Group Averages	1981	1982	1983	1984	1985	1986	Basic Point Change 1981-1986
New York banks	3.61	3.92	4.41	4.56	4.79	5.05	144
Southeast banks	5.91	5.93	5.72	5.77	5.96	5.97	6
Texas banks	5.75	5.62	5.77	5.67	5.81	5.85	10
California banks	3.83	3.85	4.33	4.56	4.50	4.52	69
Western banks	4.62	4.63	5.00	5.11	5.11	5.36	74
Top fifteen banks	3.86	4.02	4.49	4.67	4.79	4.97	111
Industry proxy	4.22	4.38	4.79	4.93	5.07	5.24	102

Source: Montgomery Securities, *The Quarterly Bank Monitor*, February 27, 1987.

Table 3. U.S. Commercial Banks'
Noninterest Income as a Percentage
of Earning Assets, 1977-1984.

Year	Interest (percent)
1977	0.67
1978	0.98
1979	1.04
1980	1.19
1981	1.30
1982	1.37
1983	1.44
1984	1.32

Table 4. Top U.S. Banks' Equity Ratio, Second Quarter 1987.

J.P. Morgan	5.96
Bank of Boston	5.02
First Bank System	4.71
Continental Illinois	4.69
First Interstate	4.46
Bankers Trust	4.12
Security Pacific	3.86
Wells Fargo	3.75
Mellon Bank	3.30
First Chicago	3.28
Chase Manhattan	2.98
Chemical Bank	2.82
Citicorp[a]	3.60
Manufacturers Hanover	2.36
BankAmerica	2.33

a. Yearend 1987.
Source: Company reports.

commitments to technology in order to satisfy customer needs and increase their own productivity. Reflecting the importance of such systems-related opportunities and investments, the 140 largest U.S. banks will spend more than $45 billion on automation and new data systems during the 1985-1990 period. Citicorp, the leader in this trend, has invested about $500 million in systems development, established 160 data centers, and installed 20,000 banking terminals.

Cost Pressures

The cost structures of banks have been changing in recent years. Deregulation of deposit rate ceilings and the heightened competition for deposits have required banks to pay market rates for a significant proportion of their funds. This trend also reflects corporate and retail customers' growing sophistication and demands for higher real returns on their deposits. In addition, the proliferation of banks' corporate cash management service has, among other effects, significantly reduced the amount of customer float in the banking system and increased the institutions' cost of funding.

Also significant in banks' cost structures has been the rising and currently high level of operating (noninterest) expenses. These reflect, primarily, increases in personal compensation and, secondarily, the higher costs of premises and technology. For example, in 1986–1987, Bank of America spent approximately $50 million to consolidate its 20 different telecommunications systems into a single, flexible network. Tables 5 and 6 portray the noninterest expense trend among U.S. banks in recent years.

Table 5. Five-Year Noninterest Expense Growth
Rates for Selected Groups of U.S. Banks, 1981–1986.

Bank Groups	Growth Rates (percent)
New York banks	15.4
Southeast banks	20.3
Texas banks	15.8
California banks	13.1
Western banks	13.9
Top fifteen banks	15.6
Money-center banks	15.6
Industry proxy	15.9

Source: Montgomery Securities, *The Quarterly Bank Monitor*,
February 27, 1987.

Table 6. Noninterest Expense/Assets for U.S.
Banks, Selected Years 1960–1984.

Year	Noninterest Expense/Assets (percent)
1960	1.93
1965	2.00
1970	2.51
1975	2.50
1980	2.51
1981	2.64
1982	2.81
1983	2.86
1984	2.94

Risk Sources

Increased interest and foreign exchange rate volatility have confronted banks with additional risk and special opportunities in recent years. Money market and foreign exchange trading transaction volumes have grown enormously. In 1986, the average volume of foreign exchange trading in the United States was $60 billion, twice the 1983 volume. This greatly increased volume provides opportunities and possibilities for loss[11] when banks serve customers and take speculative positions themselves.[12] Exemplifying the related income opportunities and year-to-year volatility is Bankers Trust Company. The following excerpt is from its 1986 annual report:

Trading Account Profits and Commissions and Foreign Exchange Trading Income

Trading account profits and commissions and foreign exchange trading income of $223.8 million in 1986 increased $101.5 million over 1985. Trading account profits and commissions of $166.4 million were $151.6 million higher than the

$14.8 million earned during 1985 and $100.6 million higher than 1984's level of $65.8 million. Foreign exchange trading income was $57.4 million in 1986. This was $50.1 million lower than the record $107.5 million earned in 1985 and $10.4 million lower than the $67.7 million earned in 1984.

Fees and Commissions

Fees and commissions of $324.1 million were $66.8 million higher than the $257.4 million earned during 1985 which were $53.8 million higher than 1984's level of $203.6 million. These increases were primarily attributable to a variety of merchant banking activities.

Thus banks have been forced to develop many new asset and liability products intended to meet customers' needs while lessening their own vulnerability to unexpected rate changes.

In recent years, problem loans to developing countries have caused banks to seek more quality in further asset expansion. In the wholesale market, the highest-quality corporate borrowers in North America and Western Europe (those able to go *directly* to public markets) are overbanked. Their corporate treasurers can *select* among alternative financings and deals offered by competing banks and negotiating effectively on price and terms. To make matters even more unfavorable for the banks, corporations are reducing the numbers of banks they do business with, and the percentage of banks' corporate customers that borrow from them has declined from approximately 50 to 40 percent.

In light of this, banks face the dilemma of how to develop adequate returns on their assets while maintaining prudent quality in their loan portfolios.[13] They also have to obtain sizable fees from trading and noncredit services to supplement asset growth as important sources of revenues. In this realm, commercial banks must compete with generally more agile, experienced, and market-responsive investment banks while seeking to develop innovative financial products that will serve fee-generating customer requirements. The skills, traits, culture, infrastructure, and orientation that supported profitable growth by commercial banks in the decades before the 1980s are *not* what is required to compete in investment banking today.

VIII. Broad Implications

The managements of banks have been strongly challenged by the significant changes in their business environment, opportunities, problems, and sources of risk. Traditional distinctions among financial institutions have become blurred as their product lines have expanded. Financial markets that were once very localized are now more national or international in scope. Banking services are unbundled more often as the delivery functions are separated from service production.

Most banks[14] were not prepared to readily meet these challenges. Now, they are devoting themselves to strengthening their management practices and capabilities as well as modifying their business definitions, goals, strategies, and organizational cultures.

The Choices For Banks' Senior Management

Senior bankers face many important choices that will influence their banks' basic goals, strategies, and operating modes for years to come. Given the complexity of the external environment, and the rapidity of important choices to be made in a relatively short time, the decision-making task and responsibilities are enormous.

Strategic Marketing Issues

At the broadest possible strategic level, should a bank's senior management attempt to position the institution *now* for where it should be, say, ten years hence by taking a bold, giant step forward?

For example, Bankers Trust decided to become a global merchant bank. Wells Fargo decided to drop most international business, pull back sharply from national corporate customers, and focus principally on home-state California retail and commercial customers.

Or should the bank advance by incremental steps, feeling its way with caution and more certainty but probably forgoing possibilities for significantly differentiating itself from competition? Senior managements require unusual insight, strong conviction, courage, and board-of-director's support to move so boldly.

With the deregulation of the banking and related financial services industry, a shakeout or "rationalization" among participants began to develop a few years ago and has recently gathered momentum with new legislatively provided opportunities for selective acquisitions, mergers, and startups across state borders. This momentum is expected to accelerate in 1990–1991 when interstate banking becomes a nationwide phenomenon. Some participants will buy others, some will merge, and some will be forced out of business by more able competitors. For individual participants, the industry shakeout brings great opportunities as well as threats and uncertainties, depending on the bank's goals, competitive strength, capital resources, market price (in relation to its book value and earnings), asset size, shareholders' objectives, and so forth. Strategically, each bank's management has to size up its survival prospects and pursue a strategy to position the institution to the best advantage.

For example, two large commercial banks have recently carried out these decisive strategic retrenchments.

1. Chemical Bank, London. In late 1987, it announced a 20 percent staff cut worldwide and selective pullbacks from international business, including the Eurobond markets. Instead, Chemical will emphasize its strengths in treasury services, foreign exchange, corporate finance, leasing, and mortgages.
2. First Interstate Bank Ltd. It recently reduced outstanding loans to major domestic companies from $10 billion to $2 billion and withdrew from fixed-rate Eurobond offerings and government securities trading.

An important industry development in the mid-to-late 1980s has been the expansion of "superregional" banks, each resulting from mergers among sizable regional banks. Table 7 lists the top superregionals as of June 30, 1987.

Table 7. Major Superregional Banks.

Bank	States	Assets ($ billions)
First Interstate	Calif., Ariz., Wash., Nev., Ore.	$51.8
Wells Farge	Calif.	44.7
PNC Financial	Pa., Ky., Ind., Ohio	32.7
Bank of Boston	Mass., Conn., Maine, R.I.	30.5
First Bank System	Minn., N.D., S.D., Mont., Wash., Wis.	28.4
First Fidelity Bankcorporation	N.J., Pa.	27.1
Bank of New England	Mass., Conn., Maine, R.I.	27.0
Sun Trust Banks	Fla., Ga.	25.6
NCNB Corp.	N.C., S.C., Ga., Fla., Md., Va.	24.6
First Union	N.C., S.C., Ga., Fla.	24.5
Shawmut National	Conn., Mass., R.I.	24.5
Fleet Financial	N.Y., R.I., Maine	24.4
NBD Corporation	Mich., Ill., Ind.	22.6
Banc One	Ohio, Ind., Ky., Mich., Wis.	22.2
Norwest Corp.	Minn., Iowa, Neb., Wis.	20.3
First Wachovia	N.A., Ga.	18.8

Source: *Wall Street Journal.*

Senior managements must also evaluate the need to compete in the *commodity-like* aspects of the banking business with commoditylike products. Thin-spread lending is the most important example. If a bank cannot earn satisfactory profits in certain market segments or geographic areas or from certain products that are undifferentiated from competitive offerings, management must determine whether it can reduce operating costs, credit losses, and cost of funds drastically to enhance profit margins. Otherwise, should it continue to offer these products?

Similarly, banks have to define their target customers and segments carefully. Each bank must reexamine its most attractive competitive possibilities and the associated profitability potential in the light of new, more intense competition, the variety of customer needs and behavior, and the varying economics and customer-serving capabilities of competitive institutions. For example, the Bank of California has decided to concentrate on banking services for wealthy persons and lending to middle-market companies. And State Street Bank has reduced the number of its branches from 39 to 6 and deemphasized banking in favor of financial data processing.

In resolving these and similar dilemmas, bank managements must determine the costs associated with given products, customers, market segments, and geographic areas. They have to weigh the potential cost to the institution of declining to offer clients the traditional commercial banking services it no longer earns sufficient returns on. Would the bank lose existing customers and business if it were to offer less than full services? What would be the overall bottom-line effect of narrowing the bank's product, customer, or geographic spread and focusing only on what it considered the most promising business?

Consider the recent reformulation of service goals at Continental Illinois.

Under its new management, the Continental Illinois Corp. will be stripped of most of its traditional commercial banking activities and will concentrate on investment banking activities. Thomas Theobald, chairman of the bank holding company, announced yesterday.

Theobald, the 50-year-old former vice chairman of Citicorp, who joined Continental in August, said the company would sell all its small Chicago-area banks, most of which had been acquired within the past year. And, like at least two leading investment banking firms, Continental will pull out of the unprofitable municipal securities business, he said.

Instead, Continental will focus on generating loans and selling them to such investors as smaller banks, savings institutions and pension funds.

Continental also will provide sophisticated money management services intended to enable borrowers, lenders and investors to hedge against swings in interest rates and exchange rates.

Theobald also said that the company and its primary subsidiary, the Continental Illinois National Bank and Trust Co., would continue to provide commercial banking services for very wealthy individuals.

"What we're trying to do is concentrate on the current needs of about 1,000 corporate relationships across America," he said in a telephone interview.

"We don't need new customers. We have to deliver a more modern product line," he added.

Because of the global character of such business, Continental will expand some of its foreign offices—probably in cities such as London and Tokyo—but will sell its offices in Brussels, Madrid, Seoul, South Korea, and Taipei, Taiwan, which are not international financial centers.[15]

Wells Fargo Bank of California offers a successful role model as an institution that has decisively and vigorously prepared itself for the new era in banking. Attesting to its success is the annual gain in its share price: up 34 percent in 1985 and up 60 percent in 1986. The bank's 1986 annual report notes

Wells Fargo embarked several years ago on a corporate strategy of reorganizing and rationalizing its operations. Strategic goals were:

- Concentrating our resources on lines of business in which we have the experience and competitive strength to excel and profit.
- Building our market presence and reputation as a major regional banking company serving California and the West.
- Focusing nationally on selected banking activities.
- Responding to our customers' needs for financial services in a timely and efficient manner.
- Controlling costs in all of our business.
- Maintaining a strong balance sheet in order to respond quickly and effectively to business opportunities.
- Building value for our shareholders.

An associated strategic question is: How far and by what means should a bank *depart* from its traditional forms and ideas of commercial banking in search of greater profitability?

A prominent example is a bank that deliberately constrains or decreases its traditional commercial lending activities in favor of potentially more profitable but also riskier[16] trading, capital markets, and other "investment banking" activities. Security Pacific, for instance, spent $300 million between 1982 and 1988 to expand into investment banking.

In the past few years, banks have taken the following steps to enhance profitability by reorienting activities:

1. Banks have become more dependent on trading for their own accounts to generate profits. In 1987, Security Pacific, for example, sold $250 billion of other companies' debt through its global securities network based in London and a New York trading operation.
2. Many banks are now selling down a portion of their risk asset portfolios to realize the following benefits: lower the costs of carrying loans; reduce the amount of booked assets with thin spreads; earn fees for distributing clients' debt instruments; strengthen the bank's capital–asset ratios; and retain the ability to service the borrowing needs of valued, highly rated clients. Loan sales by major U.S. banks grew from zero in 1982 to more than $50 billion in 1986.[17]
3. Market volumes have increased enormously, which largely reflects the introduction of new instruments such as financial futures, traded options, Eurobonds, note issuance facilities, currency and interest rate swaps, and forward rate agreements. The total volume of interest rate and currency swaps increased from approximately $10 million in 1981 to $100 billion in 1985.

In search of new customers and means of making money, a bank may choose to diversify into capital market and trading activities, new geographic markets, or new countries, or it may choose to go "down-market." Management must then assess how much additional institutional competence will be required to limit risks and earn profits when operating with relatively unfamiliar markets, customers, and transactions. Efforts to develop new business can go awry, as the following examples indicate:

- In 1985, Bank of America lost $95 million with allegedly fraudulant mortgage-backed securities. The bank had no previous experience in acting as escrow agent and trustee for pools of mortgage loans. Therefore, it did not adequately assess the nature and extent of the associated risks.
- In mid-1987, the Morgan Bank's London office reportedly lost heavily on a $500 million perpetual floating rate note issue that it underwrote. Estimates of Morgan's Euro losses ranged from $20 million to $80 million before taxes.
- During the October 1987 stock market crash, First Options of Chicago, Inc., acquired approximately one year earlier by Continental Illinois Corp., reportedly lost $90 million.

Where can a bank obtain skilled traders, dealers, and risk managers?[18] Who will determine risk limits and new politics and strategies to contain risks? How will the new-look financial services and activities *fit* into the existing bank culture, compensation schemes, and structure? How will the bank convince prospective customers that it has the needed capabilities? Figure 2 shows how Continental Illinois has advertised its capital-generating capabilities.

Figure 2. Advertisement for Continental Bank.

What happens if your company doesn't expand wisely?

If your company doesn't have ready access to capital, you could run into trouble as you expand.

That's why Continental Illinois has committed over 200 banking professionals worldwide to matching companies like yours with people who have capital to offer.

In fact, last year we closed over three times as many capital-generating deals as we did the year before.

Why are so many companies now working with Continental Illinois? Probably because we're ready to be very creative in finding the right way to raise cash for each organization.

We'll look at private placement of debt or equity and everything in between, mergers, acquisitions and divestitures, bond issues, syndicated loans, receivables financing, leveraged leasing, and asset swaps.

And we're willing to use any combination of these options to get you the capital you need, when you need it, on terms that agree with your business.

So if your company has an opportunity to expand, call Continental Illinois at 1-312-828-6772.

We'll help keep a good thing from blowing up in your face.

Continental Illinois
We make money work.

Continental Illinois National Bank and Trust Company of Chicago

Table 8. Participation of Various Banking Institutions in Selected National Securities Markets, 1986.

	London GBDᵃ	London SEᵇ	New York GBD	New York SE	Tokyo GBD	Tokyo SE
Citicorp	x	x	x	x	x	x
BankAmerica			x	x	x	
Chase Manhattan	x	x	x	x	x	
Bankers Trust	x		x		x	
Security Trust	x	x		x	x	
Morgan Guaranty	x		x		x	
Merrill Lynch	x	x	x	x	x	x
Salomon Brothers	x		x	x	x	
Morgan Stanley	x		x	x	x	x
Goldman Sachs	x		x	x	x	x
American Express	x	x	x	x		
Barclays Bank	x	x			x	
National Westminster	x	x			x	
Midland Bank	x	x	x			
Klienwort Benson	x	x	x			
Mercury Int. Group	x	x		x	x	x
Paribas		x			x	
Deutsche Bank	x	x		x		
UBS	x	x		x		
Swiss Bank Corp				x		
Credit Suisse	x	x			x	
Nomura		x		x	x	x
Daiwa				x	x	x
Nikko				x	x	x

a. GBD = Government Bond Center.
b. SE = Member of Stock Exchange.
Note: Many banks are represented through part-owned subsidiaries. Most U.S. banks are members of the New York Stock Exchange through limited service discount broking subsidiaries.
Source: *Financial Times*.

To ensure prudent management of the bank's overall risk–return parameters, these considerations must be dealt with before the bank ventures too far into new areas. But the world will not stand still while banks learn their way in the new-look financial arena. In fact, one half of all debt raised in the United States is done through securities, and some estimates place this as high as 80 percent by the year 2000.

Table 8 shows how commercial banks of various nationalities are pushing to develop global capability in the securities markets. In general, the pattern has been to acquire status as stockbrokers in London, primary bond dealers in New York, and licensed securities dealers in Tokyo.

J.P. Morgan is currently the leader among U.S. commercial banks in making the transition to investment banking. As of late 1987, net loans accounted for less than 50 percent of Morgan's balance sheet. In the past four years, investment securities increased from 10 to 18 percent of total assets, and trading account assets doubled. New interest income now provides one half of total income. Noninterest income from corporate finance fees and trading account activity accounts for one half of total income.

Similarly, Bankers Trust Company shed its retail banking and credit card operations business in the late 1970s and forced itself through a dramatic cultural change, skill reorientation, and new organizational structure to emerge with a deal-maker orientation and capability. Between 1982 and 1985, Bankers Trust's fees and commissions increased from $126 million to $257 million and now account for an increasingly important part of the bank's total income.

Market-Responsive Management Practices

Beyond these important strategic choices, bank leaders must also bring about important changes in their institutions' management style, culture, and systems. There are no readily available models for these changes. Great courage, creativity, and attention are required to determine the best possible course and the methods for its pursuit.

We believe the most desirable changes for commercial banks incorporate the following:

- The entire officer corps must be energized and trained to be market focused, customer oriented, forward looking, more competitive in spirit, task oriented, creative, willing to take more personal accountability, act more decisively, and adopt a bottom-line orientation. Consider this example.

  Wells Fargo Bank experimented successfully in 1987 with being "marketing oriented." It adopted the philosophy that "the customer is always right" and that "very few customers are going to rob the bank with adjustments." Hence, when a customer comes into a branch with a problem or complaint, the tellers and customer service representatives are authorized to settle the problem on the spot. During the six-month experiment, the bank's branch employees have given $300,000 in on-the-spot adjustments, and customer and employee goodwill have gained.[10]

- Banks must organize more around customers' needs and activities.
- Significant improvements in banks' cost accounting and management information systems are needed as bases for strategic and tactical decisions as well as sound financial transactions. They are also needed to monitor and guide the composition of the bank's loan portfolio.
- Leadership at the top must be visionary, strong, decisive, strategically oriented, and able to provide subordinates with models of desirable behavior.
- The organization must behave strategically at all levels, setting goals for actions and using data for analysis of markets and resource choices, developing priorities, and specifying implementation processes for goal fulfillment.

Table 9. Percentage of Noninterest Expense to Pre-Tax Earnings, 1981–1986.

	1981	1982	1983	1984	1985	1986
J.P. Morgan	0.82	0.83	0.76	0.73	0.81	0.84
Top fifteen banks	2.28	2.72	2.29	2.59	2.91	3.09

Source: Montgomery Securities, *The Quarterly Bank Monitor*, February 27, 1987.

- The bank should have performance standards for individuals and business units as well as impartial performance reviews and direct rewards for performance. This is part of a systems approach for implementing bank strategies throughout the organization and guiding officers to be more individually responsible and accountable.
- A bank must be able to liquify and reposition its asset portfolio if the assets do not meet its current risk return or strategy criteria. The requisites for meeting this standard are appropriate management information systems, leadership commitment, trading skills, and distribution capability.
- A bank must trim its non-interest expenses in order to compete strongly in terms of economics, strategic flexibility, and adequate return on capital. Lasting cost reductions can be effected with slimmed-down management structures, closure of unprofitable facilities, tighter control of expenses, and greater reliance on computer technology.

  For example, in late 1987 Mellon Bank announced plans to cut approximately 2,000 positions and froze wages. Similarly, Chemical Bank began a reorganization to eliminate 10 percent of its work force, closing 25 New York branches and 16 foreign representative offices.

Exemplifying the potential for effective control of non-interest expense in a bank's overall profitability equation is J.P. Morgan. The bank's percentage of non-interest expense to pre-tax earnings is plotted in Table 9 for the period 1981–1986, compared with a weighted average for the top 15 United States banks.

Marketing Issues for Management

Following on the principal strategic and managerial concerns, what are the important marketing challenges and issues that face commercial banks today? In the broadest sense, they relate to *significantly modifying* the value systems and management practices of most institutions to become (1) more *externally* focused and (2) more ready to deliver competitive value in the marketplace.

Promulgating more *externally focused* values and management practices is intended to provide for

- More attention to customers
- More alertness to competitors and closer analysis of their behavior
- An institutional willingness and ability to be more responsive to the requirements of customers and thrusts of competitors

To deliver *competitive value to the marketplace,* banks must develop and introduce new products and services; sell them more aggressively and effectively; and offer better delivery systems, more competitive pricing, and enhanced capabilities to meet customers' needs and solve their problems. This goes far beyond the traditional bank practice of providing broad, generic product lines and expecting customers to select what they want.

The foregoing guidelines for modifying a bank's value systems and management practices translates into a series of important and highly challenging questions and issues for each institution. As we observe the current commercial banking scene and look ahead to the probable marketplace preoccupations of bank management, the following major issues and questions will be likely to predominate:

1. Where are we today in the marketplace?
   a. How do our customers and prospects view us given the many changes in customers' needs and behaviors, the new competitors in the marketplace, and the new forms of competition? This question must be answered for a bank's traditional business lines and for each new line of business.
   b. What is our market share and market position vis-à-vis available business and important competitors?
   c. Where are we now making money, and where are we not making money? Presumably, 20 percent of the customers provide 80 percent of the profit (the 20-80 rule) in most market segments, lines of business, and business units. Strategic decisions about what business our institution should be in and where and how to allocate resources for the future requires *facts* about the economic implications of these choices.
   d. How does our institution compare with competition? Do we and our competitors have any "natural" advantages in strength of reputation and relationships with customers when we operate as indigenous institutions competing with "foreign" institutions? What are our overall competitive strengths and vulnerabilities in products, delivery systems, relationships, capital strength, and so on?
2. What do our customers and prospects need, want, and value in financial services? In seeking to answer this question, the bank must define customers and identify meaningful market segments.[20]
3. Who should our target market be? In identifying its customer base, the bank should consider both currently available business and future trends in customer needs and competitive offerings.
4. What should we choose to provide as "value" to targeted customers, and what specialized marketing approaches should we take to compete successfully for desired business? The answer to this critically important question will determine how the bank should *position* itself in the minds of its target customers and how it might *distinguish* itself from other institutions in products, delivery systems, relationships, service orientation, pricing, reliability, and so on.
5. How should we *implement* our chosen strategy? What new products should be developed? What will the roles of sales and relationship managers be? How important will it be for them to know customers and how to sell the bank's products and capabilities? How will the bank maintain a clear focus on customers to ensure that over time it will be fully responsive to their needs and values?

IX. Conclusion

Institutions that succeed in going forward will have to overcome their negative qualities that are legacies from the past (high overhead, bureaucratic management style, and so forth) and act appropriately competitive in the new marketplace. Both of these performances require

1. Selecting the right course of action based on market facts, realistic self-analysis, and reasonably correct prognostication about the future
2. Implementing the chosen paths with careful yet flexible management approaches that combine a customer-focused outward vision and internal devotion to delivering superior value to the target market

Banks that are too far behind in market position and management capabilities or whose economics are too far out of line with today's demands will not endure. Banks that are decently positioned and possess alert management have a fighting chance to endure—possibly in a merger with other financial institutions or banks whose *combined* muscle, market position, and reconstituted economics ensure competitiveness. Banks that are relatively well positioned in the marketplace and that for years have been adroitly managed for the deregulated era will be the winners, provided they do not grow too quickly through horizontal diversification and lose control of their economics and abilities to deliver superior value to designated customers.

X. Notes

1. Wholesale generally refers to clients that are corporations, banking institutions, and governments.
2. Any competitor from *another* banking jurisdiction, for example, from another state or country.
3. Thomas Rideout, "First the Bad News, Now the Good News," *ABA Banking Journal*, October 1987.
4. For example, in 1986–1987, expansion-minded Security Pacific Bank invested $1.7 billion to acquire companies that included five out-of-state banks.
5. In mid-1987, U.S. commercial banks' exposure to the five biggest Latin American debtor nations totaled $72 billion.
6. Lowell Bryan, "The Credit Bomb in Our Financial System," *McKinsey Quarterly*, winter 1987.
7. For example, in 1983, Morgan Guaranty *shrank* holding company assets by 1 percent and permitted only 5 percent growth in 1984.
8. For example, in September 1987, Citicorp raised $1.2 billion in a new equity issue, Manufacturers Hanover raised $276 million, and Bankers Trust raised $250 million.
9. For example, in late 1987, Japanese investors agreed to purchase $350 million in Bank of America notes and preferred stock, with both issues convertible into the Bank's common shares.
10. J. Richard Fredericks, "Darwinian Banking—Chapter Two," June 1987, Montgomery Securities Institutional Research.

11. For example, the Bank of America, with $141 million pretax income from currency trading in 1986, reported $26 million in unreconciled trading accounts in 1987, reflecting the huge volume of such transactions. In November 1987, Den Norske Creditbank, Norway's largest commercial bank, suffered a $92.5 million unrealized portfolio loss through trading in stocks and equity-linked instruments in foreign exchange that exceeded the limits set by management.

12. Several of these challenges are heightened in *international* banking, where virtually all international liabilities are interest bearing, and the proportion of interest-rate-sensitive liabilities in relation to total liabilities tends to be higher than the proportion of domestic liabilities. (The latter reflects the heavy proportion of interbank liabilities, the comparatively short-term nature of nonbank deposits, and the widespread use of variable interest-rate clauses in longer-term funding.) These two characteristics have a major bearing on the profitability of international business. Since average funding costs tend to move in close synchrony with marginal costs, the pricing of international loans is set on a "marginal" basis to minimize the impact of fluctuations in interest-rate levels on bank profitability. Concurrently, banks try to hold at a satisfactory level the differential between interest-rate-sensitive liabilities and assets.

    A recent example is First Bank Systems, the 16th largest U.S. bank holding company. It had been an aggressive participant in recent years' bond markets. But in 1987, it lost *$700 million* on its bond portfolio.

13. In recent years, when the difference between a BBB and an AAA credit in fixed-rate bond yields was approximately 100 basis points, the difference in yield between two such credits for a floating-rate bank loan was only 25 basis points. See Bryan, "The Credit Bomb in Our Financial System."

14. The few exceptions are banks with highly developed managerial systems that enable them to be adaptable, flexible, forward-looking, and competitive.

15. *New York Times*, October 29, 1987.

16. The "riskiness" of foreign exchange today is reflected in the variability of related quarter-to-quarter earnings experienced recently by major U.S. banks.

Money Center Banks' Foreign Exchange Profits.

	Third Quarter 1987 ($ millions)	Change From Second Quarter (percent)
BankAmerica	$24.0	−42.9
Bankers Trust	71.3	−29.5
Chase Manhattan	51.7	−14.9
Chemical New York	28.4	−23.2
Citicorp	79.0	−38.8
Continental Illinois	4.9	−40.2
First Chicago	12.3	−55.0
Irving Trust	8.6	−33.8
Manufacturers Hanover	7.1	−65.4
J.P. Morgan	26.4	−50.8
Average	$31.4	−36.3

17. Bryan, "The Credit Bomb in Our Financial System."

18. Even in *familiar* trading activities, banks encounter unexpected and difficult operational problems. In 1987, Irving Trust Co., a major foreign exchange trader since the 1920s, had to take a "sabatical" from interbank dealing because 9 of the bank's dealers were recruited in a package deal by E.F. Hutton.
19. Robert Metzger, "Creating a Marketing Culture at Your Bank," *Bankers Monthly*, August 1987.
20. Harris Bankcorp in 1984 conducted focus group research that encompassed 6 major market segments and 80 business customers to learn how they thought and made decisions about banking services. Later, the bank's management formulated as its mission statement, "We want to be the most customer-responsive, relationship-oriented provider of financial services to those markets where we choose to compete."

2

The Savings and Loan Industry

Richard W. Nelson
Vice President and Chief Economist,
Federal Home Loan Bank of San Francisco

Most savings and loan associations (S&Ls) are specialized financial institutions that serve the markets for real estate finance and insured savings. However, participation in the industry is not determined by the functional business performed but by organization under a charter as a savings and loan association. Savings and loan charters have been liberalized to permit associations to engage in various financial businesses, with some S&Ls expanding beyond the markets for real estate finance and insured savings. Further, some savings and loan associations are owned by nonfinancial firms.

Today, the S&L industry faces several serious challenges that will likely dominate management's attention. In this chapter, we discuss these marketing and managerial challenges in the context of the industry's origins, its current structure, and the financial crisis that has shaped these issues.

I. Origins and Early Development

Although their charters restrict the activities they may engage in, S&Ls have emerged as specialized institutions for largely economic rather than regulatory reasons. The first S&L was organized in 1831, following closely the establishment of commercial banks in the late 1700s. Early S&Ls were cooperative associations in which individuals pooled their savings to finance the construction of their own homes. These associations expired after each member of the association was able to build a house. As a result, they were conceived in highly specialized terms.

Within this context, a specialized charter or bylaws made economic sense as a method of protecting the interests of the members of the cooperative.

S&Ls soon became self-perpetuating institutions that accepted funds from savers whether or not they desired to finance their own housing. Demand for housing and financial savings increased rapidly with the development of towns and cities in the United States. The S&Ls' continued specialization in these lines of business was consistent with their early environment.

As specialized institutions, S&Ls were not affected by early federal banking legislation. The National Banking Act of 1863 provided for federal charters for commercial banks, introduced the federal government in bank supervision, and established a national currency backed by federal government securities. Congress was unconcerned about S&Ls because they had not been involved in note issuance, as the commercial banks had been. In 1913, the Federal Reserve Act established the Federal Reserve System and further extended federal supervision of commercial banks. Again, congressional concern revolved around the currency system and its role in the banking and economic crises of the late 1800s and early 1900s. S&Ls were not involved.

The Great Depression had a serious effect on S&Ls and triggered the extension of the federal government into regulation of the industry. In 1932, the Federal Home Loan Bank System was created to provide a central credit facility for home financing institutions and federal charters for S&Ls. In 1934, only one year after the creation of the Federal Deposit Insurance Corporation (FDIC), the Federal Savings and Loan Insurance Corporation (FSLIC) was created to insure the deposits of S&Ls. In the years that followed, S&Ls came to be viewed as instruments of a national housing policy, along with the Federal National Mortgage Association (Fannie Mae), the Government National Mortgage Association (Ginnie Mae), and the Federal Home Loan Mortgage Corporation (Freddie Mac).

II. Markets and Competitors

Savings and loan associations held financial assets of $1.2 trillion as of yearend 1986[1] (see Table 2-1). In total financial assets, S&Ls ranked second among all types of financial intermediaries, behind commercial banks (with $2.6 trillion in assets), and ahead of life insurance companies (with $900 billion in assets). S&Ls hold about 15 percent of the total assets of all private financial intermediaries in the United States. This figure is the broadest measure of their market share since all financial assets are substitutes for one another to some extent. Broadly defined, the S&Ls' market share has been relatively stable in recent years, rising a little during the 1970s and falling slightly during the 1980s.

S&Ls remain highly specialized in mortgage finance, with 70 percent of their assets invested in mortgages and mortgage-backed securities. Although among the most specialized of all financial institutions in this country, S&Ls nevertheless face stiff competition in the mortgage markets from other, less specialized financial institutions.

Table 1. Total Financial Assets Held by Private Financial
Institutions in the United States, Yearend 1986 ($ billions).

Commercial banks	$2,581
Savings and loan associations	1,158
Life insurance companies	905
Private pension funds	635
State and local government employee retirement funds	470
Mutual funds	414
Finance companies	412
Other insurance companies	346
Money market mutual funds	292
Mutual savings banks	239
Credit unions	166
Security brokers and dealers	78
CMO issuers	65
Real estate investment trusts	8
Total	$7,769

Source: Board of Governors of the Federal Reserve System, Flow of Funds
accounts, financial assets and liabilities, yearend 1963–86.

About $670 billion of the S&Ls' $870 billion mortgage-related portfolio is
in home mortgages. S&Ls hold about 39 percent of the nation's home mortgages,
either directly or in the form of mortgage-backed securities, and are the largest
investors in this market[2] (see Table 2–2). The S&Ls' share of this market has
declined from around 50 percent in the mid-1970s but is only slightly below its
level of the early 1960s. The chief S&L competitors in this market are commercial
banks and mutual savings banks.

Growth of mortgage-backed and derivative securities has been the major development in the home mortgage market in recent years. These are capital market
instruments backed by mortgages or, for derivative securities, by mortgage-backed
securities. Most are issued by the government-sponsored agencies, Fannie Mae,
Ginnie Mae, and Freddie Mac, and are traded as commodities in national markets.
The growth of mortgage-related securities was driven by several factors, including
the desire to (1) broaden the market for mortgages, (2) increase their liquidity,
(3) reduce credit risk through a government guarantee, (4) separate and redistribute
the risks of holding mortgages, and (5) develop specialized financing vehicles for
portfolio investors.

S&Ls acquire mortgage-backed securities by swapping mortgages that they
originate with the federal mortgage agencies or investment banks and by purchas-
ing them on the open market. About 25 percent of the S&Ls' total home mortgage
portfolio was held in the form of mortgage-backed securities in 1986, up from
about 4 percent in 1979. The rapid growth of these instruments coincides with
and is related to rapid growth in reverse repurchase agreements, most of which

Table 2. S&Ls' Share of Selected Markets.

	1986 Mortgage Holdings ($ billions)		Market Share (percent)			
	Total Outstanding	Held by S&Ls	1986	1980	1970	1963
Home mortgages						
Excluding mortgage-backed securities	1,667.4	485.6	29.1	43.0	41.5	41.3
Including mortgage-backed securities	1,667.4	667.4	38.5	45.1	41.5	41.3
Multifamily residential mortgages	246.3	80.4	32.6	26.8	23.0	19.3
Commercial mortgages	554.0	119.5	21.6	17.7	13.4	12.9
Consumer credit	50.6	723.0	7.0	4.5	2.3	2.5
Other business credit	24.0	1,302.2	1.8	0	0	0
Small time and savings deposits	1,966.0	719.8	36.6	41.0	35.4	38.9
Including money market funds shares	(2,258.1)		(31.9)	0	0	0
Checkable deposits	637.8	40.3	6.3			

Sources: Board of Governors of the Federal Reserve System, Flow of Funds accounts, financial assets and liabilities, yearend 1963–1986; Federal Home Loan Bank Board, combined financial statements, FSLIC-insured institutions, 1986.

are secured by mortgage-backed securities and provide a significant source of financing for S&Ls. Individual S&Ls use their mortgage-backed securities in various ways. Some S&Ls use them as their principal source of investments; others as a method of converting mortgage holdings into more liquid investments with less credit risk.

Derivative mortgage securities represent further attempts to refine and extend the market for mortgages. Most are secured by mortgage-backed securities and divide the cash flows from these securities in ways that separate identifiable components of risk. Thus the risk of holding mortgages can be redistributed among investors, including S&Ls. Collateralized mortgage obligations (CMOs) for example, address the risk of early repayment of mortgages and translate cash flows into short-term tranches with relatively little prepayment risk and longer-term tranches with greater prepayment risk. Interest only and principal only strips (IOs and POs) separate ownership of interest payments and principal payments from mortgage-backed securities, redistributing both prepayment risk and reinvestment risk. Senior–subordinated structures have been developed to concentrate credit risk. As with mortgage-backed securities, S&Ls purchase those instruments on the open market as additions to their portfolios and use them to sell off risks in the loans that they originate.

S&Ls also are the largest holders of multifamily residential mortgages and have increased their share of this market significantly since the early 1960s. At yearend 1986, they held about 33 percent of this market, competing chiefly with commercial banks, insurance companies, and mutual savings banks. S&Ls have also increased their share of commercial mortgages to 22 percent but still rank third in this market behind commercial banks and life insurance companies.[3]

Although S&Ls remain major portfolio lenders in the mortgage markets, some of them have become more like mortgage bankers. These associations specialize in originating and servicing loans rather than holding loans as portfolio investments. Thus their market shares must be measured by originating and servicing volume rather than by portfolio holdings.

In the insured savings market, S&Ls compete with commercial banks, mutual savings banks, and credit unions. S&Ls' share of insured time and savings deposits is about 37 percent, making them the second largest supplier behind commercial banks. Money market mutual fund shares are very close substitutes. U.S. government securities and other financial assets sold in small denominations are also competitive instruments. S&Ls have a relatively minor penetration (6 percent) in the market for transactions deposits, which is still dominated by commercial banks.

S&Ls participate in many additional markets. They have become increasingly involved in real estate development. S&Ls began extending nonmortgage business loans in the 1980s but still have only a 2 percent share of this market.[4] The associations' share of consumer lending has increased significantly since the early 1970s but is still at only 7 percent. The volume of auto loans and credit card loans, which S&Ls began to offer during the 1980s, has grown particularly rapidly, and today makes up about 40 percent of their total consumer loan portfolio. S&Ls also make home improvement loans, education loans, and mobile home loans.

III. Industry Structure and Regulation

As of yearend 1986, there were about 3,132 S&Ls in the United States, operating from about 20,287 offices.[5] Office location determines the geographic market an S&L competes in for much of its business because convenience is so important to most retail customers in mortgage and deposit markets and because local expertise is important in underwriting most types of mortgage loans. Most S&Ls operate relatively few offices and thus compete in relatively narrow geographic markets.

Federal law does not restrict interstate branching by federally chartered S&Ls as it does by federally chartered commercial banks. Nonetheless, the Federal Home Loan Bank Board generally has restricted interstate branching by S&Ls in accord with standards applicable to commercial banks, and most S&Ls operated within state boundaries before 1980. Since then, most states have moved to regional or national branching for state-chartered S&Ls and commercial banks. Forty-three states had authorized some form of interstate expansion as of early 1988. Twenty of them permit acquisition of S&Ls within the state by companies that operate nationwide, and 23 limit acquisitions to companies operating in specified regional areas.

S&Ls vary considerably in size. At yearend 1986, 2,077 S&Ls—about two thirds of the institutions—had total assets ranging between $25 million and $250 million.[6] These are small institutions; they operate from few offices and are oriented toward local markets. There are 385 even smaller associations with assets under $25 million. At the upper end of the spectrum are 539 institutions with assets ranging from $250 million to $1 billion and 219 associations with assets exceeding $1 billion. Those with the most assets generally operate extensive branch networks and serve broad geographic areas.

About 60 percent of S&Ls are mutual organizations, owned by their depositors. Mutual organizations span the entire asset-size range but are more heavily represented among the smaller institutions. Many of the stockholder-owned institutions are owned by holding companies. Unitary S&L holding companies (companies that own only one S&L) are unrestricted in their activities, but multiple S&L holding companies are confined by law and regulation to a specified range of activities. S&L holding companies range from pure holding companies owning one or more associations and having no independent operations to large industrial firms like Weyerhaeuser and Ford Motor. Before the 1980s, commercial bank holding companies were not permitted to own S&Ls, but since then, they have begun acquiring the associations.[7]

S&Ls are organized under charters from either the federal government or 45 of the 50 states. Slightly over one half of the associations hold federal charters, and their powers are determined by federal law. They are subject to regulation by the Federal Home Loan Bank Board and must be insured by FSLIC. The greatest concentrations of state-chartered S&Ls are found in Texas, California, Ohio, New Jersey, Illinois, and Pennsylvania. The powers of state-chartered associations are determined by the varying laws of those states. All but about 300 relatively small, state-chartered associations have chosen to be insured by the FSLIC and are subject to its regulations as well as those of the state banking agencies.

Before 1980, the S&L charter was generally quite limited, precluding most consumer and business lending or the offering of demand accounts. However, some states, like Texas, gave S&Ls broad powers to invest in real estate. Landmark federal legislation in 1980 (the Depository Institutions Deregulation and Monetary Control Act) and 1982 (the Garn-St Germain Act) liberalized the federal charter significantly, adding the powers to engage in consumer and business lending and to offer demand deposits.

Most states extended these powers to the associations they charter. Some states, particularly Arizona, California, Florida, Louisiana, Mississippi, North Carolina, Ohio, and Texas, went considerably further than federal law by giving S&Ls broad authority to engage in practically any business through service corporations. More restrictive FSLIC regulations limit the ability of state-chartered associations to exploit these broad powers, and federal tax law continues to provide lower taxes for S&Ls that specialize in holding housing-related loans or investments.[8]

IV. Crisis: 1980–1982

Savings and loan associations came under extraordinary financial pressure between 1980 and 1982 as interest rates rose to unprecedented levels. The aggregate net income of S&Ls began to fall in 1980 and turned negative in 1981 and 1982, with the industry reporting losses of more than $4 billion in each year. The cumulative losses during those two years alone represented 28 percent of the industry's capital as of yearend 1980. Tangible capital (valued at book) fell from 5.8 percent of total assets at the end of 1979 to 0.8 percent at the end of 1982. At the peak of the interest rate cycle, the market value of the assets of almost all S&Ls fell below the market value of their liabilities, thereby precipitating economic insolvencies.

Many associations did not survive the crisis. The number of S&Ls had been declining since the mid-1960s, but the decline accelerated after 1980. By the end of 1984, the number of S&Ls had decreased by an additional 20 percent.[9]

The associations' vulnerability to crisis stemmed from traditional industry practices. In the 1950s and 1960s, most S&Ls simply funded long-term, fixed-rate mortgage loans with savings deposits. The long-term, fixed-rate, self-amortizing loan had become established as the industry standard during the Great Depression and was popular with customers.[10] Adjustable-rate mortgages were not authorized for federally chartered S&Ls until 1979. Though the risks of holding a portfolio of fixed-rate mortgages were not unnoticed, they were generally discounted in relation to the low interest rates that had prevailed in the 1930s, 1940s, andd 1950s, the formative years for most S&L executives.

Rates paid on deposits were subject to regulatory ceilings, but ceiling rates could not guarantee both low-cost deposits and the availability of deposits in the face of higher market rates.[11] By the late 1970s, there were large outflows (disintermediation) from commercial banks, S&Ls, and mutual savings banks into U.S. Treasury securities and money market mutual funds. The initial reaction of the regulators was to authorize new market rate accounts, beginning with the six-month certificate in 1978. The creation and sale of this and subsequent newly authorized accounts posed tremendous marketing challenges during the period.

Interest rate ceilings were phased out between 1980 and 1986, and the money market deposit account was created in 1982. These regulatory developments permitted a sharp rise in rates paid by S&Ls through 1982 but did not cause the increase in the cost of funds. In the face of higher market rates, disintermediation would have been extensive without degradation, and the costs of capital market funds, if available, might have exceeded those of the deregulated deposit instruments.

V. Relief and a Second Crisis

Interest rates declined substantially in late 1982, relieving the pressures on margins and raising the market value of S&Ls' assets. Net income turned positive in 1983 and increased substantially through 1985. But these increases came with greater volume. Industry profitability never returned to pre-1980 levels. Further, the capital positions of most associations were greatly weakened.

The problem of rebuilding financial strength and restructuring portfolios was probably manageable for most S&Ls in 1983 and 1984. Unfortunately, many associations expanded aggressively. Many of their new investments, particularly in real estate development, were highly risky and ill-fated to begin with. Regional economic crises resulting from the plunge in oil and agricultural prices in 1984 and 1985 exacerbated serious credit problems and helped precipitate another crisis in the second half of the 1980s. Reflecting this crisis, the industry's aggregate net income dropped sharply in 1986 and became a large loss in 1987.

The second crisis, unlike the first, affected only part of the industry. Most S&Ls remained profitable, often achieving record earnings and making significant strides in restructuring operations to reduce risk. But by March 31, 1987, nearly 20 percent of S&Ls had negative tangible net worth.[12] Most of the industry was healthy, but some of it was unhealthy. Instead of failing, most of the unhealthy associations were permitted to continue operating under the protection of federal deposit insurance.[13]

VI. Managerial and Marketing Challenges Ahead

The crises of the 1980s have raised major issues for the S&L industry. These include the viability of the traditional thrift strategy and the federal deposit insurance system S&Ls have depended on. Deregulation has introduced opportunities for both geographic and product diversification as well as for redesign of deposit products. The environment is changing, and significant managerial and marketing challenges lie ahead.

The situation confronting S&Ls varies considerably from institution to institution. Many associations continue to labor under problems of the past. They must work out problem credits, replace assets booked at lower interest rates with higher-yielding assets, and raise new equity capital. Associations also face longer-term issues concerning the appropriate tradeoff between profitability and risk, including the appropriate amount of equity, the extent of interest rate risk desirable, and the extent to which they should diversify their portfolios against possible credit risks.

Interest rate risk can be reduced through hedging operations (forward and future contracts, swaps, caps, and so on) with little impact on customer relationships. Alternatively, S&L management can restructure in fundamental ways that affect customers and, therefore, depend on successful marketing efforts.

For instance, many S&Ls have shifted their portfolios toward adjustable-rate mortgages. Some have expanded consumer and business lending activity, which generally involves shorter maturities. On the other side of the balance sheet, deposit structure could be lengthened, or greater use could be made of longer-term, wholesale sources of funds such as Federal Home Loan Bank advances and mortgage-backed bonds instead of traditional retail sources of funds.

Experience has shown that S&Ls can successfully market adjustable-rate mortgage loans. At S&Ls nationwide, these loans averaged about 54 percent in 1987. It was even higher in California, where S&Ls have had greater experience with adjustables and have undertaken particularly aggressive marketing strategies.

However, consumers have apparently taken to adjustables somewhat reluctantly and only where they offer significant interest rate savings over more traditional fixed-rate loans. The popularity of adjustables in 1987 is due in part to the unusually steep yield curve, which raised considerably the relative cost of fixed-rate mortgages. With the development of mortgage-backed securities, pricing of adjustable- and fixed-rate loans is determined in a national market. The implication is that individual institutions have little control over the differential between adjustables and fixed-rate loans. Thus institutions seeking to reduce interest rate risk through a strategy dependent on adjustable-rate lending may find it difficult to make such loans in an unfavorable interest rate environment. At that point, the institution may have to choose between hedging and selling fixed-rate loans to achieve interest-rate sensitivity targets.

Current adjustable-rate mortgages are tied to several indices. Among them are various U.S. Treasury bill rates and the Cost of Funds Index for S&Ls in the 11th Federal Home Loan Bank district, published by the Federal Home Loan Bank of San Francisco. Most adjustable-rate mortgages have both annual and lifetime caps that prevent the interest rate from adjusting completely to increases in market rates. As structured to date, these instruments still leave S&Ls exposed to considerable interest rate risk. Substantial increases in mortgage payments also could precipitate defaults if the borrower was unable to bear the risk. Thus it seems likely that S&Ls will continue to experiment with both the pricing and design of new mortgage instruments.

Branch strategy is another area posing major marketing challenges to S&L executives. Office expansion occurred very rapidly in the 1960s for commercial banks and S&Ls, largely reflecting economic and population growth as well as depositers' growing demand for convenience. But during the 1960s and 1970s, office expansion was encouraged by ceilings on interest rates that led S&Ls and other depository institutions to reward customers by offering (unregulated) convenience rather than (regulated) interest payments. Identifying the real demand for convenience and restructuring existing branch networks within efficient marketing strategies are major challenges. The task is complicated by the move toward interstate branching. Some commercial banks and S&Ls have embarked on an aggressive nationwide branch strategy and hope to gain advantages from cost economies or customer demand for nationwide access to services.

Changing technology, particularly in computers and telecommunications, presents further challenges to S&Ls. Automated teller machines (ATMs) are now part of most associations' retail strategies. Commercial banks, S&Ls, and money market mutual funds use toll-free 800 numbers to raise deposits by telephone. Home banking is being used experimentally although still at minimum levels. New ways of delivering deposits and loans will likely become available with further technological development. The successfully competitive institutions will use new technology to provide conveniences that customers desire at the lowest cost.

The demise of regulatory ceilings on deposit interest rates offers extensive opportunities for redesign and repricing of deposit instruments. It was largely regulation that imposed on the industry the deposit instruments introduced during the

1970s and early 1980s, including six-month certificates, small-saver certificates, retail repurchase agreements, and money market deposit accounts. Much effort went into structuring and marketing these instruments, but they were not tested relative to instruments that were precluded by regulation. The potential for significant distortions of demand is evident from the massive shifts from six-month certificates to money market deposit accounts after the latter were authorized in December 1981. Now that interest rate ceilings are gone, several innovations have been developed, including accounts tied to stock market indices. Pricing of savings accounts relative to money market deposit accounts is also at issue.

Penetrating the markets for consumer lending and business finance also poses challenges. In these highly competitive markets, customer relationships are very important. Underwriting consumer and business credit requires an expertise different from real estate lending. Thus successful expansion in these areas requires long-term strategies and considerable investment in human resources.

The need to recapitalize FSLIC presents particular difficulties for S&L executives. Depositer confidence in the FSLIC has remained strong but depends ultimately on the U.S. government's willingness to resolve the problem of insolvent S&Ls. Further, many S&Ls have had to pay higher interest rates than have non–S&L competitors.

To date, remedies have included imposing a special deposit insurance assessment on S&Ls. If continued, this assessment would likely erode the associations' competitive positions or weaken their ability to raise new capital. Some associations have reacted to this by converting to charters as commercial banks or federal savings banks that may be insured by the FDIC rather than FSLIC. A one-year moratorium on these conversions imposed by the Competitive Equality Banking Act has only postponed this problem.

Ultimately, solutions to the FSLIC problem will require infusions of public funds. Also possible, however, are merger of the FDIC and FSLIC, changes within the Federal Home Loan Bank System, and additional assessments on the industry. All of these developments would signficantly affect S&Ls.

S&L executives appear destined to operate in a dynamic environment during the 1990s. Probably no single strategy is appropriate for all associations, and individual S&Ls will face much uncertainty about which is best. Thus individual institutions are likely to take different paths and will have to devise managerial and marketing strategies appropriate to their own situations.

VII. Notes

1. Data are from the Federal Reserve System, Flow of Funds accounts, yearend 1986. These data exclude assets at offices outside the United States. Assets in foreign offices are small for S&Ls but significant for commercial banks. The Flow of Funds data also exclude nonfinancial assets and financial assets held within the same sector as the issuer.
2. As discussed later, individual S&Ls compete in local geographic markets where market shares may differ from the nationwide shares discussed here.

3. All these data pertain only to the S&Ls themselves and exclude assets held by non-S&L subsidiaries of S&L holding companies. They also fail to consolidate fully the assets held by subsidiaries of the S&Ls. In both cases, the effect is to understate market shares.
4. Included here are business loans not elsewhere classified reported by commercial banks, nonfinanical commercial paper, and finance company loans. Including corporate bonds, which are clearly a substitute source of financing, would lower S&Ls' share further.
5. The number of associations and offices reported differs somewhat in various sources. Data here are from the U.S. League of Savings Institutions, *Savings Institution Sourcebook,* 1987.
6. Data are from the Federal Home Loan Bank Board, *Combined Financial Statements of FSLIC Insured Institutions,* 1986.
7. The Bank Holding Company Act, as amended, did not specifically prohibit the acquisition of S&Ls. However, the Board of Governors of the Federal Reserve System consistently interpreted the S&L business as an activity that had been traditionally separate and denied applications for these acquisitions by bank holding companies. This policy began to change in the 1980s when the Board approved acquisitions of failing S&Ls by bank holding companies to acquire healthy S&Ls. This proposal has been opposed by trade groups in the S&L industry and by the Federal Home Loan Bank Board.
8. Federal income tax was first imposed on S&Ls in 1951. The tax advantages they enjoyed through specializing in housing finance, however, were greatly reduced by the Tax Reform Act of 1986.
9. Previously, the number of S&Ls had fallen from 6,300 in 1960 to 4,592 in 1980.
10. This form of mortgage financing did not become similarly dominant in other countries. In Canada, for example, five-year balloon mortgages were popular. As a result, Canadian housing finance institutions were much less severely affected by high interest rates during the 1980s.
11. Ceiling rates on deposits were imposed on commercial banks that were members of the Federal Reserve System (Regulation Q) during the 1930s. The ceiling rate, however, was generally above the market rate during most of the subsequent decades. Ceiling rates were extended to S&Ls' deposits in the 1960s although S&Ls were permitted to pay a differential above the rate paid by commercial banks.
12. See Bert Ely, "The FSLIC Recap Plan Is Bad Medicine," an unpublished paper, Ely & Co., September 23, 1987. Based on reported financial data, Ely identified 551 S&Ls with negative tangible net worth. The aggregate shortfall between tangible assets and liabilities of these associations was $16 billion. This figure probably overstated the economic net worth of these institutions because they valued assets at book rather than market.
13. This problem became more intractable as the losses mounted and eventually grew larger than the resources of FSLIC, which could not close the insolvent institutions. The Competitive Equality Banking Act, enacted in August 1987, provided $10.8 billion in cash for FSLIC over a three-year period, partially addressing this problem. Most of this amount, however, represented capitalization of future insurance premiums by S&Ls, leaving FSLIC without future income. Moreover, some estimates of the size of the problem are in the vicinity of $50 billion and rising the longer the problem goes unsolved.

3

Consumer Finance:
Next Generation Marketing Strategy

Richard P. Kotz
Executive Vice President
Marketing and New Business Development, Bond Investors Guaranty

During the post-World War II period through the 1970s, the U.S. consumer finance industry grew and prospered. Large "national" and major regional firms such as Beneficial, Household Finance, AVCO, and Dial Finance together with hundreds of smaller, more localized institutions borrowed money at 6 percent or less and loaned it out at 20 percent or more, primarily *unsecured*, to lower "mass-market" borrowers. Margins and profits were high. Market shifts and competitive pressures were relatively low.

The 1980s ushered in structural changes that forced the reconsideration of the entire consumer finance marketing formula of the three preceding decades, which had centered on high interest rates, high accessibility (via extensive retail branch office networks), and high levels of personal service. Deregulation of the financial services industry, significantly higher cost of funds (the prime rate climbed briefly to just over 21 percent in 1981), and high inflation together with evolving customer needs and a changing competitive landscape all meant the consumer finance industry had to cope with more fundamental marketing challenges in the last 8 years than in the preceding 80.

I. The Consumer

Table 1 shows the demographic profile of a typical consumer finance customer in the mid-1980s. From the base line shown in Table 1 there were demographic variations by type of loan, (see Table 2).

Table 1. Demographic Profile of a Typical Consumer Finance Customer.

Age	40
Sex	Male
Annual income	$28,000
Education	High school, some college (42 percent)
Profession	Wide variety, slight "blue collar" skew (13 percent owners, professionals, managers)
Married	More than 90 percent
Children at home	More than 68 percent
Two wage earners	More than 60 percent

Table 2. Demographic Variations by Loan Type.

	Personal Closed End Loan	Personal Revolving Loan	Real-Estate-Secured Loan
Age	Younger	Average	Older
Sex	More female	Average	More male
Income	Less	Slightly more	More
Education	Less	Slightly more	More
Marital status	More single	Married	Average

Through thick and thin, general consumer borrowings have increased steadily over the past decade (see Figure 1). Consumers' attitudes toward loans and borrowing have also evolved as their indebtedness has increased. As the data below[1] shows, some feelings haven't changed that much.

Consumer Attitude	*Percent*
Conservatism	
▪ Believe you should live within your means	96
▪ Don't believe in buying things unless I have the cash	59
Preference for a personal loan	
▪ Bank	45
▪ Credit union	27
▪ S&L	12
▪ Finance company	1
Importants needs in personal borrowing	
▪ Clear information	89
▪ Easy to deal with	87
▪ Good reputation	85
▪ Competitive interest rates	83
▪ Local office	63
▪ Previous loan	41

Figure 1. Total Consumer Debt, 1974–1985.

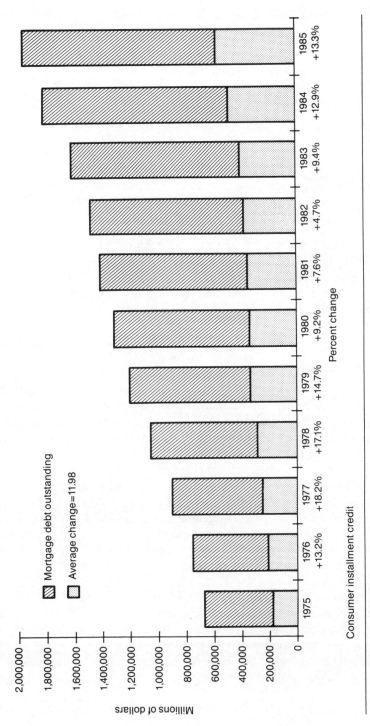

Source: *Federal Reserve Bulletin.*

Major borrowing concerns
- Confusing terminology   80
- Process too slow   77
- Inconvenient hours   76
- Application too complicated   65
- Rejection possibility   60
- In-person application   45

However, other consumer attitudes have evolved.[2]

Confusion
- Agree the variety of financial products and services is
  confusing   77

Convenience
- Agree it would be very convenient if I could obtain all my
  financial services from one provider   80

As Table 3 shows, customer and noncustomer attitudes toward consumer finance companies are particularly revealing. Generally more knowledgeable than ever, the consumer finance customer of the 1980s is (1) coping with change and confusion, (2) not happy with the credit process or financial institutions, (3) looking for less hassle and additional tangible personal benefits, and (4) cautiously ready for new directions.

II. The Competition

Perhaps the primary force behind the need for consumer finance marketing adjustment in the 1980s has been the change in the number, kind, and intensity of the competitors for mass-market credit and related financial services.

Traditional finance companies have become more aggressive in the following areas: new product introductions (VISA cards tied to home equity loans, combination personal and real-estate-secured credit line accounts), pricing closer to S&L competition (particularly on "bread and butter" real-estate-secured loans in highly competitive states like California), use of technology (ATM access to revolving credit), and distribution experimentation (augmenting retail offices with direct response marketing by mail and telephone).

Banks rediscovered the predictability and profitability of mass-market consumers as margins contracted in the commercial lending side of their business and Third-World loans soured.

Captive finance companies like General Motors Acceptance Corporation and Ford Credit began to branch out into consumer lending for other goods besides automobiles, leveraging their customer lists and rapport and their considerable financial resources. In particular, home equity lending (including first-mortgage origination, pass-through, and servicing), has been enormously attractive to this group, which also includes the major insurance companies, many of which have mortgage banking subsidiaries.

Table 3. Attitudes Toward Finance Companies.

Finance Companies Have/Are	Total U.S.	Finance Company Customer	Noncustomer	Difference
			(percent)	
Highest interest rates	69	79	68	+11
Cold, impersonal	46	43	47	−4
Least trustworthy	45	40	46	−6
Least competent	34	36	34	+2
Easiest to borrow from	30	50	26	+24
Fastest approval	23	42	20	+22
Willing to tailor terms to my needs	13	29	11	+18

Source: *The Money Study*, 1985. Reprinted by permission.

New *nontraditional* competition for the mass-market credit customer market has also emerged among the large chain retailers, for example, Sears Roebuck, K Mart, J.C. Penny, Safeway, Kroger, and 7-Eleven. These firms are adding credit and related financial services to their vast retail networks to differentiate themselves from smaller specialty stores (their arch rivals), build store traffic, and improve store profitability per square foot. Although consumers say they are interested in one-stop shopping for financial services, they may not yet be persuaded that the major chain retailers can provide what they want. Asked if a retail store could do a good job of providing many financial services, only 35 percent of consumers believed Kroger could, 40 percent believed J.C. Penney could, and 42 percent believed Sears could.[3]

Finally, the strategic marketing partnership has become a factor in determining who gets and keeps which financial services customers. Metropolitan Life's 1986 arrangement to share the Reader's Digest Association's subscription list for targeted direct mail solicitation is a prime example of this kind of joint venture. It may well become commonplace as additional firms recognize that it is possibly more cost-effective and time-efficient to gain market access through such arrangements.

This keen competition for the mass market in consumer financial services produced a tremendous increase in advertising expenditures as everyone struggled to gain a bigger slice of the pie. From 1980 to 1985 alone, national media expenditures for financial services marketing more than doubled (see Figure 2).

With the addition of local media spending (which is at least equal to national spending), the mass-market consumer has been bombarded with an unprecedented quantity and variety of credit and related financial services communications. Some confusion, even fatigue, was inevitable.

Amid all the new competitors and their expanded marketing activities, two trends have emerged.

1. *Promotionalism.* Elements of traditional packaged goods marketing (teaser rates, trial devices, coupons, customer "clubs," and other promotional approaches)

Figure 2. Financial Services Total Media Spending by Category, 1983–1985.

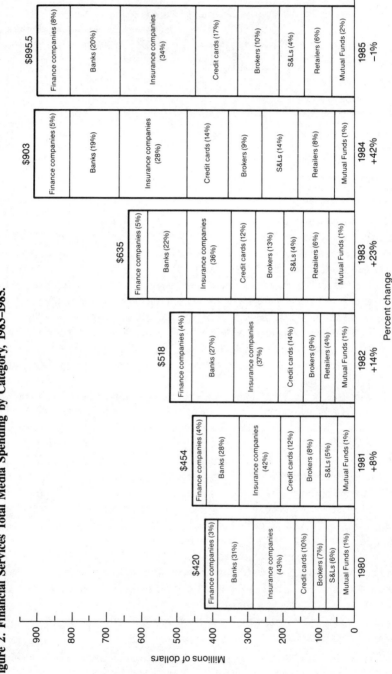

Source: BAR/LNA Multi-Media Service as compiled and published by Leading National Advertisers, Inc. Reprinted by permission.

have pervaded the marketplace in recent years and change, perhaps forever, the staid and historically gentlemanly way of marketing financial services. (Even branch offices have taken on a "money merchandiser" look, with banners and balloons galore.)

2. *Homogenization.* All the institutions competing for the mass-market consumer have begun to sound and look alike. The consumer finance companies have become more banklike in their product offerings and distribution approaches. The banks have begun to look more like consumer finance companies with their new emphasis on mass-market credit customers and friendly personal bankers to serve them.

Clearly, the world is changing, exacerbating old problems and creating new opportunities for the consumer finance industry.

III. Problems and Opportunities

Problems

In the 1980s, consumer finance marketers are operating in the following marketplace context:

- Some residual negative image as the "lender of last resort"
- Higher prices (interest rates) than competition
- Static customer base and high turnover
- More intense competition than ever from both traditional and nontraditional sources
- Bank continuation as the "gold standard" of consumer acceptance for mass-market credit needs
- Technology lag—with fewer in-office PCs and ATMs than competitors have, consumers perceive consumer finance companies as lacking modernity
- Poor marketing information systems
- Aging U.S. population—prime consumer finance customers tend to be younger

Opportunities

Balancing the problems are the following leveragable opportunities:

- Established, extensive "retail" distribution system
- Experienced, service-oriented loan office staff
- Fast and friendly service reputation to build on
- Sizable (though static) customer base
- Large, unused mass-market credit capacity to tap, particularly home equity loans
- New products and services to distribute through existing branch loan offices
- New nonretail distribution and niche marketing possibilities

IV. Strategic Issues

In this context the strategic issues facing consumer finance marketers are basic and far-reaching.

Figure 3. Marketing Strategy Spectrum.

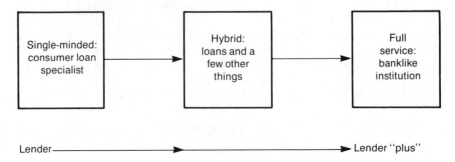

1. How to attract and keep more new customers
2. How to keep current customers longer and get more revenue per customer
3. How to differentiate their firms from other financial services companies in general and other consumer finance firms in particular
4. How to defend against nontraditional competition (K Mart, for example) and more promotional marketing tactics
5. How to manage with narrower profit margins
6. How to add more value to consumer credit products
7. How to define and establish the right long-term position in a new, changing marketplace
8. How to decide whether a push or a pull marketing approach is appropriate for the future

V. Strategic Alternatives

Consumer finance companies have considered several strategic marketing alternatives ranging from consumer loan specialists to banklike institutions (see Figure 3).

Several pilot programs are under way at the bank end of the strategic spectrum (for example, Beneficial's experiment with a savings bank in Florida chartered by the Federal Home Loan Bank Board and the Household Bank test markets in California and Maryland). Although the jury may still be out on these programs, they represent a significant strategic marketing change from the traditional consumer finance operation by offering products from both the asset and liability sides of the balance sheet.

The marketing strategy development challenge boils down to these key questions.

1. Who will prefer to buy products and services from the consumer finance company of the future?
2. Why will these consumer finance products and services be perceived as better than those offered by any competitive source?

Figure 4. Psychographic Segmentation—Lifestyles and Financial Attitudes.

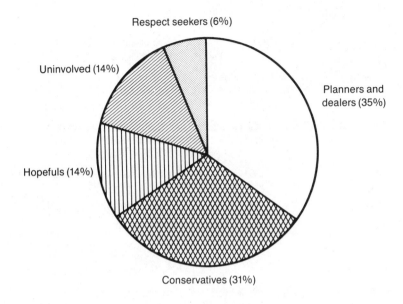

Respect seekers (6%)

Uninvolved (14%)

Planners and dealers (35%)

Hopefuls (14%)

Conservatives (31%)

Source: *The Money Study*, 1985. Reprented by permission.

VI. Long-Term Strategy Development

In working out optimum customer targets, consumer finance marketers must realize that even though people have the same demographics (age, sex, income, and so on), they may have different attitudes about credit and other financial services. *The Money Study*, a national probability market research project completed in the mid-1980s, segmented by financial attitude the U.S. adult population into five groups (see Figure 4).

The segment labels are unimportant. The salient point is that, demographically, the "average" consumer finance customer (male, age 40, high school graduate, $28,000 annual income) is represented in *each* of the financial attitude segments. But because of considerable differences among the various segments (see Table 4), there will likely be significant variations in responses to marketing approaches and product offerings among those of similar demographic but different psychographic, or attitudinal, profiles.

Another important strategic consideration is the life cycle of the consumer. As people move from the young-adult to grandparent stage of the life cycle, their needs for credit and other financial services change (see Figure 5).

An auto loan, personal credit line, or basic checking account straightforwardly marketed might be appropriate for a new beginning, hopeful. Conversely, a home

Table 4. Psychographic Segmentation.

Segments	Lifestyles	Financial Attitudes
Planners and Dealers (35%)	Spend heavily but within means Live well	Plan and manage Credit active Save and invest Take "reasonable" risks
Conservatives (31%)	Price conscious Homebodies	Bank oriented Avoid risk Don't want financial advice
Hopefuls (14%)	Spend more than save Price conscious	Insecure, need and want help Credit active Discontent with banks
Uninvolved (14%)	Overspend Indulge	Indifferent toward all financial affairs Credit active Dislike banks
Respect seekers (6%)	Do-it-yourself types Renters	Risk-adverse Insecure Credit active Need help from financial institutions

Source: *The Money Study*, 1985. Reprinted by permission.

Figure 3–5. Consumer Credit Life Cycle.

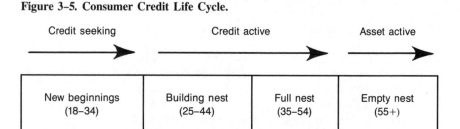

equity credit line with VISA card access or a variable-rate CD aggressively marketed would probably work better with an empty nest, planner and dealer. A particular challenge for consumer finance marketers is that their customers often "graduate" to banks at about age 45 as they gain credit confidence and begin to have a positive net worth.

Whatever attitudinal segments may be targeted within the broad mass-market for credit and other financial services, certain marketing facts of life seem inescapable for consumer finance companies.

1. There will be an interest rate disadvantage of at least 100–200 basis points between banks and S&Ls.

2. Given the limitation of their technology, information systems, and planning resources, finance companies will not be able to pioneer sophisticated new products and services broadly.

3. Because of a somewhat unfavorable image, high prices, and inexperience with delivering sophisticated financial products (investment products, financial planning, and so on), consumer finance companies cannot expect to appeal to more upscale customers. These people are strongly entrenched with banking and brokerage institutions, very fickle, difficult to please, and unwilling to pay finance company interest rates.

Therefore, consumer finance companies will most likely have to stick with their traditional mass-market customer base; offer a limited, credit-oriented product line; and compete on service. But what kind of service and how should it be delivered?

More than anything, mass-market customers across all attitudinal segments seem to want to deal with a financial institution whose people are

- Empathetic
- Knowledgeable
- Responsive
- Caring
- Professional
- Clear-speaking

The essence of consumer finance marketing strategy is realizing that *how* a loan product is explained or delivered is much more significant than *what* the credit product is, including (within reason) the interest rate charged. If consumer finance customers feel you are not just extending credit but helping them enhance their lives in important, personal ways (a new roof, a college education, an ailing parent's medical bills), they will become loyal, satisfied, repeat purchasers.

To execute this kind of marketing strategy well, it is necessary to do the following:

1. Loan office staffs must be trained to be competent in both product knowledge and "customer care."
2. Loan offices themselves must look and operate like places where average folk can feel comfortable in discussing anxiety-evoking financing matters and taking on debt.
3. Marketing communications should seek to reassure prospective clients that they will be treated with the responsiveness and respect they want and deserve.
4. Computer-based direct mail programs should systematically and preemptively address the ongoing credit needs of *current* customers to minimize account turnover.
5. As many ways as possible should be found to meet customers in person (so that the staff training and comfortable office ambience can pay off).
6. Niche marketing programs to women, Hispanics, and empty-nest older couples should be tested aggressively.
7. A market research program to track customer awareness, attitudes, and satisfaction over time should be followed religiously.

In summary, for the foreseeable future, consumer finance marketing strategy should be centered on the concept that the process *is* the product.

VII. Notes

1. Synergistics, 1984.
2. Synergistics, 1984.
3. Synergistics, 1984.

4

The Marketing of Mutual Funds*

James S. Riepe
President, T. Rowe Price Investment Services, Inc.

"Now...for one day only...all of our inventory has been marked down...no sales charges...free exchanges and new low minimums...just $99 will buy you shares in our practical Money Maker Fund...or shoot for the stars in our sporty Maximum Capital Gain Fund...don't delay...stop by today and collect double coupons!"

You say you've never heard a mutual fund hawked like this before? You're right. You never have and you never will. But as we explain in this chapter, some of the techniques used to market mutual funds are not so different from those used in distributing consumer goods, such as toothpaste or shampoo or television sets. Like the manufacturers of these items, sponsors of mutual funds strive to differentiate their products and instill recognition of their brand name in the consumer. They seek to build customer loyalty and generate repeat business. And their goals are the same as those of any other business: increased sales and profits.

But the marketing of funds also differs in some very important ways because of the unique characteristics of this product. *Like* other consumer products, funds offer their buyers the promise of future benefits. *Unlike* other products, the nature of the benefits is less predictable. As a result, fund marketers must adapt their skills to fit the demands of a dynamic investment environment.

Although mutual funds are not found in department stores or car lots, they are marketed through a variety of distribution channels. The fund sponsor may market *directly* to you, the consumer, as L.L. Bean sells through its catalogs. Funds may also be distributed through *intermediaries* or middlemen who, in turn, sell

*The author would like to acknowledge the assistance of Jane Nelson in preparing this article.

to the end user. For example, many fund sponsors employ wholesalers who market their funds to retail brokers; the brokers then promote the funds to investors. A parallel might be drawn with Sony, which hires a sales representative to persuade Macy's to carry Sony TV sets. Macy's, of course, has its own salespeople who sell to the customers. Some fund sponsors may have *captive sales forces* that market their own funds directly to consumers. These are, in effect, "factory store" operations in which the sales force sells its own company's proprietary products.

Before taking a closer look at the marketing process used by mutual funds, we need a firm understanding of the mutual fund product—what it is and how it evolved. We want to show the crucial differences as well as the similarities between the marketing of mutual funds and shampoo or TV sets.

I. Mutual Funds: The Nature of the Beast

In its simplest form, a mutual fund is a vehicle through which an investor is able to acquire a pool of securities. Each investor in a mutual fund holds a share of that fund's assets in proportion to the cash he or she invested in the fund. Fund investors share the expenses of operating the fund and, in turn, share the investment returns that the fund generates in the form of current income or capital appreciation or both.

An important difference between a mutual fund and a typical consumer product is that the benefits accruing to the buyer (investment returns in the case of funds) are *variable*. Changes in the value of the fund's investments are passed directly through to its shareholders, reduced only by the fund's operating expenses. By pooling their monies in a mutual fund, investors gain several advantages, the most important being (1) diversification, (2) professional management, and (3) low cost.

Since the first funds were created in our country more than 60 years ago, these investment vehicles have evolved from a small cottage industry into a very substantial, mature segment of the enormous financial services industry. In fact, mutual funds now represent one of the four major repositories of individual household savings, along with demand and savings deposits, direct securities investments, and insurance reserves.

Today investors can choose from *more than 2,500 individual mutual funds,* covering a wide range of investment objectives. In addition, there are nearly 300 individual fund managers or sponsors, ranging from those with a single fund to the very large mutual fund "families" that offer up to 100 different funds. As a result of the wide acceptance of funds by individual and institutional investors, the industry has grown from infancy in the early 1920s to more than $800 billion by mid-1988 (see Table 1).

Reflecting the generally risk-averse nature of individual investors, combined with the generally higher yields available from fixed-income investments, the fund industry has experienced its greatest growth in fixed-income products. Predominantly a common stock fund industry until the mid-1970s, the business has swung materially in favor of more conservative investments that promise high current

Table 1. Number of Funds and Total Industry Assets.

Year	Number of Funds	Fund Assets ($ billions)
1940	68	0.4
1950	98	2.5
1960	161	17.0
1970	361	47.6
1980	564	134.7
1982	857	296.6
1984	1246	370.6
1985	1531	495.5
1986	1843	716.3
1987	2324	769.9
1988[a]	2608	796.2

a. As of 8/31.
Source: Investment Company Institute, Washington, D.C. Reprinted by permission.

Figure 1. Distribution of Total Net Assets by Type of Fund.

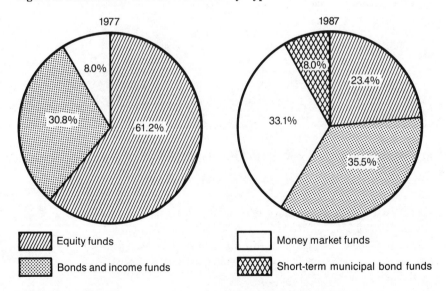

Source: Investment Company Institute, Washington, D.C. Reprinted by permission.

income and less fluctuation in principal value. We are now largely a fixed-income fund industry, with equity or common stock funds currently amounting to less than one quarter of total assets (see Figure 1).

II. Fund Managers: The People Who Bring You Mutual Funds

Since mutual funds are just corporate shells, usually lacking employees or assets other than portfolio securities, the fund manager (or sponsor) plays the key role in their operation. Generally, there are two types of mutual fund managers: independent and captive. The *independent* managers may be either privately held or publicly owned. Customarily, they do not have their own distribution systems but depend on others to sell their funds. A large percentage of industry assets is controlled by *captive* managers whose funds are distributed almost solely by an affiliated sales force. These managers are usually owned by large brokers or insurance companies.

The mutual fund manager operates under a contract with the fund, which is negotiated with each fund's independent directors (those directors not affiliated with the manager) and approved by fund shareholders. In a nutshell, a manager customarily performs four primary tasks for a mutual fund:

1. *Creates and pays for new funds.*....The manager develops and formulates the fund's investment concept, absorbs the organization expenses, and frequently subsidizes operating expenses until the fund grows to an economic size.
2. *Distributes fund shares.*....This effort significantly influences (1) the operating expense ratio of the Fund and (2) the Fund's profitability to the manager.
3. *Provides investment advice.*....The manager selects securities to be purchased and sold for the fund's portfolio, ultimately determining the investment success of the fund.
4. *Services and maintains shareholder accounts.*....This function is performed either directly by the manager or indirectly through a third party whose activities are overseen by the manager.

In this chapter, we focus on the first two of these functions: product development and distribution. If these are not executed successfully, there is no need for the others.

III. Shareholders: Who Are They?

Every good marketer knows that to sell successfully, you must first understand your customers and their needs. The increasingly sophisticated marketing techniques used by mutual fund providers attest to the industry's growing knowledge of the characteristics of its more than 30 million shareholders.

In 1986, the Investment Company Institute (the industry's primary trade group) conducted a major survey to pinpoint shareholder characteristics. Among the principal findings were:

- Six out of ten shareholders hold managerial or professional positions.
- Three in ten are retired.
- Sixty-eight percent are college graduates (compared with 21 percent of the general population), and three in ten have completed graduate school.
- Diversification was the chief attraction of mutual fund investing, and investment performance was the criterion generally used in selecting a particular fund.

Table 2. Characteristics of Fund Shareholders (1986).[a]

	Direct Market Purchasers	Sales Force Purchasers	All Respondents
Median age	50.3 years	53.7 years	52.4 years
Median household income	$50,300	$45,100	$46,400
Male financial decisionmakers	78.2%	73.0%	74.5%
Completed graduate school	39.8%	31.2%	33.6%
Moderate risk-takers	64.5%	54.7%	57.2%
Employed	69.6%	60.8%	63.5%
Retired	26.0%	34.4%	32.0%
Total household amount invested in funds (median)	$39,900	$37,300	$37,500

a. "Shareholders" refers to the primary financial decisionmaker in households owning funds.
Source: Investment Company Institute, Washington, D.C. Reprinted by permission.

The survey also compared characteristics of customers who buy funds sold directly to investors with those who buy from a salesperson. These characteristics, listed in Table 2, help explain the recent success enjoyed by sales force marketers. Customers who bought funds from a salesperson were somewhat older, more risk-averse, and less knowledgeable about investments than those who bought from direct marketers. Not surprisingly, these investors were attracted to the burgeoning offerings of fixed-income funds that accompanied the favorable interest rate environment of 1983–1986. They were also less apt to make independent decisions and more inclined to rely on a broker or other sales agent to recommend a specific fund product.

IV. Marketing: The Fight for Shelf Space

The challenge of selling a mutual fund today is similar in some ways to the challenge of selling breakfast cereal. Indeed, investment managers often hire packaged goods marketing experts to plot their sales strategies. They reason that a person who can secure and increase the shelf space that a supermarket allots to Old Brand Flakes or New Brand Flakes has the marketing know-how to boost mutual fund sales. After all, the mutual fund field is also crowded and competitive—and many funds look alike to investors.

Because the variety of distribution channels is expanding, it is helpful to again divide them into their two main categories: (1) sales requiring *intermediaries* and (2) *direct sales* to end users.

Selling Through Intermediaries

This is the oldest approach to selling mutual funds and accounts for more than two thirds of mutual fund sales today.

Usually, the intermediary is a salesperson, often a stockbroker, insurance agent, or financial planner. The salesperson may be *directly employed* by the mutual fund

Figure 2. Mutual Fund Industry Assets, Yearend 1987.[a]

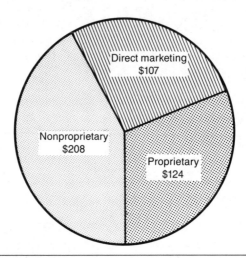

a. Assets in billions of dollars (excludes money market funds).
Source: Investment Company Institute, Washington, D.C. Reprinted by permission.

provider, as when a Dean Witter broker sells a Dean Witter mutual fund. Or the salesperson may act as *agent* for the provider, as when a Dean Witter broker sells a Putnam or Franklin fund.

Until recently, the most common intermediary was a stockbroker acting as independent agent. (A number of insurance agents sell mutual funds as part of a financial planning approach but have yet to become major factors in the distribution process.) Such brokers select mutual fund investments for their customers from among a smorgasbord of funds provided by both large fund complexes, such as Franklin and Putnam, and smaller ones, such as Templeton. Fund sponsors employ wholesalers to market the funds to brokerage firms—to secure shelf space, as it were.

But with the growing popularity of funds in the 1980s, brokerage firms saw an opportunity to earn annual management fees in addition to sales commissions by creating "store-brand" mutual funds. In an amazingly short time, these so-called *proprietary* funds captured a hefty slice of the mutual fund pie—nearly 30 percent of bond and stock fund assets by the end of 1987 (see Figure 2).

Attesting to the power of financial incentives, which we detail later, it is estimated that proprietary funds now account for no less than 50 percent—and as much as 80 percent—of total mutual fund sales by some of the nation's largest brokerage firms. The downside of this increased emphasis on proprietary sales is the question it raises about brokers' objectivity in recommending investments to their clients.

As mutual funds have proliferated, funds offered through sales forces have had a definite advantage over the direct marketing sector in reaching the general

Figure 3. Fund Sales by Method of Sales and Investment Objective, 1987 (by percent).

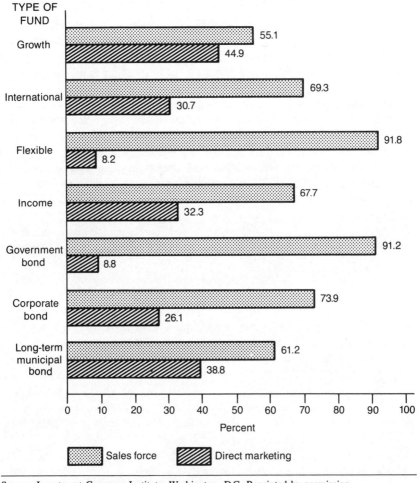

Source: Investment Company Institute, Washington, D.C. Reprinted by permission.

public. Presumably, a salesperson has personal knowledge of a consumer's financial needs and can explain the advantages of a certain fund. Figure 3 illustrates the recent success of sales intermediaries in selling fixed-income funds. In 1986, funds distributed through sales people accounted for 74 percent of total industry sales and a phenomenal 97 percent of some $53 billion of government bond fund sales, the fastest growing segment. In 1987, this percentage was slightly lower because these funds lost some of their luster. In contrast, equity fund sales by the sales force sector was closer to its traditional 60–65 percent share.

In recent years, a new type of intermediary has emerged: the deposit-based institution. Although generally prevented from selling mutual funds by federal regulations, banks and thrifts have designed ways to circumvent those restrictions and offer funds to their retail customers. Typically, third-party funds are used, but a few of the largest banks have made judicious use of loopholes and become de facto sponsors funds.

In addition, a growing number of banks are broadening the investment menus of their trust departments by using mutual funds. Trust officers find they can benefit their customers by gaining access to a wide variety of professionally managed investment alternatives without bearing the fixed costs of creating such expertise in house.

In another approach, several banks and thrifts have assumed the role of the traditional, independent commission-based agent. This new source of revenue is particularly appealing to depository institutions in search of additional fee income. Under a variety of agreements, the institution will permit a mutual fund provider to sell funds directly to its customers, sometimes right in the bank lobby. Some banks and thrifts have formed new entities to act as conduits in marketing mutual funds as well as other investment products provided by third parties, such as life insurance.

The last major intermediary we discuss is definitely not the least influential—the employer. Employer purchases of fund shares can be made directly or on behalf of employee retirement plans. Reflecting the tremendous growth in defined contribution retirement plans, mutual fund managers now market directly to employers who offer these plans as an attractive employee benefit. The plans include profit sharing and money purchase pension arrangements, 401(k)s, 403(b)s, and SEP-IRAs. (The ugly-duckling tax code names don't help the marketers.) Such plans are gaining favor with corporate managements because they limit the employer's retirement plan liability to a known amount (a fixed percentage of employee compensation), and being voluntary, they offer a meaningful benefit to employees at little cost to the employer. Mutual funds, in turn, are ideal vehicles for these plans for several reasons: the employer allows the employee to direct the allocation of the contribution; mutual funds offer a variety of investment options; and funds can be purchased and redeemed daily for maximum flexibility.

Figure 4 illustrates the tremendous growth in the institutional market since 1970. Institutional investors range from bank trust departments to employee retirement plans. In 1987, these investors accounted for more than one third of total mutual fund assets.

Selling Directly to the Investor: The No-Load Funds

Although a few fund sponsors, like T. Rowe Price, have always marketed directly to the public, the direct marketing era gained momentum in the 1970s. Several factors came together during that decade to change the traditional distribution methods.

- Consumerism, defined here as "seeking greater value for each dollar spent," was increasingly embraced by the public.

Figure 4. Total Institutional Assets in Mutual Funds.

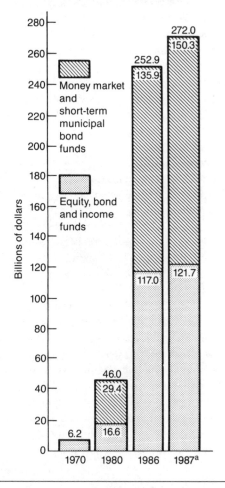

a. Preliminary.
Source: Investment Company Institute, Washington, D.C. Reprinted by permission.

- Sales of income funds increased as equity prices languished, highlighting for fund buyers the unfavorable effect of deducting large up-front sales charges from their investments.
- The broker distribution system and its individual brokers sold fewer funds and turned to other more salable investments. (This trend was sharply reversed in the mid-1980s.)
- Direct marketers of nonfinancial products, like L.L. Bean and Horchow, were proving that at least some of the public was willing to make purchase decisions without face-to-face contact.

Several major fund complexes, including Fidelity and Vanguard, converted from the broker distribution system to direct sales. Unlike selling through intermediaries, direct marketers have little personal contact with their customers. They cannot meet the customers or make recommendations and arguments favoring one investment over another. Direct sellers tend to be the industry's low-cost providers because they don't have to pay any fees or commissions (loads) to any intermediary; hence they are often called no-load funds (see Figure 5).

Direct marketers rely on print advertising, radio and TV, mail, telemarketing (still rather new), informative communications, and word of mouth. It is a more passive form of selling in that potential investors must take the initiative in calling the fund sponsor, obtaining a prospectus and sales literature, and sending or wiring the money. Direct sellers view their existing customer base as the most promising source of sales for new products.

To nurture this customer base and attract new customers, the direct sellers have developed sophisticated telecommunications centers and data processing systems. With the latest in computer technology and on-line information at their fingertips, the direct marketing telephone representative can explain the features of the funds offered for sale, dispense information, market new products, and fill shareholder requests. Typically, the no-load fund complexes offer convenient telephone exchange and redemption services to their shareholders, along with such features as systematic investing through payroll deductions or automatic bank account debits—all free of charge.

As direct marketing costs rise, however, and overall competition becomes increasingly fierce, some direct marketers have backed away from the pure no-load dogma. At the same time, the high loads charged by the funds distributed through sales forces have met with increased resistance from investors, forcing many of these funds to find less obvious, though seldom less costly, ways to reward their salespeople. Indeed, the load funds can hardly reduce financial incentives to their sales forces, whether proprietary or third party, without jeopardizing their claim to shelf space. Thus some mutual fund sponsors now appear to be engaged in what John C. Bogle, chairman of the Vanguard Group, has characterized as an unusual type of price war—a war to raise, not lower, prices.

V. Pricing: What Is Its Importance?

We have been taught that a low-cost strategy leads to success. Michael Porter, a Harvard Business School professor who specializes in analyzing competition in different industries, suggests that achieving low cost relative to your competition is a way to cope successfully with competitive forces. Yet as we noted, the high-cost load funds distributed through salespeople have dominated the industry. This occurs because in the fund industry, it is the distribution cost, not the manufacturing cost, that separates one competitor from another. The method of distribution, then, is the primary factor in setting pricing in the fund industry. Yet the pricing arena, until recently, has been one of the most sensitive and least explored aspects of our business.

In comparing funds to typical consumer goods, we can point out a significant difference. Mutual funds must disclose to the buyer any distribution fees being

Figure 5. Pyramid of Temptation.

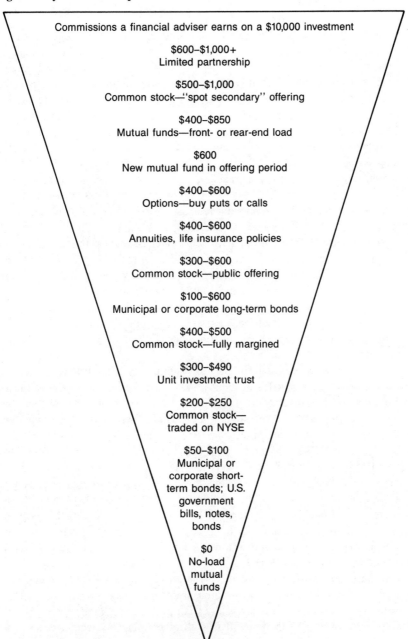

Commissions a financial adviser earns on a $10,000 investment

$600–$1,000+
Limited partnership

$500–$1,000
Common stock—"spot secondary" offering

$400–$850
Mutual funds—front- or rear-end load

$600
New mutual fund in offering period

$400–$600
Options—buy puts or calls

$400–$600
Annuities, life insurance policies

$300–$600
Common stock—public offering

$100–$600
Municipal or corporate long-term bonds

$400–$500
Common stock—fully margined

$300–$490
Unit investment trust

$200–$250
Common stock—
traded on NYSE

$50–$100
Municipal or
corporate short-
term bonds; U.S.
government
bills, notes,
bonds

$0
No-load
mutual
funds

Source: Mary Calhoun, *The Guide to Investor Protection*, (Newton Lower Falls, Mass.: Overture Publishing, 1987). Reprinted by permission.

paid—an unbundled price. But how many shampoo buyers know what part of the price is for promotion?

Until recently, up-front commissions as high as 8.5 percent of the amount invested (paid on purchase) were taken for granted. The commission rewarded the salesperson and his or her firm for their marketing efforts. Now, for reasons just mentioned, many funds are experimenting with a variety of pricing techniques that are often confusing, if not misleading, for the investor. (To help investors make comparisons, the Securities and Exchange Commission now requires mutual funds to disclose fees and expenses in a standardized table in each fund prospectus.)

Sometimes the load or sales charge is split in two, with part deducted from the purchase price and part from redemption proceeds (a back-end load). Another pricing wrinkle eliminates all front-end loads but applies a stiff back-end load, which declines the longer the shareholder remains in the fund and reaches zero in some cases.

A fee that can hurt shareholders' returns while seeming to be insignificant is the so-called 12b-1 fee (named after a regulatory statute). This fee of up to 1 percent is deducted *annually* from net fund assets in addition to the standard management fee charge. It pays for ongoing expenses of marketing the fund to new shareholders and may include an annual fee (or commission) to the salesperson as long as the customer's assets remain in the fund. Thus, existing shareholders in many 12b-1 funds are subsidizing the acquisition of new shareholders.

Perhaps the most insidious fee is a sales charge applied to the regular reinvestment of dividends and capital gain distributions. (Fortunately, this is not a widespread practice.)

An interesting response to the pricing dilemma has been offered by several traditional broker-distributed fund sponsors who have created two groups of funds, each with a different pricing structure. One emphasizes front-end loads, and the other emphasizes back-end and annual fees. This is the "You can pay me now or pay me later" approach which leaves the fee decision to the investor.

Some formerly no-load funds are stepping gingerly into this ring. They have imposed low (3 percent or less) loads on their best performing funds, on the theory—probably correct—that investors are willing to pay more for good results or at least for what they hope will be good results. A few have added 12b-1 distribution fees. Others now charge for services that were formerly free, such as switching from one fund to another within a group. The number of so-called pure no-load fund managers is shrinking; among the largest are T. Rowe Price; Vanguard; and Scudder, Stevens and Clark.

Because these pricing experiments are quite new, there is no body of evidence concerning their effect on sales. But there is substantial documentation that the presence or absence of sales charges does not prevent or guarantee good investment performance. We also know that if all other things are equal, funds with higher costs will perform worse than those with lower costs. All this can be related back to value.

Peter Drucker reminds us that a "customer buys the satisfaction of a want," and that, in turn, represents value. Hence if a fund investor received value from a salesperson's advice about which fund to buy, perhaps the additional distribution costs built into that product were worth paying. Correspondingly, if the buyer of a no-load fund feels capable of making his or her own purchase decision, payment of additional distribution fees would not represent value.

XI. The Role of Trust: Mutual Funds Do Differ from Shampoo

Having couched much of this discussion in terms of products and compared funds to televisions and cereals, let us now stress the critical difference between a mutual fund and a typical consumer product.

Virtually all providers of goods and services want to deliver good quality. Mutual fund managers are no different. But a financial investment is *not* a consumer product with identifiable, measurable consistency of performance. Johnson & Johnson's baby shampoo always looks, smells, and performs the same from bottle to bottle. Colgate toothpaste tastes and looks the same from tube to tube.

In contrast, mutual fund managers cannot make any promises about the future performance of the investment. They can talk only about how funds have performed *in the past* and assure us of the professional expertise of the managers and their general expectations. No one—not the fund manager, not the investor—can predict the course of financial markets. Even money market funds, which maintain constant principal value, have fluctuating rates of return. Unlike bank products, which guarantee a specified interest rate for a specific period without loss of principal (thanks to deposit insurance), mutual funds, by definition, pass through to the shareholder the fluctuations in the underlying investment's value. Hence the benefits of fund ownership are unpredictable and will vary.

What is it, then, that mutual fund managers can offer to investors? They offer *hope*—the hope of achieving acceptable investment returns on the shareholders' money. They offer *service*—tending to the shareholders' investments, doing the things investors would otherwise have to do themselves. But perhaps most important, they offer *trustworthiness*—ultimately, shareholders are entrusting their money to the fund manager and, even though the returns are inherently unpredictable, investors trust the managers to act in the shareholders' best interest.

This sense of trust, in turn, flows through the distribution system and affects how funds are marketed. Thus sales agents hope the potential investor has enough faith in their judgment to commit assets on their recommendation. The direct seller, without benefit of a personal relationship with the customer, faces a harder task. The fund-sponsoring organization must develop a reputation for integrity and service and communicate that, along with the fund's investment characteristics, in a way which will persuade some investor to send a $10,000 check in the mail to an essentially nameless, faceless investment manager.

No, it's not at all like selling shampoo.

5

The Life Insurance Industry

Richard J. Borda
Vice Chairman, National Life Insurance Company

I. Industry Overview

To understand the life insurance industry in the United States, a knowledge of its dimensions is helpful.

At the end of 1986, more than 2,000 legal reserve life insurance companies were in business in the country. Almost 95 percent of them were stock companies owned by stockholders; the rest were mutual companies owned by their policyholders.

The combined assets of those companies totaled more than $937 billion, and life insurance in force exceeded $6 trillion. In 1986 alone, more than $1 trillion of life insurance was purchased, reflecting the industry's continuous growth trend.

Not surprisingly, insurance in force has shared in this growth. Of the three major lines of life insurance sold today—ordinary, group, and industrial—only industrial has declined in sales and insurance in force. Ordinary in-force life insurance increased from slightly more than $1 trillion in 1975 to more than $3 trillion in 1986. Group life insurance showed a similar surge, increasing from approximately $900 billion to more than $2.8 trillion during the same period. Benefits payments exceeded $68 billion during 1986, almost three times the amount paid out ten years earlier.

More than one million people are involved in selling and servicing life insurance. That work force is almost evenly divided between home office personnel and the agents, brokers, and service personnel in the field. At least one company is domiciled in each state in the country. The stock companies are chiefly in the South and West, whereas the mutual companies predominate in the Midwest and Northeast.

Life insurance is owned by 85 percent of American families in an average amount of about $75,000. Approximately 70 percent of adult Americans own some form of life insurance. The income of life insurance companies is derived primarily from two sources: premiums paid by policyholders and earnings on investments. In 1985, more than $113 billion in income came from life insurance premiums and annuity considerations, and more than $67 billion was derived from investment income.

Since part of each premium dollar is invested in the economy, the life insurance industry is a major source of capital for the country. The four major components of the industry's assets prove the importance of this funding source.

1. Corporate debt issues, the largest segment, total more than $341 billion, or 36 percent of total assets held.
2. Mortgages total $194 billion, or approximately 21 percent of total assets.
3. Government securities total $145 billion, or 15 percent of assets held.
4. Corporate stock holdings total $91 billion, or 9 percent of the aggregate of assets held.

Among industries that have developed in the United States, life insurance is a relative newcomer. To be sure, there were life insurance companies in the United States in the late 1700s but only a handful. Not until the latter half of the 19th century did the industry begin to grow, modestly but steadily. Its great burst of growth has come since World War II. The number of companies has increased from some 473 at the end of 1945 to more than 1,000 in 1955 and more than 2,200 today.

This industry growth has produced three tiers of companies. Less than 1 percent are "mega" companies, 5 percent are large to medium-size businesses, and most are small companies. This tiering is even more obvious when assets, insurance in force, and new business are analyzed. In 1986, 39 percent of the assets were held by the ten largest insurers. These same ten companies accounted for almost 30 percent of the insurance in force and 24 percent of the new business volume. The top-ranking company had $103 billion in assets, whereas the 100th-ranking company had $1.6 billion.

Clearly, the industry is dominated by relatively few companies, perhaps the top 5 percent, and even within that group, there are significant differences in size. Despite the differences and by almost any measurement, life insurance is an industry of major importance in our economy; it directly and indirectly affects almost all American people.

II. Market Profile

As the decade of the 1980s comes to a close, the dynamics of the marketplace are forcing important changes on the life insurance industry, which is under pressure of increased competition, shrinking profit margins, and escalating costs. To cope with these forces, the industry must shift from the comfortable practices of the past to a more dynamic, more demanding, faster-paced way of doing business. The need to move from complacency to a "survival of the fittest" mode is a new experience that portends a shakeout for the life insurance industry, which may be similar to developments within the overall financial services industry.

One of the more significant influences on the insurance marketplace has been the movement toward the deregulation of financial services. This has had a profound effect on life companies and their customers. Barriers to competition have been lowered, fostering increased competition from companies outside the insurance industry. Commercial banks, securities firms, manufacturers, and retailers, along with insurance companies, are all vying for consumers' discretionary dollars. At the same time, the insurers themselves have been offered opportunities to expand beyond their traditional business lines.

Besides widening the marketplace, deregulation has provided increased opportunities for diversification and development of new revenue sources. This change is critical because substantial risks are associated with reliance on limited products and markets. Avoiding these risks is the prime motivation of many financial institutions that seek diversification.

The erosion of "jurisdictional boundaries" has reduced the industry's ability to protect itself by excluding outside competitors. The insurance industry, like banking, has been something of a club with everybody observing the rules of membership. Not any more. The membership is changing, and so are the rules.

Deregulation has also affected the consumer, who now has more sources than ever to select financial services from. Deregulation has freed pricing mechanisms from the artificial regulations of the past, allowing the marketplace to decide price. Therefore, it has become even more important for insurance companies to be competitive.

Today's consumers are forcing change in the marketplace because they are better educated, more informed, and more discriminating in their choices of financial products and services. Consumers are no longer content to assume a passive role but, increasingly, are forcing business to be more responsive to their needs. Many in the industry have to make major changes in how they do business to respond to and, more important, anticipate these new consumer needs. Life insurers can no longer develop products in a vacuum and expect them to sell. Understanding the marketplace and responding to its needs are essential to remaining viable in today's environment.

The once-comfortable profit margins of the life insurance industry are now a thing of the past. Forces converging on the industry are reducing profit margins to dangerously low levels.

A major element in the erosion of profits has been the life companies' need to compete with the savings products that other financial institutions are marketing. Life insurance policies with high cash value features and investment-oriented products like universal and variable life insurance require competitive returns, particularly as consumers become more sophisticated and aware of what is available in the marketplace. In striving to maintain an edge on the competition, insurance companies have allowed profit margins on these products to erode through interest rate crediting wars. Many companies have been willing to forgo profit as the price for retaining market position. Solutions to this dilemma have yet to be found, and profits continue to deteriorate.

Another concern related to the industry profitability is the threat on the legislative front. The disposition toward regulation of risk selection, as shown in the movements for unisex pricing and bans on AIDS testing, reflects further pressures on pricing flexibility that could reduce profitability.

As elusive as the solutions seem to be, these issues must be dealt with to restore respectable profit margins.

Operating costs have escalated as companies have recognized that survival in today's competitive marketplace requires installing modern technology, improving customer service, and employing highly skilled personnel. Moreover, distribution costs, particularly the sales force commission structure, continue to exert pressure on ever-shrinking profit margins, while start-up costs of new agencies and new agent subsidization cause further drains on capital. All this poses a difficult question for management: Should the company save costs and sacrifice service, or should it improve service and increase costs? If the pundits are right, and increased customer service is the key to the future, the dilemma of costs versus services looms as a major challenge to life insurance companies.

III. Keys to Success

To compete successfully in this new environment, life insurance managers must address several important issues. The greatest challenge is to recognize that fundamental changes are taking place within the industry. Resistance to change is an instinctive response that is reinforced when historically there has been as little change as there has been in the life insurance business.

Management unwilling or unable to adjust to the changing environment will stagnate and eventually disappear, much like the dinosaur.

A second issue is financial health. Central to the growth and success of any company is its financial strength. Increased competition has caused a significant erosion in the profit margins of life insurance companies. Worse yet, companies in the life insurance industry appear willing to risk ever-declining profit margins to maintain market share, a strategy that has plagued the property and casualty companies.

The heightened volatility of our financial markets makes investment income as well as investment portfolios increasingly vulnerable to market forces. In such an environment, adequate surplus must be available to absorb the shock.

In the final analysis, profit is essential for increasing surplus, and a healthy surplus is essential for sustaining growth and remaining competitive.

Controlling expenses has come to the forefront as a major issue. Though much lip service has been paid to controlling expenses, little has been done about it. During the past few years, corporate America has undergone a substantial restructuring, striving to reduce operating expenses in order to improve competitiveness and increase profitability. Whether this goal has been achieved in all cases is open to question. But clearly many expenses have been brought under control, and corporate earnings are on an upward trend.

A company that seeks to remain competitive in the life insurance industry has to rein in expenses. This is a major challenge because of the industry's costly distribution systems and bias toward cumbersome, bureaucratic organizational structures.

The ability to provide superior customer service is a vital ingredient in a life company's recipe for success. Of financial services, today's consumer is more sophisticated, more aware, and more demanding. Further, he or she has more diversified opportunities for placement of discretionary funds than in the past. Where there are no significant difference between products and prices, quality of service will often be the decisive difference between sellers.

To provide superior service well-trained personnel and computer systems support are needed. As life insurance products become more varied and complex, sales and support personnel must be able to quickly and accurately answer their customers' questions and solve their problems. Company personnel must be well-trained and adequately informed to provide the service required by today's discerning consumer. Increasingly, the quality and efficiency of the communication between customer, agent, and home office is becoming critical to selling and retaining customers.

Market selection is a strategic decision that affects a company's chances of success or failure. Today, many companies, uncertain about their role in the marketplace, are experiencing an identity crisis. The possibilities vary widely and range from serving as a financial supermarket to acting as a niche player. Some companies have already elected their strategy. For example, Boston's John Hancock Mutual Life Insurance Company has opted to become a financial supermarket, expanding beyond traditional life insurance to financial services such as property and casualty insurance; equipment leasing and financing; retail and institutional securities brokerage and underwriting; investment management; real estate investment, brokerage, and management and consumer banking.

Sears Roebuck illustrates how some retailers are entering the financial services market. Sears now owns an investment firm (Dean Witter), a real estate company (Coldwell, Banker), and an insurance company (Allstate Insurance). Underlying this financial supermarket strategy is the perceived need to develop new sources of revenue and avoid the risks inherent in a single-line business.

At the other end of the spectrum is the niche company, such as Houston's American General Corporation. This company has become a leading specialist in selling industrial or "debit" insurance, a life insurance product with modest face value that is sold largely in rural and small-town areas where the agent usually collects the monthly premium at the policyowner's home. This market has been shunned by many insurers, but American General has been amply rewarded by capitalizing on the scant competition in this area.

Also related to market selection are the changing demographics of our population, which represent a major challenge to the life insurance industry. The baby boomers, that sizable market segment born in the decade following World War II, are entering into middle age with changing financial requirements. There is growing evidence that this group relies less on life insurance for financial security and is turning more to investment-related services to meet its financial needs. The life insurance industry must develop new products and services to ensure that this market is not lost to competitive providers of financial services.

Another important demographic change is the aging of our population. Senior citizens (no longer a euphemism for oldsters) are a growing and important market segment in our society. Companies that provide financial services to attract the considerable resources of this group can capitalize on the aging of America.

The changes in the marketplace are forcing life insurers to make some difficult decisions about the future direction of their business. The once-clear distinctions between various providers of financial services are blurring, whereas the consumer's needs and options are expanding. Careful thought and skilled execution will be needed to give optimal direction to corporate resources and energies. The race for survival will allow few false starts.

IV. Principal Marketing Challenges

As the life insurance industry looks toward the future, it faces challenges in market selection, customer needs, cost-efficient distribution, and image improvement.

Market selection, an important strategic decision, is fundamental in setting a course for the future. Capital is a vital resource that must be allocated judiciously in committing to market segments. Market selection is a high-stakes game. For many companies, success or failure will depend on this choice.

Determining consumer's needs requires greater attention. In the past, the common practice was to develop a product, and then persuade the customer that it suited his or her needs. Today's consumer is not content with that arrangement. The buyer now has more choices, is more aware of those choices, and will select the one that best meets his or her needs. Responsiveness to consumer needs is critical to sales success in today's market environment.

To attract customers, the company must produce products that meet their needs. This requires a close working relationship between corporate marketing personnel and product developers, an arrangement often absent from life company operations. As investment-oriented products come into wider use, the investment department becomes a third party in this relationship. Moreover, products must come on stream more rapidly because the product life cycle is shortening. Innovation and flexibility are becoming critical attributes for the successful life insurance company since a more dynamic marketplace requires adapting rapidly to competitive and economic changes.

Companies need to develop a more cost-effective distribution system as profit margins shrink and costs escalate. Personnel costs are rising, but personal contact is still the chief method for marketing life insurance products. The individual salesperson is still needed to sell life insurance although other distribution systems are coming into wider use, notably group insurance and direct response marketing. The saying, "Insurance is sold, not bought," seems to hold true. The traditional relationship between agent and client will probably become more critical as products become more complex and consumers demand more service. But the challenge will be to minimize costs while maximizing the agent's productivity.

The life insurance industry is also challenged by the need to improve its public image. Recent studies by the American Council of Life Insurance (ACLI), as well as other surveys and studies, revealed an increasingly negative attitude among consumers about the industry. Life insurance companies are often perceived as more concerned with selling their products than with the welfare of the consumers they sell to. There is doubt about the ethical standards of life insurance companies as well as the motives and practices of the agents selling their products. The value of life insurance versus other financial products is also in question.

ACLI's research indicates that while the insurance industry's image is deteriorating, a potential major competitor, the commercial banking industry, is increasing its lead in this area. In safety, honesty, and trust, banks consistently score higher than life insurance companies. This could become particularly troublesome as the banking industry pushes for insurance powers and the right to compete in this market.

The image issue is not new, but it is acquiring greater significance as the boundaries separating the life insurance industry from other financial service competitors begin to erode and the consumer's spectrum of product alternatives broadens.

V. Conclusion

The U.S. life insurance industry is experiencing a secular change that is shaking its very foundations. At a recent annual meeting, the chairman of the Life Office Management Association stated that the life insurance industry has gone "from 100 years of complacency into shock and disarray." A restructuring of the entire financial services industry is under way, and life insurance companies, like it or not, have been caught up in the currents of change. Increased competition, within and outside the industry; shrinking profit margins; changing markets; escalating costs; and other factors are challenging life company management. The survivors will be those companies that are responsive to the marketplace, cost conscious, and profit oriented.

VI. Notes

1. American Council of Life Insurance, *1987 Life Insurance Fact Book Update* (Washington, D.C.: American Council of Life Insurance, 1987), p. 36.

6

A Macroview of Private Banking:
Marketing Challenges and Choices

Thomas J. Wacker
President, Royal Trust International Limited

I. Introduction

Private banking is becoming a commonly used term as commercial banks, even investment banks, look for ways to leverage their considerable overhead and thereby improve profits. Actually, the business is as old as banking itself. The earliest banks were set up as private operations through which the activities of their shareholders were channeled. Indeed, many of today's most famous houses began as private investment vehicles.

However, the select group of privately owned Swiss banks must be credited with defining the term *Private banking* as it is used today. A general definition of private banking is: Providing a convenient, confidential, and comprehensive program of personal financial counseling, structured to meet the investment, banking, and estate planning needs of wealthy individuals. This chapter presents a wide-ranging discussion of

- "The wealthy"
- The range of financial (and other) services provided to them
- How the services may be provided
- The bank's strategic considerations in offering these services

A global perspective is taken rather than focusing on the major geographic cross sections.

What Is Private Banking?

Most organizations choose private banking services criteria that fit their particular positions in the market, taking into account their current client base and the segmentation of its top tier for special attention. Usually, this first cut is done on the basis of net worth or net investable assets. Income level is sometimes also considered. The reasoning is that a current or potential client must have enough money to manage or a sufficient demand for services to justify the attention required.

For example, a prospective client must have the potential to deliver $500,000 in investable assets to the organization within 12 months.

The next segmentation is more complicated and is frequently determined by the organization's location, strengths, weaknesses, traditions, culture, market strategy, and so on. The following classifications are commonly used:

1. Geographic location: local, regional, national, or international
2. Product preferences: active or passive investors, frequent borrowers, wealth preservers
3. Client buying approach: as determined by psychographic analysis based on profession, age, sex, hobby, or other characteristics that can often be identified by surveys
4. Source of wealth: inherited, earned, won at the race track

This list is far from comprehensive, but it indicates that private banking can be structured to offer services to many different types of people. Some financial institutions do not adhere to current high net worth or income as a criterion. Persons likely to make the grade in the foreseeable future are often included, pursuing a strategy of "hook them while they are young and relatively poor."

Why So Much Interest in Private Banking?

The true private banks have been in operation well over two centuries. Banks like Citibank, Chase, and the big Swiss banks have pursued the business internationally since at least the mid-1960s. But it has been fashionable only since the end of the 1970s, when profit margins on traditional commercial banking business came under extreme pressure. In the 1980s, this condition was exacerbated by the drying up of attractive financing opportunities in the developing countries. Many banks found it no longer made economic sense for their international organizations to carry on traditional activities. The keen interest in private banking stems from the recognition that overhead for these operations is largely in place, and many of the market contacts are the same as those used in traditional commercial banking.

Other financial institutions concluded that private banking made sense for different reasons. Economic growth and personal prosperity have increased remarkably over the past ten years in the OECD countries, specifically, in the United States, Germany, France, Japan, and the newly developed countries in Asia. Banks with retail networks, investment banks with private clients, brokerage firms, and so on in these locations have found themselves with many wealthy clients. This discovery, coupled with an awareness of intense competition for the business, has spurred many banking firms to provide special services for private clients.

Other financial organizations recognized that by providing differentiated services to wealthy or potentially wealthy clients, they could productively integrate the specific product skills found in various functional divisions. These skills included lending, investment, trust, foreign exchange, merchant banking, and international funds transfer. Thus private banking represented an opportunity to increase earnings as well as a vehicle for more fully using and integrating the institution's existing infrastructure.

While others were gradually entering or backing into the business, the smaller Swiss banks, followed by the Big Three, expanded private banking as a core business that they knew to be profitable in its own right. Their success is not surprising.

Who the Clients Are

The most important segmentation for private banking seems to be geographic. Domestic markets in almost every country differ significantly from one another in many important respects. The international (cross-border) market represents a separate and distinct challenge.

A standard approach is to adopt a broad-based less selective strategy in the home market and a product-based strategy for the rest of the world. In the U.S. and Canadian domestic markets, private banking is oriented much more toward lending and the use of effective leverage than in the international market, where investment is normally the chief product. Domestic markets differ considerably, and only the largest institutions will be able to operate comfortably in more than one of them. For example, Citibank is now pursuing private banking in many domestic markets around the world.

Number of Clients

In any domestic market, an array of official and unofficial sources provide information about the chosen market segments. But none of these sources provides precise information about the number of prospects. For example, there are great gaps in information about prospects with high net worth because most of these people do not wish to be identified, except when they want special or unusual service.

Even more difficult is quantifying the cross-border market. One consultant advises that the best way to determine the size of the global private banking market is to analyze international capital flows, particularly the errors and omissions account. Sadly most of the funds going into the international private banking market come from countries experiencing political and economic instability.

Most recent studies confirm that the private client market in OECD countries and elsewhere is large enough to allow more players. One estimate is that this market has more than $600 billion in investable assets, of which $150 billion to $175 billion originates in Asia. This amounts to a great business opportunity for private bankers who add significant value to their services. The question is how to develop the business.

What the Client Wants

It is important to identify the services clients are willing to pay for. Successful private banking operations have several characteristics in common.

1. A highly relationship-oriented approach, with account managers developing rapport with their clients. In these circumstances, the importance of continuity cannot be overemphasized.
2. Maintaining strict confidentiality in dealings and utmost discretion in handling transactions in public markets. The Swiss secrecy code and similar laws in Singapore underscore this requirement.
3. The ability to customize products and personalize services to meet the individual needs of private clients. This can be a problem for large bureaucratic organizations with established policies and procedures. Private clients want things to be done their way and, within the bounds of propriety, they usually get what they want.
4. Advice in tax minimization and, where possible, tax avoidance. Wealthy clients in both the domestic and international arenas expect their private bankers to help them achieve this goal. Close collaboration with lawyers and tax accountants is required because there is always the danger of stepping over the legal line in enthusiastically trying to assist the client. Good management practices and sound judgment are the principal safeguards.

Product requirements vary by markets. In the North American market, creative and flexible lending is the principal product. The international market usually requires full protection of the principal sum and only secondarily measures return on investment. It is also customary for an international client to set aside a certain sum for higher risk investment or even to gamble in the market. In the latter case, it is essential that the banker provide expert advice on the equity and foreign exchange markets. Often, venture capital opportunities can be placed with international private clients once their basic desire for security is satisfied. Private placements are usually welcome as special opportunities for investment. These alternatives cover the entire spectrum of risk.

Understandably, an entrepreneur is readier to take risks in his or her home environment than with "secure assets" that have been geographically diversified. However, these tendencies are manifested differently in each location. In large countries like the United States, there are major differences among regions, for example, between the Northeast, the Southwest, and the West Coast. National cultural characteristics can also be important when private bankers decide which product line to offer. Asian clients tend to keep approximately 50 percent of their investments in markets close to home, sending the balance to Europe or North America.

Within geographic markets, the segmentations (active or passive investors, inheritors, earners, psychographic analysis, profession, age, sex, and so forth) are often considered the main determinants. Once the markets to attack are decided, intelligent market research will help settle which product lines to offer.

The Product Range

The chief categories of private banking products are as follows:

1. Investment
   - Private portfolio management (local and cross-border)
   - Commingled funds (unit trusts, mutual funds, and so on)
   - Real estate (commercial and residential)
   - Venture capital
   - Private placements
   - Precious metals
   - Fine art, antiques, and bloodstock
2. Banking
   - Current accounts (in various currencies)
   - Deposit options
   - Cash management and funds transfer
   - Credit cards
   - Automatic bill paying
   - Foreign exchange trading (often speculation)
   - Accurate, timely consolidated statements of account
3. Credit
   - Overdrafts and personal lines of credit
   - Securities loans (Lombard loans)
   - Mortgages (multi-options, locations, and currencies)
   - Letters of guarantee or credit
   - Project finance (real estate and oil and gas are most common)
4. Trust and advisory
   - Trust and foundation arrangements (asset protection)
   - Private investment company administration
   - Tax planning
   - Estate planning
   - Property management
   - Economic research

Some years ago, any laundry list of private banking products would have included a section on personal services such as walking the dog while the master was traveling, handling the education expenses and many of the parental duties for children attending boarding school, and buying jewelry and other personal items, often delivering them in another country. Today, there seems to be a shift from personal service requests to professional product knowledge. This is not to say that the occasional demand will not be made.

Another change in delivery of private banking services is that many clients seldom visit the premises. Nowadays, private bankers usually visit their clients. Those working in the international market must travel a great deal. When they are in their offices, they often accept instructions over the telephone. Therefore, private banking premises should be tastefully decorated, but they need not be lavish. Indeed, a sophisticated back office is more important than a fancy reception area. The former will be needed to support the automation required for quality order execution, whereas the latter may be considered ostentatious.

Segmentation Analysis

Table 1 shows the customer requirements and services offered in the private banking market. The vertical axis categorizes clients by personal characteristics and investment objectives, uses these criteria to identify preferred service levels and products, and then identifies the complexities of the distribution system.

The horizontal axis catagorizes the types of services offered as (1) traditional service; (2) transaction service, which is less "warm-nosed" and tends to be more structured and impersonal; and (3) specialized service, which is "cold-nosed" and often related to investment banking.

Table 1 is not intended to pigeonhole clients but to focus on variations in services and approaches to offering them to the target market. It can also be used to help determine which private banking market to aim for, to develop a viable pricing strategy and then to arrange the appropriate staffing.

The Competition

Striking differences exist between domestic and international private banking. The domestic market tends to be dominated by both the large organizations and numerous niche players in any specific country, region, or location. In general, organizations operate only within their domestic environment, where they are formidable competitors. In the international arena, there are only a few big players.

1. Swiss banks
   - SBC
   - UBS
   - Credit Swiss
   - Private banks (Lombard Odier, Pictet, Julius Baer, and so on)
2. American banks
   - Citibank
   - Morgan Guaranty
   - Chase Manhattan
3. British organizations
   - London merchant banks
   - Lloyds/Coutts
   - Insurance companies

The Japanese and Canadians are not yet significant competitors in international private banking. But they have some very capable niche players, as do the Germans and the French.

In many markets, lawyers, accountants, and financial advisors are often used as banking intermediaries. Thus they develop strong relationships with prospective private banking clients and are excellent sources of business. In the United States, Citibank offers members of these professions, particularly lawyers, special banking services as an incentive to make referrals.

Investment banks and stockbrokers are also active in private banking during their dealmaking. However, they have a basic problem: They are perceived to be partial to recommending investment in deals that they originate. To minimize these

Table 1. The Private Client Market.

Segment Differentiation	Traditional Service	Transaction Service	Specialized Service
Defined by			
Personal characteristics	■ Confidentiality ■ Security ■ Requires full relationship management (A/O continuity is crucial) ■ Warm-nosed ■ Deals directly with bank ■ Global investment diversification	■ Cold-nosed ■ Security, confidentiality, and relationship management are less critical ■ Global investment diversification ■ Often deals through intermediaries	■ Driven, aggressive ■ Cold-nosed ■ Global investment diversification ■ Demands high level of professionalism ■ Willing to take risk ■ Prestige-conscious
Investment objectives	■ Reasonable competitive performance acceptable ■ Short- to medium-term orientation ■ Moderate to low risk tolerance ■ Generally cross-border oriented	■ Short-term orientation ■ High to moderate risk tolerance ■ Cross-border oriented ■ Performance-oriented	■ Dealmaker ■ Capital formation ■ Short-term focus ■ Leverage-oriented ■ High return expectations
Determines needs			
Service level	■ Periodic access ■ Periodic asset allocation counseling	■ Continuous asset allocation counseling ■ Frequent access	■ Expects immediate action ■ Contact with private banker and at times with product specialists
Products	■ Custom or simplified fiduciary services ■ Full range of traditional private banking products, primarily deposits and portfolio accounts	■ Real estate ■ Merchant banking ■ Emphasis on nondiscretionary global securities trading, foreign exchange, precious metals, and margin lending ■ Custom or simplified fiduciary services	■ Merchant banking products ■ Access to global products ■ Credit (clean or partly secured) ■ Real estate ■ Custom fiduciary services
Identifies delivery system			
Distribution complexity	■ Moderate on product usage ■ Moderate to high on personal attention	■ High on personal attention due to importance of fast response time and information needs ■ High on product usage	■ Requires seasoned account manager and senior attention ■ High due to product complexity

conflicts of interest, most investment banks have separated their asset-management from their deal-origination functions. In some cases, it may be impossible to eliminate potential conflicts since investment banks and brokers derive most of their revenues from commissions. The majority of investment banks confine themselves to offering specialized services to private clients.

What Is Needed to Succeed

The strong, consistent commitment of the institution and its top management to private banking is critical to its success. A successful private banking business can take years to build up because it is based on strong personal relationships. Therefore, the institution needs top-quality, dedicated people with the skills required for high-level performance. As the business has become more popular, salaries of trained private bankers have skyrocketed. The best performers among them will bring clients into the bank and expect to earn as much as investment bankers with the same level of experience.

Certain institutional characteristics are critical to the success of private banking. One is a corporate culture oriented to service and flexibility in dealing with clients. Also necessary are a sound capital base, a good corporate reputation, and a physical presence in the key locations. To be effective in international private banking, even the smallest-scale operation needs offices at least in London, Switzerland, Hong Kong or Singapore, and New York or Miami. These locations should be supplemented with some capability in a respected offshore banking center like the Channel Islands.

Caribbean locations are also acceptable, but they have lost some of their appeal beacuse of a perceived association with racketeering, tax evasion, and the narcotics trade.

Issues Confronting the Organization

Prudent Policies and a Code of Conduct.   Integrity, professionalism, judgment, and discretion are particularly important in private banking. Know your customer, the basic law of banking, also applies. Here are a few applicable rules:

1. The bank must be satisfied that the client's primary source of income is legitimate.
2. Currency is accepted only when the bank is fully satisfied that the source is legitimate. Even then, each transaction should be closely monitored.
3. The bank should avoid dealings with prominent public fugures.
4. Bank representatives must not involve themselves in moving funds out of countries that impose exchange controls unless they fully comply with these controls.
5. Verbal and unsigned instructions should be handled in a prescribed manner. Account statements not sent directly to clients should go into a separately controlled "Hold All Mail" file.
6. Strict confidentiality and informantion security standards must be in place.

Credit Policies and Procedures. These must be flexible enough to accommodate customized transactions. Extensions of credit to private banking clients should be fully secured and priced to cover the additional administrative overhead. However, the collateral often includes such assets as unlisted shares, works of art, bloodstock, antiques, and unusual real estate. The client frequently does not disclose the purpose of the loan. Such situations call for intelligent and creative private bankers. The most challenging transactions will arise in the specialized service category.

Reputation. This is perhaps the most valuable asset of any financial organization. In private banking, it is frequently at risk.

For example, there are varying estimates of the amount of Third-World debt that has been gradually "recycled" into private accounts in safe-haven locations. No one knows the exact amount, but estimates run into the tens of billions of U.S. dollars. It seems safe to say that a large portion of these funds was not earned legitimately by the current holders. That many large banks are on both sides of these transactions has not been lost on fiscal authorities in the less developed countries, the International Monetary Fund, and world public opinion. Therefore, caution is recommended in handling private funds from LDCs.

Another risk arises when foreign financial institutions attract legitimate investment funds as well as professionally qualified people away from the LDCs that need both so desperately in their home markets. The rationale for this is that people and money will gravitate toward opportunity, and the challenge is for the LDC government to create an environment to retain both. Again, the private banker should maintain a low profile and exercise good judgment. The risk of criminal involvement poses the greatest danger to the reputation of a private banker. Vigilant managment and strict policies should guard against this pitfall. Certain transactions are simply not worth the risk. But even the most careful organizations will be caught out at times. When this happens, the institution must take decisive corrective action, backed up by a professional public relations effort.

Private Banking. This takes on an elite status in a financial organization because of the very nature of its client base and the way its business is conducted. Salaries and prerequisites are often higher than normal, and some organizations will find these disruptive. Frequently, companies will be unable to accept the organizational consequences. In the mid-1970s, for example, many commercial banks that entered the investment banking business found it to be an alien culture. Most of their ensuing disappointments were caused by this fundamental incompatibility.

Organizational Disruption. This is also likely to occur when a private banking operation is set up within an established functional or geographic structure. The problem arises because private banking, depending on its target market, product line, and distribution system, normally needs a wide focus. Clients will demand that private banking be linked to the entire organization. This means another segmentation across the existing businesses and structures, supported by a management information system that allocates costs and attributes revenues credibly. Without such a system in place, management will not know how to value private banking as a discrete business, and the private banking staff will not have a basis for incentive compensation.

Top managment must give private banking strong support from the outset to ensure that the existing power structure gives up part of its turf to make room for this new venture.

Strategic Marketing Choices

Global.   Only a few players can engage in private banking in many domestic markets and all the key international centers. This strategy generally encompasses the traditional, transaction, and specialized services—essentially an everything-for-everyone strategy.

Citibank is the most prominent practitioner of this strategy. Losing focus is the chief danger in this broad approach. In the very early days, when private banking was a part of Citibank's Trust Group, the services offered were almost entirely traditional. When private banking became part of the Investment Banking Group, there was greater emphasis on transaction and specialized services. Now that private banking is managed by Citibank's Personal Banking Group, a wide-ranging, locally directed distribution system is encouraged. There are many ways to achieve the same objectives, with a healthy divergence of opinion along the path.

Chase Manhattan is following a similar strategy, with less emphasis on domestic markets outside the United States.

Selective Approach.   In this case, a large organization would have a more limited distribution network and offer a narrower range of products. The Big Three Swiss banks appear to follow this strategy. Their main product is private portfolio management in Switzerland, with attendant banking and estate management services. This pattern has been maintained for many years and is likely to be soon followed by others. Private banking in Switzerland is marketed as a defined product, offering the protection of Swiss secrecy laws, Swiss discretion, professional ability, and an environment with a long banking tradition. However, many Swiss private banking clients are now focusing on below-average investment performance, rather high fees, and somewhat tarnished secrecy codes. Responding appropriately to these pressures is the challenge now confronting the Swiss banks.

Morgan Guaranty and some of the London merchant banks follow variants of this strategy.

Small Operations with Select Client Lists.   Many relatively small private banks with extremely select client lists are found in Switzerland, Luxembourg, Vienna, London, New York, and a few other locations. These firms usually have a highly professional but exceptionally narrow product offering. Often they provide highly customized services. Probably the best U.K. examples of these private banking business are Morgan Grenfell and N.M. Rothschild. Merrill Lynch Private Banking follows this strategy in the United States, with lending, private placements, and investment banking as the core products. Others operating in this group on a smaller scale include accountants, lawyers, financial counselors, and private portfolio managers.

A Chain of Boutiques.   This strategy is practiced notably by American Express. Its units include Boston Safe Co., Trade Development Bank, Sherson Lehman Hutton, American Express Asset Management, and American Express Bank. Private banking operations work effectively with American Express' travel and entertainment credit card operations for comprehensive client service within an extremely interesting franchise.

Royal Trustco, a Canadian example of this approach, has linked several different providers of personal financial services in an efficient global private banking network.

In both examples we have a network of separate corporations working effectively in concert to offer specialized private banking services.

II. Conclusion

Private banking is currently a fashionable business that many banks have been practicing successfully for years. It can provide an organization with a virtually risk-free return by leveraging existing capability and infrastructure to provide more personalized services. However, it must be done properly, with an appropriate strategic direction and correct implementation. The market is limited by definition, but huge in dimension. Competition abounds. It is not likely that the absolute earnings from private banking will ever be a primary source of income for a large organization. But if the business is handled properly, resulting earnings will be very high quality in both consistency over time and realization of targets for return on assets and equity.

7

Marketing Mutual Funds to Institutional Investors

Bradford K. Gallagher
President, Fidelity Investments Institutional Services Company

I. Overview of the Mutual Fund Industry

The phenomenal growth of the mutual fund industry has been the most compelling story in the financial services industry during the 1980s. From $135 billion at the beginning of 1980, mutual fund assets surged to $716 billion by the end of 1986. Fueled by the historic bull market, mutual funds have literally changed the way both individuals and institutions invest.

The rate of growth in institutional markets has been even more rapid than in retail markets. Institutional holdings in mutual funds represented $46 billion at the beginning of 1980. By the end of 1986, institutional assets accounted for more than $253 billion, or 35 percent of the total mutual fund industry.

The amount of mutual fund assets under management is impressive enough, but that reflects only one part of the growth. The surge in assets under management has been matched by an equally impressive jump in the number and variety of funds. There are now more than 1,800 mutual funds, surpassing the number of companies listed on the New York Stock Exchange. Today, mutual funds cover the full spectrum of investment disciplines, offering vehicles to suit the investment needs of virtually any institution.

II. Recent Trends in Financial Markets

The equity explosion of the 1980s has increased the growth possibilities for investors. But along with rising opportunities has come greater risk. The institutional investor, often acting in a custodial or fiduciary role, must be particularly sensitive to the business of risk management. Moreover, the proliferation of new products and derivative investments (for example, zero coupons, junk bond issues, mortgage-backed securities, and stock index futures) has opened up territories previously unexplored by many institutional entities.

The accelerating movement toward globalization in the financial marketplace has increased the need for information and capabilities that extend to the international arena. The so-called Big Bang in the United Kingdom opened the door to further integration of the world's financial markets. Investing today is a 24-hour global race, with starting gates in New York, Tokyo, and London. To enter this race, an institutional investor must have trading and research capabilities that meet the requirements of the international marketplace.

All these trends have been noted by the mutual fund industry. Indeed, mutual funds have flourished because they have recognized the needs of individuals as well as institutions in this fast-moving age and heeded the call for enhanced services. Where risk has been the issue, mutual funds have offered diversification. Where investment expertise has been needed, the funds have offered professional management. Where transaction costs have been a concern, mutual funds have offered cost-effective participation and easy access to a spectrum of financial products.

III. The Institutional Environment Today

Increasingly, institutions are turning to mutual funds as an investment option, thereby creating many new opportunities for providers of institutional services. Banks and other fiduciaries, corporations, universities, foundations, and government agencies are now among the institutions utilizing mutual funds. Thus the need for specialization in the various segments of the institutional market has become more important.

As new opportunities have arisen, the environment has become more competitive. Investment managers now range from full-service providers of brokerage and mutual funds to boutiques with specialties in specific investment disciplines.

IV. The Nature of the Institutional Investor

Marketing to institutional investors requires a thorough knowledge of the institution and its particular needs. The relationship between customer and vendor is necessarily close. The need to demonstrate skills and cultivate the business relationship at the point of sale is critical to the ultimate success of the relationship for both parties. Familiarity with a client's business and the nuances of the particular industry enables the provider of financial services to be more responsive to a customer's needs.

V. Marketing Mutual Funds to Institutional Investors

To be a successful participant in today's institutional market, we at Fidelity begin with the simplest of axioms: Know your customers and respond to them. That is the clearest path to success. But in that broad mandate, there are several narrower areas of focus.

■ Quality Products and Services. We offer a comprehensive range of investment products and services that answer the demands of customers and reflect the high quality that institutions require. We must be sufficiently flexible in designing programs to tailor them to meet changing market conditions as well as individual customer specifications. We also invest heavily in the future of the business through the development of new products and customized delivery systems. These delivery systems are designed to facilitate client trading and account inquiries with attendant specialized reporting capabilities.

■ Highly trained, focused professionals. Products must be offered with the support of well-trained and experienced marketing professionals. To the institutional customer, dealing with professionals well-versed in various market niches is vital in establishing the confidence required for a sound business relationship. By building a highly trained, experienced team around discrete institutional markets, we have created a high level of specialized expertise. This is an outgrowth of the realization that the needs of a small corporate investor may differ considerably from those of a large banking institution or a tax-exempt foundation. We have thus organized vertically integrated business units around each individual market segment to develop distinct areas of expertise.

■ Market orientation. This market-segment orientation represents a significant departure from the traditional view of product management, which organized itself around products or brand names. Frequently, the product-first approach meant marketing the same product to every customer, regardless of their profiles. History demonstrates that the product-first approach is inadequate in today's sophisticated institutional markets. Instead, we at Fidelity have put the market, and therefore the customer, first. Products are custom-tailored to respond to the needs of the particular market segment and ultimately the needs of the client.

We use our market-segment approach to target major markets within the institutional customer base: banks, corporations, tax-exempt institutions, insurance companies, government agencies, investment advisors, and broker-dealers.

■ Entrepreneurship. We encourage new ideas, aiming to foster an entrepreneurial spirit throughout our market management team. That spirit epitomizes the Fidelity corporate culture. Our marketing team is designed to remain as close as possible to our customers, for we believe this closeness will generate novel approaches to customer needs. We believe innovation grows out of listening to customers and developing new ways to serve them. The customer, therefore, is the centerpiece of our efforts.

A closer look at two institutional markets, the banking and corporate sectors, will show how marketing strategies must be molded to suit each investor.

The Banking Sector

Mutual funds provide attractive products for banks in both the trust and retail areas.

At Fidelity, we offer institutional equity, fixed-income funds, and money market funds that enable banks to supplement their common trust funds. Through mutual funds, bank trust departments can avail themselves of investment management expertise, extensive research capabilities, and a wider range of investment products.

Considering the increasingly complex nature of investment, a mutual fund relationship gives banks access to a diversified product line that can expand as client needs and market conditions dictate.

The use of mutual funds is also cost-effective. By turning to mutual funds to supplement their investment expertise, banks are relieved of the expense that layers of research and systems can entail.

Although Fidelityis, first and foremost, an investment management business, we offer extensive operational and marketing support services to complement our investment services.

On the retail side, consumers are increasingly selective in their choice of financial products. Many banks have recognized the appeal of mutual funds as a device for expanding relationship banking. Though the Glass-Steagall Act prohibits banks from underwriting mutual funds, many view relationships with mutual fund companies as a valuable way to expand the range of products they can offer their retail customers.

When the banks offer the products of investment entities with a high market profile, like Fidelity, introducing the funds to bank customers is much easier. Through Fidelity's ACCESS Program, we offer a wide selection of our retail mutual funds with complementary marketing and operational support services.

We recognize that banks retain a close and often emotional link to the consumer, offering traditional services and a high degree of trust. Our arrangements with banks represent an additional distribution channel for each of us as well as an opportunity to reach an otherwise unattainable customer who often feels most comfortable doing financial business within the confines of his or her local bank's branch office.

The real strength of this arrangement is that it takes into account the diversities of financial consumers with varied investemnt personalities and seeks to serve these persons in a reassuring environment. Bank customers are often less venturesome with their money. As new investors in mutual funds, they may find more comfort in choosing among funds that are offered in the familiar financial setting of their local bank.

Clearly, the regulatory climate is changing. With legislators and regulators chipping away at Glass-Steagall, banks may soon be able to offer funds of their own. But we are confident that banks will continue to rely heavily on the expertise and services of outside mutual fund companies.

The Corporate Sector

Another major area of concentration for mutual funds is the corporate sector. Here the market is highly diversified, varying according to company size and the services required.

In today's fast-moving markets, corporate managers recognize the value of having experienced investment professionals at their disposal. Fidelity has devoted much energy to developing the corporate market.

A major area of emphasis in the corporate sector is providing defined contribution plan services, particularly the burgeoning market for 40l(k) plans.

Adopted in 1980, the 401(k) plan has grown into the most popular retirement vehicle among corporations. Indeed, more than 90 percent of *Fortune* 500 corporations offered their employees 401(k) plans in 1986. These plans derive their popularity from the distinct advantages that they offer to both employee and employer.

Since contributions are based on a percentage of salary or payroll, employers have the advantage of knowing with much certainty what the amount of these contributions will be. Moreover, since the plans are employee directed, the employees absorb the investment risk.

For employees, 401(k) plans have the advantage of permitting a greater sense of participation and control over their retirement income decisions, instead of leaving them to be made arbitrarily by an anonymous investment manager.

Garnering a share of the 401(k) market requires a particularly strong effort to establish client trust and confidence in the money manager. Assigning retirement assets to a money manager may entail a lengthy evaluation by the corporate client, involving judgment of investment performance, record keeping, and employee communications services.

At Fidelity, we mount a comprehensive effort to give our client all the tools needed to provide the best program. Because selecting investment options for a 401(k) plan may take some time our initial sales contacts demonstrate the wide range of vehicles and services that Fidelity places at the client's disposal. Fidelity's high market profile is a distinct advantage in this respect. Our considerable resources in research capabilities and experience in portfolio management are considered substantial assets. In subsequent consultations, we work closely with the client to tailor a program to its needs.

Besides actual money management, there are the equally important matters of handling individual accounts, delivering investment information to employees, and providing a range of related services. Implementing these programs at the corporate level may require considerable planning and staffing To complement our investment management services, we have spent considerable time and money to develop innovative, responsive record-keeping services that enable employee participants to make daily telephone exchanges among Fidelity funds as market conditions or personal investment goals warrant. Moreover, employees receive periodic statements on the status of their fund accounts. A growing number of companies are opting for this convenient feature.

Because employees need adequate information to make their investment choices, it is important to give them thorough factual background about investment vehicles and characteristics. Most corporations have personnel dedicated to handling employee retirement plan inquiries, but they may require assistance in explaining specific features. We are available at all times to answer questions from administrators or employees. Finally, employees need periodic reports about fund performance, portfolio holdings, and investment strategy. We make a major effort to provide employees with timely investment data, such as investment updates and annual reports, and human resources personnel with the materials needed to explain programs to participants.

Marketing mutual funds, whether 401(k) or cash management services, to the corporate sector is a sometimes complicated process that may entail a relatively long lead time from initial sales contact to completed agreement. We have found that patience and diligent attention to the aforementioned details support the sales process and demonstrate Fidelity's commitment to a high standard of service.

VI. Institutional Client Service: A United Effort

At Fidelity our primary strength is our people. The institutional investor expects to do business with knowledgeable and skilled personnel. For that reason, we stress complete professionalism in every aspect of our client service efforts. We have a highly motivated and responsive team of professionals. Whenever possible, we hire people with relevant experience. We then conduct an ongoing series of training sessions and sales conferences to update our marketing and sales professionals on new developments in the market, new products and services, and consultative sales approaches.

Our goal is not only the immediate sale but also a continuing relationship. We regard a large part of our sales job as an educational responsibility. Thus we assign sales specialists, by geographic region, to the various market segments to ensure that a customer in any given segment will receive the expert attention he or she requires for the occasion. Equipped with a comprehensive knowledge of our product line, performance history, fee structure, and service capabilities, the sales representative can tailor the appropriate product to each customer.

Our marketing managers and product managers focus on identifying and responding to needs in the marketplace. In turn, they develop sales, marketing, and research materials that will support the sales team in the field as well as the marketing programs of our clients. Working in tandem with sales representatives, we keep our marketing effort as close as possible to our customers and their needs.

We regularly attend trade shows to introduce our capabilities to new institutions. And we periodically invite clients to participate in Fidelity-sponsored investor conferences. During these conferences, customers articulate their concerns, and we give institutional investors a closer look at Fidelity's resources and capabilities. Finally, we advertise in trade and professional journals to build our corporate image and broaden prospective client awareness of our products and services. However, at the institutional level, nothing can supplant the value of professional-to-professional contact.

VII. The Future: Staying Competitive in a Competitive Universe

The mutual fund industry has enjoyed remarkable prosperity. It is always hazardous to predict the future of financial markets, but clearly it will be a formidable challenge to sustain the industry's recent growth. Perhaps the only certainty is that change and innovation will continue to alter the financial landscape. Increased market globalization, round-the-clock trading, more widespread securitization—all these will likely help shape our financial future.

Amid a whirlwind of change, therefore, the companies that prosper in the future will be those that demonstrate these three time-tested strengths.

1. Listening carefully to customers. The customer may be the single best source of ideas. Companies that listen to customer descriptions of their needs and improve services accordingly will maintain their market strength.
2. Keeping products versatile. Companies must structure their products and services with a built-in flexibility to meet a wide variety of institutional needs. They must invest heavily in the future of the business by developing new products and delivery systems.
3. Sticking to the knitting. Companies must maintain a commitment to high quality in existing products and services. They should avoid diversifying outside their areas of expertise at the expense of existing businesses and customers.

By remaining committed to professional expertise, high-quality products and services, and responsiveness to client needs, mutual funds companies will ensure themselves a spot in the institutional marketplace.

8

Marketing Financial Services Overseas

Michael Coles
Former Chairman, Goldman Sachs & Co.

I. Introduction

The approach to marketing financial services overseas described in this chapter is based largely on my experiences as an American investment banker responsible for much of his own firm's international activities from the mid-1960s to the mid-1980s. This period covered the birth and development of the global financial marketplace.

In this chapter, we address (1) establishing corporate objectives, with an emphasis on the long-term health of the company as a whole, not only its offshore business; (2) determining the products to be marketed and setting priorities according to anticipated benefits; (3) selling the selected product line, by whom and to whom; and (4) measuring results, with attention to published league tables.

The overall conclusions are that (1) the international business of an American investment bank must always be the servant and never the master of the primary domestic business; (2) the international business exists only to preserve, and we hope strengthen, the domestic base; and (3) the key to a successful international marketing strategy is to determine the penetration needed in each significant business area so that offshore activity provides optimum benefit to the whole.

II. Setting Objectives

In overseas business, as with most other human endeavors, it's helpful to have a clear idea of what you hope to achieve before you start out. Three possible objectives come to mind immediately.

1. To develop a new area of profitable business
2. To protect an existing profit base
3. To keep up with the competition

Each of these is arguably a sensible reason for a financial institution to seek overseas expansion of its business, but each deserves critical examination before its adoption as an institutional objective.

The financial services business is not like manufacturing. An industrial manufacturer can often export the product of surplus capacity with little or no increase in overhead. Industrial exports may prove at least as profitable as domestic sales and frequently more so. But in the area of financial services, providers often find that their business margins, and hence revenues, are lower overseas, whereas costs and associated risks are considerably higher than they are accustomed to at home.

> Keeping a security analyst in Tokyo costs at least twice the inflated salary he or she earns in New York, and investment bankers admit that profits in these new markets are years away.[1]

In the banking business, particularly if proper account is given to risk, offshore activities are generally much less profitable than domestic ones. Moreover, today, when the dollar's value compared with other major currencies is declining, the offshore financial services industry finds itself in the worst of all possible worlds: Its costs, largely for people and occupancy, are mostly measured in foreign currencies without an offsetting increase in revenues, which are still largely dollar-denominated. Protecting an existing profit base is a more readily defensible international business objective.

> Amalgamated Foods Treasurer Bob Jones has approval from his Board to raise $200 million of medium-maturity debt. He calls a few of his closest investment bankers to get rate ideas. He may even ask for firm bids. Banker A quotes him 9 percent, and Jones questions this, saying that at least two others are quoting 25 basis points less for issues in the Eurobond market. Banker A says he wouldn't know anything about that, 9 percent is a domestic quote. "We aren't involved in the Eurobond market."

Will Banker A get a call the next time Jones wants to come to the market? Since domestic and international debt markets are now virtually inseparable, a firm without an international presence cannot even pretend to be involved in underwriting and distributing corporate debt.

A second example may be less obvious but, given the profit potential, possibly more important.

> Bill Smith, CEO of Consolidated Beejams, has decided to sell his Wicket Division. He calls some banker friends to seek buyer ideas and possible marketing strategies before selecting one of them to be his agent in the transaction. Banker A submits a list of potential buyers, all of them domestic. Banker B, on the other hand, submits a well-thoughtout list in which European and Japanese names are prominent. When Banker A is asked why his list is deficient in this respect, he says his firm has little contact with foreign companies.

Banker A's tenure in the merger business, domestic or international, is likely to be short.

In today's global environment, an investment banking firm can maximize profits by concentrating on a purely domestic business, with the likelihood that it will suffer significantly in anything but the shortest-run perspective. Alternatively, the firm can go totally overboard in committing assets overseas and face a long-run erosion of profit margins. Arguably, the secret of successful international penetration is to expand overseas enough to exploit one's domestic profit base to its maximum potential, and then stop. It is difficult to achieve this balance without deciding how much is enough. Even before the dramatic events of October 1987, the income statements of major investment banking firms were beginning to reflect the negative effect of too costly and too rapid expansion into overseas markets.

Keeping up with the competition is an international business objective that should not be dismissed too lightly. Admittedly, it is usually unwise to assume there must be merit in an activity simply because the competition is undertaking it. Consider, for example, the rush to set up offices in Germany to underwrite deutsche mark issues. The most frequently heard argument for doing so was if they are doing it, we must too, or we'll be left behind. This is hardly a compelling reason for making a very expensive entry into a highly competitive marketplace where both form and substance seem to favor the domestic players.

Although blindly following the competition can be a mistake, there are also good reasons not to remain aloof from an overall trend. First, it is desirable to be in a position to capitalize on significant economic or structural changes. For example, during the 1960s and 1970s, Japanese securities houses were developing global networks that contributed little to their overall profitability and may indeed have reduced it. It is doubtful whether even the Japanese would claim to have anticipated either the speed with which their country has become a major capital exporter or the magnitude of such wealth. But their global presence, maintained for years despite almost certain marginal profitability, enabled Japanese brokers to capitalize on this cash glut and become, overnight, among the leading intermediaries in the international marketplace.

On a smaller scale, during the period of Mitterrand-led socialism in France (1978–1985), business in that country provided little opportunity for foreign intermediaries. Short-term profit considerations might have dictated a reduction or even elimination of coverage of French clients. But a longer-term view would have anticipated the possibility of a right-wing renaissance, accompanied by a wave of privatization. The firms that had the staying power to continue coverage, maintaining relationships in both the public-sector companies and the supervising government agencies, had great advantages in competing for privitization business against those firms that had left the field and later sought to return.

An analysis based solely on profit considerations may adversely affect the organization, which after all, consists of people with all of their normal but sometimes illogical drives and frustrations. However well-reasoned the narrower strategy may be, the sight of a competitor conducting worldwide activities in a high-profile, jet-set manner may cause some of a firm's most loyal, best, and brightest talent to think the grass may indeed be greener elsewhere.

Also key in selling intangible services like investment banking is recognizing that perception may be just as important as reality in the eyes of the buyer. Professor Samuel Hayes III at the Harvard Business School has cited as a key for success in investment banking "the perception that the firm can deliver a quality service." Even if the issuer has no need for international services and is unlikely to develop them soon, he or she may prefer, because of image alone, to deal with a firm that has a well-developed global reach.

A practical approach to setting international objectives should concentrate first on protecting (and let's hope extending) an existing profit base. Absolute profit expectations will be conservative, whereas market-penetration targets and related commitments of people and material assets will be carefully measured on the premise that a well-planned, somewhat limited approach will provide better long-run returns than one of unbounded worldwide expansion. Careful attention will be paid to long-term global trends, balanced by senior management's constant reminders that trees do not, and probably will not, grow to the sky. In the 1970s, many people made plans assuming that oil prices would exceed $75 per barrel by 1990, and they were badly burned. Even today, those same people are probably making significant international dispositions expecting that Japan will continue to be the world's largest creditor well into the next century.

Ample evidence supports the thesis that international business should extend and protect the domestic base rather than be structured as an independent activity. During the 1950s and 1960s, the main thrust of New York-based international investment banking was carried out by firms whose senior partners had been brought up in the exclusive and patrician atmosphere of pre-World War II (and even pre-World War I) international banking. Firms like Dillon Read, Kuhn Loeb, Smith Barney, Harriman Ripley, and White Weld dominated what little international business was done. First Boston was making some inroads in Latin America and the Far East. Morgan Stanley, capitalizing on its House of Morgan connections, was doing some (but not much) international business. Salomon Brothers; Goldman, Sachs; and Merrill Lynch, on the other hand, were going about the unglamorous and at times grubby business of consolidating their domestic bases. Sidney Weinberg and William Salomon were quite content to leave to the Dillons, Schiffs, and Ripleys the heady business of ocean travel and wining and dining heads of state. The rest is history. As their domestic bases dwindled in stature, so did the overseas credibility of the international houses. The lesson is clear: A firm cannot remain powerful internationally without the benefit of an equally powerful domestic presence.

III. Product Management

Three product categories might fit into an international marketing plan designed to achieve some or all of the objectives outlined above.

- Category I. The most desirable products, whose characteristics are such that the firm should do everything it reasonably can to maximize its share of the market concerned.
- Category II. Products with less desirable characteristics, which would be avoided altogether if they did not provide some essential support to other areas of the business.
- Category III. Products with some superficial attractiveness which, on closer examination, are found to add nothing to the business overall or to have a possibly unfavorable effect.

One danger of the international financial services business is the ease with which both senior management and international executives can persuade themselves that a product belongs in a category different from the one that rigorous analysis would properly assign it to.

What characterizes a Category I financial product? Clearly, it should be a high-margin product with a reasonable life expectancy derived from structural or practical barriers to entry. Clearly, too, the firm providing it should have a clear-cut advantage over its global competitors, including a leading position in a well-developed domestic market.

A good example of a Category I product is the business of executing international mergers and acquisitions, provided that the firm offering the service is a leading contender in either the U.S. or British merger markets. Although the leading Japanese securities firms have achieved a strong position in the international capital markets, they still have a long way to go before achieving a similar position in international mergers. They are not hampered by inherent technical shortcomings. Rather, the concept of a merger market as such is still largely alien to the Japanese domestic industrial scene.

Despite the setbacks of October, 1987, the still poorly defined concept of international equities could be another Category I product, provided that the firm seeking to manage such issues is (1) based in a country with a flourishing domestic equity market, (2) has a leading position in it, and (3) has the sales force needed to project their position internationally. There are some notable exceptions, but evidence indicates that the future of international equities will belong to U.S., Japanese, and British firms. The domestic equity markets of these three countries together account for about three quarters of world equity values. Possibly even more telling is the commitment that leading U.S., Japanese, and less so, British brokers have made to building extensive offshore sales networks.

Although the Eurobond market has become the world's largest single market for corporate and public-sector debt, it arguably remains a Category II product. Although few would enter these shark-infested waters willingly, no firm can compete today in the business of raising capital unless it is prepared to do so globally.

Investment bankers conduct two basic businesses: assuming client risk and enhancing client values. Risk assumption relates chiefly to the liability side of the client balance sheet, particularly the issuance of securities in public markets. Value enhancement relates chiefly to the asset side of the corporate balance sheet, focusing on corporate reorganizations, acquisitions, divestitures, and so on.

Although value enhancement now provides the most profit and entails the least risk, it is difficult to attract clients if you are not also willing to work on the liability side of the balance sheet, which means assuming risk.

In the eyes of most users of investment banking services, there are some risks that an investment bank must be able to assume if it is to have any credibility as a full-service institution. At the top, or close to the top, of such a list is public offerings of debt. To put it another way, there is still room (some would say an increasing amount of room) for a firm offering a high-quality boutique financial advisory service. But when a firm goes beyond that to offer a wider range of services, it must proceed on a broad front or perish—hence the many firms that seem willing to spill blood in the Eurobond market.

Why is the Eurobond market so unattractive? First, it is incredibly competitive. In each of the world's major domestic corporate debt markets there are, at most, half a dozen viable competitors for a piece of debt underwriting business. In general, these competitors meet one another on roughly equal terms. They are equally regulated, finance themselves in the same markets, and are, by and large, subject to similar long-term motivations. They operate within the same economic framework. From time to time, individual firms may do something stupid, but there is little motivation for long periods of real foolishness, and there is much market discipline to prevent it.

In the Eurobond market, on the other hand, there are probably at least a couple of dozen credible contenders for any piece of business. These contenders come from very different economic and regulatory backgrounds, are motivated in very different ways, and have widely differing approaches to measuring success or failure. At any given moment, there is ample reason for any one of them to behave unwisely, and there are conditions that lead to extended periods of severely competitive silliness.

Further, the Eurobond market is remarkably flexible and free-form. New instruments and adaptations of old ones (particularly instruments that straddle different markets or involve different currencies) are more likely to emerge first in the Eurobond market. This willingness and ability to innovate provides an attractive environment for financial entrepreneurship. But it also creates a frenzied atmosphere of high tension that is designed, it is probably fair to say, as much to provide a marginal, short-lived competitive edge as to serve any long-term client interest. This aspect of the market offers another reason why one must be in it, however reluctantly. Absence from the Eurobond market will distance a firm from the cutting edge of financial creativity and thus diminish its overall ability to compete.

In recent years, client loyalty has eroded markedly in domestic markets but has become virtually nonexistent overseas. Clearly, the international debt markets have become the forum of choice to try out new providers of investment banking services.

Why, are international equities placed in the favored Category I, whereas international debt is relegated to the undesirable Category II?

The answer hinges on an understanding of the different characteristics of debt and equity. Except for little-used tap issues, debt securities (1) are sold in a single, finite transaction; (2) have their own characteristics of maturity, coupon, and covenants; and (3) develop their own trading markets. Although investment bankers always try to tell their clients otherwise, an unsuccessful debt transaction (provided it is not one of a string of them from the same issuer) will have little or no impact on the value of past or future issues and will normally reflect much more on the reputation of the lead manager than that of the issuer. The responsibility for issuing debt may well be vested at quite a low level in the corporation. Cost-conscious treasurers will be tempted, and probably wise, to accept the lowest firmly underwritten bid they receive even if their knowledge of the market leads them to believe it cannot be resold other than at a loss.

Equity, on the other hand, is fungible. No one has yet invented Euro-equity or an Asia-equity or been able to design something that can properly be called equity and still be tangibly distinguishable from extant shares. An unsuccessful issue of international equities will immediately affect the value of extant shares, which value will automatically be reflected in the home trading market. Chief executives are usually very sensitive to the value of their company's shares. It is an important measure of how good they are at their jobs and may be a significant component of their compensation or personal net worth. Small wonder that the decision to issue equity and the choice of manager of the issue is usually made by the chief executive officer. And a wise CEO will look far beyond the house that promises to do the job at the lowest apparent cost.

A Category III product meets none of the criteria specified for the first two categories. This type of undesirable product does not defend any domestic profit base because it is not marketed domestically. It does not provide any domestic skills you can export, nor any competitive standing you can trade on for marketing. It probably has an apparent profitability, or you wouldn't be looking at it seriously, but even that benefit may be overstated. Possibly the biggest attraction of a Category III product is that it aims for a sizable market that others consider important—the keeping up with the Joneses syndrome.

One area of business that fits this description is the syndication of commercial bank loans, which had a brief and unhappy vogue as an investment banking product in the 1960s and early 1970s. Investment bankers were tempted by what was then a large, very visible international business that seemed both glamorous and profitable. More important, the commercial banks seemed content to allow investment banks to get the mandates and put together the deals while they provided the money. But after a few years, the commercial banks quite sensibly asked why they needed the investment banks to intermediate in what was an increasingly competitive business. It took a few more years for investment banks to realize that they couldn't compete since they brought nothing unique to the part except their wits. When transactions involved offering several billions of dollars to Brazil, having money to lend (which investment bankers didn't) meant a lot more to clients than any amount of wits.

The story didn't end there. In the 1980s, the quality end of the syndicated loan market changed into a securities market because of the development of revolving underwriting facilities (RUFs) and Eurocommercial paper. Investment banks felt at home with these products. Their willingness to commit capital was important for success, and they brought considerable sales skills and trading experience to this market. Moreover, the growth of other activities such as real estate and facilities financing and leveraged and management buyouts, all requiring access to bank financing, meant the ability to work globally with bank credit and lending officers was once again an important investment banking skill. Finally, through the growth of so-called merchant banking, investment banks became lenders themselves, using their capital to provide bridge financing in connection with mergers and similar transactions. It is dangerous to assume a Category III product will not, at some later date, graduate to a more desirable class.

Though difficult, categorizing a given product is essential for a successful marketing effort. Flexible thinking is also required.

For example, an offhand analysis of the deutsche mark bond market by an American-based investment bank would probably place this product in Category III. But the bank's management might realize later that its growing expertise in foreign exchange dealing and currency swaps provides a capability with respect to synthetic deutsche mark securities.[2] Marketing these instruments requires a knowledge of the underlying trading market in deutsche mark debt and creates a more compelling rationale for at least upgrading the business into Category II. However, it leaves open this question: To be a credible factor in trading deutsche mark bonds (which can be done quite effectively as an add-on to an existing dollar bond trading capacity in London) does one also need to incur the significant incremental expense of being in a position to lead-manage new issues (which, under current German regulations, requires a substantial presence in Germany)? The key is knowing when to stop.

IV. How to Sell the Product

A sensible investment banker (one who has decided to follow the rules set forth in this chapter) will probably market only the first two product categories. The organization's Category I products, by definition, will be among the very best available in the world markets. Its Category II products should be of respectable quality and, to the users, virtually indistinguishable from comparable products offered by leading competitors.

> One of the distinguishing characteristics of the Eurobond market, cited earlier as an example of a Category II product, is that it's highly competitive. The smart player in that market will strive to deliver a first-class product but will plan his solicitations so that the resulting volume of activity will be enough to give him reasonable credibility in the market but not so much as to cause him to lose money.
>
> Ideally, this business will involve only those clients for whom the provision of otherwise unattractive services will permit realization of the investment banker's broader strategic objectives.

To successfully market products that will meet the requirements of the strategic plan, the investment banking organization must deal with such key questions as

To whom are we selling? What kind of people should staff the sales force? Where should they be based? How should they be supported? How well are they doing?

One investment banking organization targeted about a thousand prospective clients outside North America. These fell into three principal groups: private-sector companies, public-sector companies, and sovereign governments and their agencies. For the investment banker, the private sector represents the most desirable clientele. Companies in the public sector don't do equity issues (except as part of the privatization process) and are not as likely as those in the private sector to make acquisitions. Sovereign governments run deficits that have to be financed, typically by a steady stream of debt instruments. Such Category II products may provide interesting tombstone advertisements and league table standings but contribute little to the banker's bottom line. However, the investment banker who is attentive to a country's debt financing requirements may find his or her organization well-positioned to obtain attractive privatization business.

This same investment bank also categorized its target list by nationality, recognizing that an international marketing strategy is likely doomed if it fails to consider differences in national character and business practices. Examining a few key countries illustrates some of the problems and opportunities.

The United Kingdom

The United Kingdom represents an attractive market for investment banking services. Language problems are minimal, communications and infrastructure are excellent, and the industrial base is substantial. The British are eager, experienced overseas investors and thus disposed to make transitional acquisitions. The political regime has looked favorably on the private sector in recent years.

On the other hand, many players are eager to get a piece of the business. The British market is highly competitive, and banking coverage of British companies is intensive. Moreover, the London merchant banks have much expertise, with head offices and support staff right on the spot and client relationships going back centuries.

Decisionmakers in British companies are very open to new ideas and willing to use new providers of investment banking services regardless of nationality.

In two critical areas, British companies offer particularly attractive opportunities to U.S. investment banks. First, they are highly desirable clients for transnational merger business. Second, British companies are accustomed to having easy access to equity and do not hesitate to go to the market with a share issue when the balance sheet warrants it. Changes in the structure of the London market and its related practices have made these companies aware that equity-raising techniques used elsewhere, particularly in the United States, may at times be beneficial. Therefore, the leading U.S. investment banks can find exciting business opportunities to manage equity issues for British companies. In this and other offshore markets, the banker operating in unfamiliar territory must be particularly careful to understand fully the risks involved and to manage them appropriately.

A well-trained, competent investment banker should be able to develop relations with, and effectively cover, British companies at all decision-making levels from treasurer to chief executive officer. In this respect, the British market resembles the United States more closely than any of the others we are discussing.

Germany

The sheer size and strength of the Germany economy would make it seem an ideal market for investment banking services. However, the very close relationship that exists even today between a German company and its lead, or house, bank must always be recognized. Although the ties are less binding than in the 1960s and 1970s, they still exist and must be accommodated. German companies differ further from their Anglo-Saxon counterparts in that, typically, the commercial side has more influence than the financial side in the review of acquisitions. A German company generally considers the appropriateness of an acquisition in relation to existing commercial plans rather than as a unique business opportunity. All other things being equal, German companies are less likely than British or U.S. companies to be buyers, and their decisionmaking is somewhat slower.

Moreover, relative currency movements have caused the performance of German offshore acquisitions in deutsche mark terms to be a lot less exciting than the British experience in sterling terms. Still, German companies do make acquisitions, and sizable ones at that. Therefore, the product must be sold to them professionally and consistently.

The management structures of German companies are much more hierarchical than those of British or U.S. companies. Typically, the chief executive officer of a German company is not a "buyer" of investment banking services. An investment banker fortunate enough to gain access to the CEO during a routine call, would soon find himself referred to the finance staff. But it is very important for the investment bank as a firm to have a relationship with the CEO. It is also highly probable that the CEO won't want a close relationship with someone who is on first-name terms with his treasurer. But being on first-name terms with the treasurer is vital if you are going to do any business with the company. Thus the need for two-tier coverage becomes apparent.

Japan

Like Germany, Japan is a prime market for investment banking services. Japan also has a well-developed domestic financial sector that can and does take care of many of the needs of its corporate clients. The structure of Japanese companies is such that they are not major borrowers in the bond markets. By contrast, Japanese banks may borrow to obtain low-cost funding via the swap mechanism, and the public sector will do so for policy reasons. Inefficiencies inherent in their domestic capital markets result in Japanese companies fondness for offering new equity issues in overseas markets. Much of this takes the form of convertible debt or debt with warrants. The Japanese securities houses compete fiercely for this business, which is thus not very profitable.

Since they have not historically been great asset buyers, Japanese corporations did not until recently make very attractive merger clients. Like the Germans, they have a rather lengthy decision-making process, which means they are not very opportunistic buyers. Noteworthy, though, are (1) the tendency of enterprises within a given industry to follow one another's lead (for example, if one bank makes a major acquisition, you can be reasonably sure that others will be considering the same move) and (2) an aggressive Japanese investor appetite for real estate, which provides exciting opportunities for investment banks with well-developed real estate capabilities.

Although there is still some unwillingness to acquire going concerns, Japanese companies have much interest in building their U.S. presence. The U.S. market, by far their largest export destination, is today vulnerable to the rising value of the yen, which affects Japanese competitiveness, and the ground swell of American protectionism, which could lead to tariff barriers or quotas. Despite some recent well-publicized acquisitions, the creation of manufacturing facilities in the United States still represents the favored method of entry. The thoughtful investment banker can find plenty of profitable opportunities in real estate acquisition, construction financing, long-term plant financing, pollution control financing, and so on. Soliciting this business is complex, involving as it does both Japan-based and U.S.-based management. Close coordination between bankers in the home office and Japan is essential.

Each of the three countries selected for detailed discussion above has major domestic financial markets of its own. These countries, among others, provide an opportunity for the well-equipped banker to maximize revenues derived from a particular client while minimizing calling costs. A strong domestic position is the most likely initial selling point for a Category I product: a major acquisition or equity issue in the banker's home market. Success in this effort can lead to international assignments to do similar work.

Finally, the bank with sufficient presence and skills may be asked to work with, or even replace, the client's own local advisors on purely domestic transactions. But such a sequential approach has its hazards. As the bank gets farther away from its domestic environment, the risks become greater and their management more difficult. This is particularly true in equity underwriting. National practices (not necessarily the most efficient) are often structured to favor the local banking system.

In our discussion of Germany, we cited two-tier coverage as an important part of successful marketing. It is worthwhile to examine the nature of this approach and how it can be made to work. Essentially, two-tier coverage implies the necessity to assign different people from different levels in the banking firm to cover their approximate counterparts within the client organization.

For example, a fairly junior person will cover the finance staff up to, and perhaps including, the finance director. A more senior person will provide coverage at the board of directors level, with emphasis on the chief executive officer. Of course, in practice, it becomes more complicated. Much more time must be spent with the finance staff than with the CEO, so more people will be needed at the junior level. These people will be specialized, probably geographically, and responsible for knowing all there is to know about the client's business and related financial needs, the investment banking firm's product line, and how the two can be meshed most effectively. He or she must be knowledgeable about the client's home country and its economic problems and opportunities. He or she must also be fluent in the local language and regularly read the local financial press.

At the more senior level, coverage can be less frequent and therefore less people intensive. General technical product knowledge is less important, but it is still desirable, as is some familiarity with the client's business and home country. Since this person will probably perform the senior role in several countries, it is hardly fair to expect him or her to speak all the languages. But that rare commodity, a multilingual senior investment banker, does represent the best of all possible worlds.

Since many CEOs in the non–Anglo-Saxon world do not readily receive bankers, how can the senior person develop the all-important relationship with a client CEO? Three possibilities come to mind.

1. The two people may have grown up in the business together. Ideally, the investment banking representative will have spent enough time in the territory and with the client so that the middle-management person he or she first called on has advanced to the senior management ranks.
2. The person in the field can ask a contact in the company to introduce his or her senior to the client CEO. Typically, this is what happens when top management in the investment banking firm decides to make a field trip. It may be a useful way for the firm's senior management to find out what is going on although it doesn't necessarily build a warm relationship.
3. Another possibility is to take advantage of the international management meetings that many top-level industrialists enjoy attending (for example, the European Management Forum, the Bilderberg Group, the Aspen Conference). When the CEO and the senior banker are guests at the same event, they are on equal footing and can get to know each other personally.

It cannot be overemphasized that the right kind of person must be involved in marketing financial services internationally. But is a bank best represented by people of its own nationality or by those of the country where the client is located? There are no clear-cut answer to this question.

Thorough training in investment banking technical skills is essential. However, we live in the age of the specialist, and it is doubtful whether any person can carry all the knowledge needed to deal with the full product range of today's investment bank. The salespeople's specialties should be their sales skills (including knowledge of the client organizations, their problems and needs) and their relationships with the key people in the client organizations. These skills should be reinforced by people with specific product knowledge. Thus, for example, a person calling on a client to discuss a merger assignment should be accompanied by a merger specialist.

The perfect salesperson will have spent time in the target country, either at school or while training. Experience proves that it is generally easier to turn a first-class banker into a good representative in the country of choice than to make a good banker of someone whose chief qualification is familiarity with the country. Where the latter approach is necessary, it makes sense to start at the entry level.

Where should the sales force be based? Is the salesperson better placed in the client's backyard where he or she can be right on top of local events and available to see the client at a moment's notice? Or is it more advantageous for the salesperson to be in a central or regional office where he or she can benefit from cross-fertilization of ideas with other bankers and product specialists, be near the trading floor and thus aware of market movements, and be more easily supervised and controlled by headquarters policies? The answer is probably a compromise.

> Before opening our firm's first overseas office, we asked the opinion of several offshore clients about the move. Almost all counseled against it. "You are a New York investment bank, and we want to deal with people from New York," was a common remark. Nevertheless, we opened the office and business increased exponentially thereafter because we could deliver a much more efficient service over more of the working day. Communications between New York and London were such that European clients were as well off as they would have been if they had been dealing with someone in New York. (Lesson: Never let your clients tell you how to run your business.)
>
> Putting people in Europe to service European clients clearly makes sense. But the wisdom of having people scattered all over the world is questionable. Experience indicates that costs go up and efficiency goes down.

There is also the question of presence, the exent to which an investment bank's clients perceive the organization as being part of their community. Nationalism is still strong in Europe, and a firm that has a presence in, say, France, will probably have an edge there over a firm that doesn't. This edge is probably reinforced by the concern that several governments (notably the French and German) are expressing about London's established leadership as the financial center of Europe. When leading investment banks move to establish offices in Frankfurt or Paris, the governments of France and Germany regard this action as a modest victory in their attempt to recover ground lost to London. It will be viewed particularly favorably if the government is involved (as it is, for example, with French privatization) in deciding who gets the business.

There are many ways to establish a presence without actually opening an office. A carefully planned program of low-key entertainment, directed as much to the social and political communities as to the business communities, can be helpful, as can unostentatious, selective support of local charities. Membership in civic and service organizations is also helpful. Senior people from the head office should be encouraged to visit the country as often as possible and get involved in these activities. Employment of a local elder statesman in business, banking, or even politics can be very useful, provided that he or she is the right person and his or her time can be used productively. Such a person can be particularly valuable in Japan.

V. Measuring Performance

Proper evaluation of performance involves two important considerations: (1) which entity is being measured and (2) who will be looking at the results.

A firm can organize its international business along either regional lines or functional lines. Carried to an extreme, regional organization means establishing an offshore subsidiary to conduct all the firm's international business. The parent acts like a shareholder. It has some say in long-term strategy and certainly in the selection of senior management but little in the day-to-day running of business. Management of foreign operations will, quite rightly, be charged with maximizing profits, and its performance will be measured accordingly. The success of the off-shore activities can be measured without considering its benefit to the domestic and international business as a whole.

Organized along functional lines, the firm's principal business segments (for example, mergers and acquisitions, equities, or fixed income) can be run globally with long-term profit maximization of the whole as the objective. Control is exercised at the center. It is probably much easier to provide the cooperation needed between, say, the equity and merger departments to arrange a partial leveraged disposition than it would be to ask the foreign subsidiary to give up a profitable piece of international business because long-term client interests are better served by executing it domesticlly. Though we, as you will have gathered, strongly prefer organization along functional lines, this approach sacrifices one key element: the ability to measure profits.

> The firm is representing a major corporate client in the auction sale of one of its divisions. The strategy is to narrow the field to half a dozen truly interested parties, and then select the best combination of price and contractual arrangements. The firm's person covering Germany must spend a lot of time canvassing that market for potential buyers. Assuming one of them is a finalist, the representative must work with the prospect to ensure that the rules of the game are fully understood and the best possible bid is placed under those rules.
>
> If the winning buyer is an American company, a strictly regional accounting would say the time of the German representative has been largely wasted. (It can, of course, be accounted for by some kind of transfer payment, but this provides only limited incentive for the offshore subsidiary to put its best foot forward.) The merger department, on the other hand, has scored a resounding victory. Accounted for along functional lines, the outcome would permit the representative in Germany to be considered part of a winning team.

Complex accounting systems designed to measure international profitability can produce skewed results. For example, strict profitability analysis might argue for dropping or curtailing a Category II product that sensible management would deem essential to the global success of the business as a whole. But if there are no profitability yardsticks for the international business, costs can run wild, and the entire organization can be placed in jeopardy.

What is the solution? There appears to be some merit in setting conservative goals based on the strategic plans of the organization as a whole, the markets to be focused on, and the penetration desired in each of them. The key to going from this point to an international profit maximization is to achieve the goals at the lowest possible cost. It sounds easy but requires enormous discipline to say "enough" instead of building up the most extensive people and capital facilities in each business area. Put simply, know what you are trying to achieve and what your costs are. Try to get where you want to go as cheaply as possible.

Users of performance measurement data appear to fall into three categories.

1. Senior management. They set long-term objectives and strategies for achieving them.
2. People on the firing line who are selling the product. They will want to know how they are doing within their territory in terms of market share as it relates to the overall product strategy.
3. The customers. They will probably want to use some objective measurement of performance to select an appropriate intermediary.

Senior management will probably use some measure of goals achieved versus costs incurred to judge organization performance. Regional representatives, functional specialists, and clients will most likely pay more attention to market share, which brings us to the question of league tables.

We need market share data that will tell us how well we are doing in moving toward the goals we have set for ourselves and that our customers will believe. We must be aware that, like it or not, our customers will read what the competition shows them. It will be designed to show the competition in a good light and us in a poor light. The first two requirements can probably be met by subscribing to an independent database with unchallenged credibility. It will give us, as a customer, the information we need in the form we need. Anyone who has gone through the incredible maneuvers required to compile coherent marketing statistics out of published league tables will know what we mean. Subscribing to Securities Data Service or a similar organization provides internal statistics that are more meaningful and believable.

In one important respect, however, market share is synonymous with published league tables because clients tend to read them. Moreover, clients are generally (and rightly) suspicious of unpublished league tables, the kind produced with a flourish and a statement like, "Here is a printout from our database that shows our firm is the clear leader in sterling-denominated convertible issues for Swedish consumer goods companies over the past three months."

This may be interesting reading, particularly if the borrower happens to be a Swedish consumer goods company interested in doing a sterling-denominated convertible bond issue. But it also compounds the three cardinal sins of self-serving league tables: too narrow a customer base, too narrow a product line, and too narrow a time frame. Competitors will show that they are leaders in convertibles or in sterling or both and that they have held that position for several years.

Published league tables can also be misleading although it is much more difficult to prove this. A particular (and fortunately infrequent) bias in published league tables is gerrymandering to suit advertising or editorial policy. By gerrymandering, we mean constructing the table definitions to create results (winners or losers) or products that suit the business or editorial goals of the publication. A good example of this might be the editorial discovery of an "international equity market."

> Much to the surprise of those who had, as a matter of course, been distributing equities widely in international markets for the past several decades, a leading financial publication suddenly "discovered" this new product. Editorial coverage of the exciting new market made better reading when the criteria for the league tables were rather narrowly defined. This had two results. First, the tables themselves became suspect (a minor bank in northern Europe was listed as one of the "Top Ten Managers of International Equities," whereas Merrill Lynch and Goldman Sachs were not on the original list). Second, a firm that wanted to appear prominently in the tables as a manager of "international equities" had to make radical changes in its methods of distributing these securities (emphasis to be placed on the composition of the international underwriting syndicate rather than on the in-house distribution of the manager). This change did not always benefit the issuer and did demonstrable harm where (as in both organizations mentioned above) the firm already had in place a strong international distribution network.

We may not like the published league tables. Indeed, we may think they are woefully wrong, but they are designed to be, and probably are, read by precisely the people we are selling to. Being at or near the top of these tables is a helpful marketing tool. Unfortunately, it is probably as important (or more important) in getting the business you don't want (Category II) as it is in getting the business you do want (Category I). Fortunately, once you have established basic credibility in the market, Category II business is awarded as much on the basis of price as market share. Thus the key is to determine the market share you want and go for it. Don't be too shaken by those perennial feature articles whose inevitable lead-in paragraph begins, "Once again Firm X, a powerhouse in its domestic markets, ranked a slothful number 15 in *Eurobond Monthly's* annual lead manager league tables, showing how little its senior management is aware of the globalization of the securities markets." Maybe Firm X's senior management is crazy like a fox.

VI. Conclusion

International business is not a panacea that will help a firm with a weak domestic base pull itself up into the major leagues. But it is clearly desirable for an investment bank to expand internationally if it already has a strong domestic business that it wishes to maintain or enhance. Such expansion must be judicious and based on a well-developed strategy involving a carefully selected product line. Senior management must recognize that only rarely will overseas expansion enhance the firm's overall profit margins. Most often, expenses will increase faster than revenues; expenses are particularly vulnerable to adverse currency fluctuations.

The focus of offshore expansion should be businesses that are (1) already dominant domestically, (2) inherently profitable, and (3) difficult to enter. The resources necessary to obtain and execute such business are scarce, and this should be recognized. Already profitable domestic business should not be jeopardized in order to expand internationally.

Territorial markets should be chosen carefully; business potential and existing as well as anticipated indigenous and foreign competition should be studied. Regional offices should be established, with a view to the infrastructures, tax climates, and cost stability in dollar terms of the prospective host countries. Key people should be concentrated in these regional offices rather than spread thinly among target countries. Marketing staff with territorial and client expertise should be supported by technical specialists. Certain countries will require two-tier coverage by senior and junior staff.

Although performance measurement is important, it should not dictate the form of organization. Overall firm performance can best be measured against predetermined objectives of market share and expense. League tables are important, but they will not necessarily provide the desired information. Subscribing to a carefully selected independent database is essential.

Evaluation of the international business should be based on its contribution to the success of the entire organization. In the long run, the best results will likely be obtained by firms that exercise restraint in their offshore activities.

VII. Notes

1. Robert E. Worton, "Upheaval Ahead on Wall Street," *Fortune,* September 14, 1987, p. 68.
2. A security in which the underlying instrument might be, for example, a dollar-denominated Treasury note that is given deutsche mark currency characteristics by means of matching forward foreign exchange transaction.

9

Positioning a Foreign Bank in the U.S. Market:
The Case of Westpac

Anthony J. Walton
Executive Vice President and General Manager,
Westpac Banking Corporation

I. Introduction

Westpac Banking Corporation, known as Australia's World Bank, was formed in 1982 through the merger of The Commercial Bank of Australia Limited with the Bank of New South Wales, Australia's oldest public company and first bank (founded in 1817).

By 1983, Westpac was already benefiting from the merged strength of these two Australian banking leaders and had become the largest financial intermediary in Australia. With its subsidiaries, Westpac provided comprehensive banking, financial, and related services through extensive consumer branch networks in Australia, New Zealand, Papua New Guinea, Fiji, and other South Pacific Islands.

At the same time, Westpac began to look farther offshore to expand its international market share. The objective was to find the customer, geographic, and product mix that would leverage its substantial corporate position in Australia into profitable business in major financial centers around the world. Specialized corporate, institutional, and investment banking business conducted through the bank's offices in Asia, Europe, and the United States were targeted as markets with the greatest opportunities for expansion.

The geographic market with great promise was the United States, where the International Banking Act (IBA) of 1978 had already opened the playing field to foreign banks. The IBA established "national treatment" for foreign banks by treating them on basically the same footing as U.S. domestic banks, subjecting them to the same restrictions, and offering the same privileges.

Further support for Westpac concentration on the U.S. market came from identifying parallel investments in Australia and, in the United States, from American and Australian corporations. Westpac's historically strong position in Australia could, therefore, serve as a natural springboard for expansion in the United States, which in turn, would support its drive to become a top-ranking bank in the global financial marketplace.

In 1983, Westpac decided to undertake a major expansion in the U.S. marketplace that would be spearheaded by its Americas Division.

The initial step was to appoint a management team with international and domestic U.S. experience. Westpac's global staff and resources were made available to the Americas Division, but the new U.S. team was asked to design its own long-term strategy, for head office approval, to position Westpac in the North American markets.

During the next four years, the Americas Division developed and implemented an aggressive, sharply focused marketing strategy that has established Westpac as the premier Australian bank operating in North America.

II. The Management Challenge

Westpac was already on the ground in the United States with a representative office in Houston, an agency in San Francisco, and a limited branch in Chicago. A U.S. federal branch in New York City functioned as the Americas Division headquarters, but its chief business was to clear U.S. dollars for the Westpac worldwide network.

At yearend 1983, U.S. assets represented only 2.9 percent of the bank's total assets, a miniscule exposure in a major world market. Westpac had no direct relationships with U.S. customers, and U.S. business was confined to small participations in loans made by other banks.

Although number one in its home country and highly creditworthy, Westpac was relatively unknown as an international player. The challenge to the Americas Division management team was to convert a foreign bank's dollar-payments-clearing operation into a top-ranking international banking operation in the U.S. market.

III. Repositioning the Americas Division

In 1982, the first strategic plan for the newly chartered Americas Division laid out the framework for the conversion and rebuilding of Westpac in the United States. The plan evaluated impending changes in global financial markets, forecast their impact on traditional U.S. banking relationships, and anticipated the opportunity for foreign banks.

The plan also took a hard-nosed look at the competition from other foreign banks, assessed the potential for new business, and set an earnings target: a return on assets of 100 basis points (1 percent) before taxes within three years.

Figure 1. Niche Marketing.

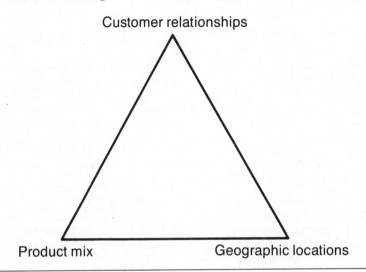

Customer relationships

Product mix   Geographic locations

The strategy strongly emphasized the triangle of concerns—customer relationships, product mix, and geographic locations—that determines the marketing strategies of all highly profitable financial institutions (see Figure 1).

IV. The Competition

The formulation of Westpac's U.S. positioning strategy began with an examination of how foreign banks already operating there defined business. The purpose of this evaluation was to find the strongest platform for success.

Our market research suggested that these foreign banks could be divided into three categories, according to their target markets.

1. Foreign banks whose primary mission is representation in the United States. They do not actively pursue corporate or institutional banking business.
2. Foreign banks that conduct banking business geared specifically to their home country and expatriate customers operating in the United States, or vice versa.
3. Foreign banks whose operations serve the home country and expatriate customers but also aim to create a wholesale and possibly retail presence in the United States. Their customers include U.S. corporations that do not necessarily have an international presence or conduct operations in the bank's home country.

Westpac determined that foreign banks in the third category showed the strongest track record for success, largely because of their flexible response to market opportunities and more broadly defined business base.

Westpac's Americas Division also forecast a realignment of the traditional line relationships between borrowers and their banks if the seemingly imminent changes in the U.S. banking environment were to occur. The securitization of the commercial lending market, the shift to a transactional approach to bank services, and the development of global capital markets were already gaining momentum. By stepping into the U.S. market with broader product lines and quality service, foreign banks would have definite opportunities to pick up market share.

By 1987, 40 to 50 of the more than 400 foreign banks operating in the United States had expanded their activities to become full-service banks. This has confirmed Westpac's strategic assumptions about requirements for success in the changing U.S. market.

V. Target Customers: The "Australian Connection" and Beyond

Given the goal of becoming a premium foreign bank in the United States, Westpac identified four preferential U.S. customer groups:

- Corporations with either a home base or an interest in Australia (These companies came to be known as the "Australian Connection" as the marketing campaign got underway.)
- Special U.S. industry groups (These companies were selected because of Westpac's strength and experience with specialized industries in Australia.)
- U.S. correspondent banks
- Customers in mainstream corporate America (This group was included when the marketing campaign gained momentum.)

The Australian Connection was an area with immediate business potential. The number of Australian corporations with U.S. operations and U.S. corporations with Australian interests proved to be even larger than originally estimated.

The U.S. corporations constituted a very large target population. In the *Fortune* 500 group of industrial corporations, 230 had operations in Australia. Clearly strong banking ties already established with Westpac Australia could open doors to these companies for Westpac calling officers in the United States. In cooperation with Westpac's corporate group in Sydney, an in-depth market research project was immediately undertaken to identify the U.S. companies already banking with Westpac in Australia and their appropriate U.S. contacts.

Westpac had established market strength in Australia with the utilities industry, the commodities industry, and top companies in the oil and gas industry. The Americas Division also targeted large U.S. corporations in these industries.

Identified corporations in these target groups were cross-referenced by credit quality and depth of domestic and international financing requirements. In developing the marketing campaign, the chief criterion for approaching the target companies was their potential for (1) building a global relationship and (2) cross-selling Westpac's financial service capabilities in other locations, particularly London and Asia.

The Americas Division also decided to tap correspondent banking, Westpac's tremendous strength in the Australian market. U.S. money center and regional banks had long been important sources of referred corporate–sovereign risk business for Westpac Australia. By expanding its loan participations in the United States and providing selected financial services to U.S. commercial and investment banks, the Americas Division could benefit from the corporate relationships these banks had established with their own U.S. customers over the years. Westpac, with its high credit ratings, could participate in funding the business its correspondent banks would solicit from their corporate clients.

VI. Niche Marketing

As part of its mission to be a premier foreign bank in the United States, the Westpac Americas Division decided to market a highly specialized mix of commercial and investment banking services. The strategy was to offer specific products and use them to (1) maximize return on customer relationships as quickly as possible and (2) penetrate the corporation's internal banking hierarchy and establish Westpac as a "line" or "house" bank.

The Americas Division adopted a produc̲-based marketing strategy based on a profile of the banking needs that had been demonstrated by target customers. The goal was maximization of profitability with high-quality customers early in the banking relationship. This can be visualized as four interconnecting circles (see Figure 2). The shaded area in the figure represents an optimal banking relationship, providing maximum return on both balance-sheet and off-balance-sheet resources.

Westpac Americas began to gain entry for the bank by cross-selling ancillary or fee-based products such as trade finance, foreign exchange, direct and contingent credit facilities, and Australian dollar and permitted investment banking services. Distinguishing itself by quality of service, Westpac moved into a line, or house, relationship with an increasing number of companies.

This niche marketing strategy for expanding banking relationships is best illustrated as a triangle, with relationships ranked from routine contacts with minimal business to lead banking (see Figure 3).

The Americas Division concluded that development of line relationships with U.S. corporations would depend primarily on the bank's service performance and product delivery. Thus commitment was made to maximize the quality of the ancillary services.

For example, Westpac Americas Division started and maintains a very active treasury group, with dealing operations in New York, Chicago, and San Francisco. Initially, our eight-member dealing team handled money market instruments, bankers' acceptances, and foreign exchange. Today, the division has forty dealers, trading in six different currencies in the spot and forward markets. They are also active in swap transactions, with increased emphasis on the full range of currency risk and interest rate management products.

The success of Westpac's global treasury capabilities is attested by its advance into the ranks of the top ten institutions in *Euromoney* magazine's 1987 survey of corporate treasurers' favorite banks for foreign exchange.

On the credit side, Westpac immediately sought U.S. long-term debt ratings so that it could offer credit-enhancement products. With little outstanding contingent liability, the bank was well-positioned and rated AA. Because U.S. banks were

Figure 2. Product-Based Marketing Strategy.

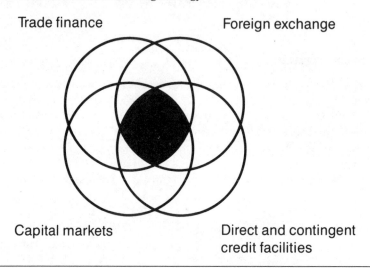

Trade finance   Foreign exchange

Capital markets   Direct and contingent
                                 credit facilities

Figure 3. Relationship Types—U.S. Companies and Their Banks.

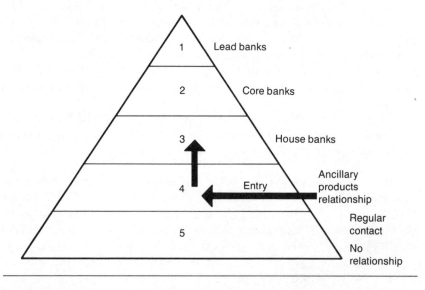

marketing limited credit-enhancement products, Westpac found an opportunity and was able to establish line banking relationships with a number of major U.S. corporations.

Between 1983 and 1987, Westpac Americas Division moved from having virtually no line banking relations to maintaining such associations with approximately 160 U.S. corporations, each with annual sales exceeding $300 million.

VII. Geographic Locations

Westpac's correlation of target customer segments and its product-based marketing strategy called for the Americas Division to expand its geographic representation in the United States. Although "bricks and mortar" offices were becoming less important as telecommunications and travel connections improved, physical proximity was essential for building awareness of Westpac's capabilities in select U.S. regional markets.

Along with New York and Chicago branches, Southern California was recognized as a gateway to the Pacific Basin trade routes. The San Francisco office was immediately converted to branch status. Adding a Los Angeles branch complemented the marketing program and provided a key link to Westpac's Australian Connection customers.

Staff capability was upgraded at the existing Houston representative office, which had been established to serve Australian customers in the U.S. Southwest. Its new objective is service to large and established oil producers.

In 1986, Westpac Banking Corporation became the first foreign bank to open a representative office in Columbus, Ohio, a major manufacturing and distribution center for U.S. industry and a hub for the Australian Connection. The flow of trade between Ohio, which has 68 U.S. companies with affiliates or subsidiaries in Australia, is significant and growing.

Initially budgeted for a loss during its first year of operation, the Columbus representative office turned a significant profit in 1987, more than justifying this strategic bricks and mortar investment.

VIII. Staff Recruiting

From the beginning, Westpac recognized that an experienced staff of professional marketing officers would be the linchpin in an effective U.S. calling program. Staffing was identified as a top priority, and the Americas Division immediately launched a recruiting effort to add approximately 50 officers.

Product and industry skills as well as geographic needs helped define specific staffing requirements. The aim was to have at least one officer in every U.S. branch or representative office who had extensive knowledge of priority banking products and the target industries. For example, energy industry expertise is a priority in the Houston office, whereas the management for the utilities industry centers in Chicago. Operating as an interdependent and highly mobile team, these officers provide Westpac with a talented and efficient network of skills.

Moreover, the expatriate representation of Australian officers in the Americas Division expanded considerably, enhancing career paths within the bank and immediately adding industry, market, and management expertise.

IX. What's in a Name?

Promoting the Westpac Banking Corporation name was a key part of the plan to expand the bank's market share in the United States.

Although the 1982 merger created an Australian bank that ranks among the top 100 worldwide in asset base and the top 50 in profitability, it also produced a portmanteau name that was not easily recognizable. Derived from "Western Pacific," the bank's geographic area of financial strength and market expertise, the Westpac name aroused curiosity but did not automatically open doors.

"Which bank is that?" every customer asked. Even those few U.S. corporations that had been established customers of the Bank of New South Wales or The Commercial Bank of Australia needed information about who and what Westpac was.

To build a public image and recognition for the Westpac effort in the United States, a marketing, advertising, and public relations program was launched at the outset. It was designed to promote the bank's strengths and to tap into Americans' interest in Australia, which has been seen in events such as the Americas' Cup Races. In the United States, Westpac Banking Corporation has been positioned as

- Australia's largest financial services group
- The provider of high-quality financial services
- A "savvy" and "aggressive" financial services group with expertise in world financial markets and a specialty in Pacific Basin finance

In each operating area, this image-building campaign has been backed by a bankwide commitment to quality products and services.

X. A Commitment to Relationship Management

Westpac's commitment to relationship banking has become the channel for delivering high-quality financial services that have repeatedly distinguished the bank from its competitors.

Many U.S. money center commercial banks have focused on transactional business, loosening the relationship ties that they had traditionally cultivated with large corporations. Westpac, by contrast, has chosen to strengthen relationships with target customers while also seeking the fee-based business that increases return on assets. Many corporate treasurers have confirmed the value of this strategy, stating that Westpac has gained an increasing share of their business because of its obvious commitment to relationship banking.

XI. Expansion Through Acquisition

The Americas Division's pursuit of line banking relationships with top-ranking U.S. corporations has been reinforced by two strategic acquisitions and the concurrent broadening of its product line.

In the summer of 1986, Westpac acquired the bullion and treasury operations of Johnson Matthey, a member of the London gold market. The new subsidiary was named Mase Westpac. Six months later, Westpac completed the acquisition of Wm. E. Pollock, a top U.S. primary dealer in U.S. government and agency securities. This subsidiary was named Westpac Pollock.

Both acquisitions are central to Westpac's capital markets strategy and are reinforced by the bank's overall global expansion into selected niche markets. Westpac Pollock gives the bank a major presence in the U.S. capital markets, and Mase Westpac complements the bank's strengths in foreign exchange, precious metals trading, and project finance.

XII. Looking to the Future

Flexible integration of commercial and investment banking services is a major part of Westpac Banking Corporation's strategy for future expansion. Westpac's frontline officers are its antennae, skilled at sensing changes in the financial marketplace.

The bank's annual marketing conference for senior line officers is an important instrument for tapping this source of information and renewing the commitment to the Americas Division. The conference provides motivation for and gives recognition to the frontline sales force. Equally important, the conference workshops and discussion groups give senior management firsthand market knowledge and the information needed to keep Westpac ahead of the competition.

Westpac has succeeded in establishing a solid foundation for positioning itself as a premier foreign bank in the U.S. marketplace. Expanding and enhancing that position will remain an ongoing challenge.

10

Commercial Bank Marketing by U.S. Thrifts

Bruce M. Lloyd
Senior Vice President, Corporate Banking, Far West Savings & Loan

I. Introduction

The entry of U.S. thrifts into the commercial banking arena has not affected the latter industry as much as many had expected. Commercial banking itself has been under enormous pressure to change, and very few of the thousands of savings and loans and savings banks have effectively responded to this opportunity. Adapting to the enormous change in the commercial banking industry requires commitment of corporate resources and willingness by management to institute creative change. Little of that has been evident among the thrifts, which in general, also lack the corporate culture to make commercial banking operations thrive.

II. No Stampede

Less than 5 percent of U.S. thrifts engage in organized commercial banking activity. The license to perform commercial banking was an "emergency" relief measure provided in the 1982 Garn-St. Germain Act. It was intended to help thrifts deal with mismatched assets and liabilities because commercial loans are generally short term, in contrast with long-term mortgages, and are made at a floating interest rate (unlike real estate lending, which except for construction loans, is generally at a fixed rate).

Thrifts have traditionally been retail, not wholesale oriented, with real estate lending (principally single-family home mortgages) their virtually exclusive asset focus.

Most U.S. thrifts are still oriented along those lines. Few are heavily involved in construction lending, income properties lending, standby letters of credit, enhancement of industrial revenue bonds, mortgage-backed securities, brokered deposits, or consumer lending (auto, mobile home, credit card, etc.). Even fewer are involved in commercial banking, and this group seems to be shrinking since the growth rate for commercial assets in U.S. thrifts peaked at 73 percent between 1984 and 1985.

III. Who Are the Players?

The few thrifts that do engage in commercial banking and certain other nontraditional businesses are, in general, big, with asset size ranging from $4 billion to $24 billion. They are generally urban and coastal (Boston–Washington corridor and Southern California) and usually publicly owned and traded, not mutual, with a holding-company structure, For example, Glenfed, Inc., runs its commercial banking unit as a direct subsidiary of the holding company, not as a division of Glendale Federal Savings.

Partly because of their size, thrifts in the commercial banking business tend to be national or regional rather than local in share ownership, lending opportunities, correspondent and investment bank relations, and so on. Indeed, several of the largest S&Ls have Eurobank lines and Eurocommercial paper programs. Their shares are traded on the stock exchanges of Europe and Japan. For example, many thrifts of varying sizes and degrees of creditworthiness have issued AAA-rated Eurobonds fully secured by mortgage-backed securities. But not all large, sophisticated, publicly owned, coastal thrifts have commercial banking operations. Fewer still have succeeded at commercial banking in terms of market penetration and profitability.

One of the best performers in share price in relation to book value is A.H. Ahmanson, whose subsidiary, Home Savings of America, America's second largest thrift, has never flirted with the idea of leaving its core business for the risks of commercial banking. The company cultivates an image of solidity and safety and emphasizes service to the retail depositer and borrower. It has been rewarded over the years with an exceptionally stable and cheap deposit base.

Another strong performer, Great Western Financial Corporation, actually planned for a commercial banking effort and hired a staff of about 40 at its Beverly Hills headquarters. But within a few months, they laid off the staff and withdrew from commercial banking. Whether Great Western's senior management foresaw the coming vicissitudes of the commerical banking industry or perceived this wholesale-oriented activity as incompatible with an overall expansion and diversification strategy based primarily on consumer and retail lending, America's third largest thrift opted our early and apparently without regret.

However, America's fourth largest thrift, California Federal Savings, principal subsidiary of Cal Fed, Inc., was heavily committed to commercial banking and has achieved some success in this endeavor. But the stock market has not rewarded its diversification, and as of this writing, its shares sell at about one half its book value.

IV. The Traditional Thrift

Until deposit interest rates were set free (albeit in a "managed" emancipation) to seek levels dictated by the financial markets, the thrift business was uncomplicated. Loans were made at the highest spread over the regulated cost of funds acceptable to the borrower. Since the cost of funds was overwhelmingly based on the gathering of retail deposits, the principal challenge to the industry was to open successful branches and attract stable deposits (amid toaster wars). On the asset side, home loans were generated by the branches or bought for the institution's own portfolio from mortgage bankers, brokers, and others.

The traditional savings institution had a local-community focus that determined the character of its customers, its competitors, and the size of the loan spread over the cost of funds. The more sophisticated savings institutions were in places like Boston, New York, and Los Angeles, where competition for deposits and loans was intense. These savings institutions had to grow larger and expand their sources of funds beyond their retail geographic areas all the way to Wall Street. They had to pursue lending opportunities that were generally real estate oriented, but also wholesale oriented, often entailing construction risks, floating interest rates, and the like.

By the time the Garn–St. Germain Act permitted commercial banking activity as a relief measure from the catastrophic effects of the freeing of deposit rates, while loan assets remained at lower, fixed rates, the "big city" thrifts were already accustomed to dealing with competition by using nontraditional measures like the following:

1. Packaging mortgage-backed securities
2. Borrowing from the Federal Home Loan Bank Board or the public- or private-placement markets against mortgage-backed securities
3. Selling jumbo certificates of deposit at higher, negotiated rates through brokers or their own money desks
4. Using state-of-the-art cash management systems in their treasury operations

About 5 percent of U.S. thrifts have entered the commercial banking field. But the proportion is much higher among the large, sophisticated big city thrifts. Here is a list, by size of reported commercial banking assets, of some of the active players in commercial banking during the past four and one-half years.

Old Stone Bank, Providence, R.I.
California Federal, Los Angeles, Calif.
Goldome FSB, Buffalo, N.Y.
City Federal, Elizabeth, N.J.
Empire of America, Buffalo, N.Y.
Crossland, Brooklyn, N.Y.
Home Federal, San Diego, Calif.
Meritor, Philadelphia, Pa.
Gibraltar, Beverly Hills, Calif.
Florida Federal, St. Petersburg, Fla.
Carteret, Morristown, N.J.

Western Savings, Phoenix, Ariz.
Glendale Federal, Glendale, Calif.
Perpetual American FSB, Washington, D.C.

Each of these institutions has a different approach and degree of commitment. Moreover, the commercial banking department, division, subsidiary, and so on in each of these and other thrifts has a very different customer base, set of competitors, and pricing or spread and fee structure from either the traditional thrift or from the rest of the company. The result can be a corporate cultural shock within the savings institution.

The customer is no longer the retail individual saver or even the middle-market homebuilder or developer. Instead, customers range from the local entrepreneur, with his or her fast-growth company, to major U.S. corporations thousands of miles away. The competition is now the regional commercial bank, the money center bank, the New York investment bank, and even the London merchant bank.

It is a more sophisticated customer, one who can "shop" his or her needs among many willing lenders with varing credit quality and pricing requirements. The commercial borrower is a user of commercial banking products like demand accounts, wire transfers, trade finance, foreign exchange, hedging instruments, and corporate trust services. More choices are available today than at any time in the history of banking because of the efficiency and globalization of the financial markets.

The effect on the savings institution is that the competition for commercial banking customers is so keen that it can require expensive responses, for example, lower credit-quality standards, lower pricing, longer tenors, and the installation of costly cash management and other banking services. If expensive responses are required, are the returns adequate? Nicheing, or selecting markets or services to specialize in in order to raise margins, has become as critical for savings institutions engaged in commercial banking as it has for the commercial banks themselves.

Most S&Ls in the commercial banking business are seeking or have found niches. But before some institutions could begin to niche, their managements threw out their entire commercial banking effort for lack of understanding or lack of profit performance commensurate with what they had experienced or were currently experiencing in their other businesses.

Along with Great Western, two other major Los Angeles thrifts have withdrawn: Gibraltar Savings with $9.6 billion in assets and Coast Savings with $7.5 billion. For all three, the reason cited for withdrawal was the low net profit compared with earnings derived from real estate or consumer lending activity. (Gibraltar retains its high-yield bond activities.)

V. Market Characteristics

The thrifts that entered commercial banking for the first time in 1983 through 1985 found the market already undergoing radical change. (Thrifts such as Old Stone in Providence and Philadelphia Savings Fund Society, now Meritor, were for legal and historical reasons, already experienced in commercial banking by the time of the Garn-St. Germain Act.) The thrifts had these same basic opportunities for profit as the commercial banks:

- The spread to cost of funds and various commitment and usage-based fees on loans
- Fee-based services such as cash management (account reconciliation, lock box, controlled disbursement, and so on)
- Demand deposit and time deposit balances
- Syndication of loans that they made, with the resulting yield enhancement as they retain part of the fees or spreads

In theory, these profit opportunities would be added to those of the traditional savings institution, along with the new powers from Garn-St. Germain, to offer auto loans, credit cards, home equity lines, and so forth. But in fact, the changes in the commercial banking business and the heightened competition have severely limited these opportunities.

VI. Loans

Since Garn-St. Germain, and even before, the larger, more creditworthy U.S. corporations, have ceased using bank loans for short-term borrowing. They will pay fees ranging between ⅛ percent and ⅝ percent for nonusage, backup lines, but the commercial paper markets are by far their cheapest sources of funds. Indeed, most large manufacturing companies have their own finance subsidiaries or function as banks do themselves, with their own interbank funds trading desks.

It is difficult for banks to compete with the efficient capital markets these corporate borrowers have access to. It is harder still for thrifts whose marginal cost of funds, excluding the retail deposit base, is anywhere from ⅛ percent to ½ percent higher than that of the money center banks.

Despite this, a few thrifts have bought "short-term strips" from money center banks. These are typically 30- to 90-day borrowings by major corporations, typically priced to the participant at a very thin LIBOR plus ¼ percent with no fees. This leaves very little spread to a thrift's cost of funds.

VII. Lending to the Middle Market

The middle-market U.S. corporation is a designation with a variety of subsets, based largely on the level of annual sales, for our purposes, say, $10 million to $300 million. This market has provided a likelier target for banks and S&Ls in their commercial banking activity. These companies generally have not had access to the commercial paper, public debt, or equity markets. This target market was also more relationship oriented, not transaction oriented as the major corporations had become. The middle-market companies were more loyal to their banks.

During th 1980s, there has been heavy competition among banks for even this middle-market, and the spreads and fees on loans have decreased. Regional banks, which did very little loan business with the major corporations headquartered in their areas, began to court the middle-market company, going farther and farther down the sales size charts for prospects. Money center banks, which had built substantial presences in regional centers like Pittsburgh, Atlanta, and Houston, justified those offices as well as their headquarters, by attacking the middle market.

Some foreign banks, particularly Canadian, British, and Japanese, have gone after the middle market along with the larger multinational companies. But most foreign banks stick to *Fortune* 500 names, foreign exchange trading, trade finance, and credit enhancement opportunities for their U.S. business.

Nevertheless, competition for the middle market has turned the prime-plus-3 percent loan of 1980 into a LIBOR-plus-2 percent loan today. It has lowered the commitment fee from 1 percent to ⅝ percent or even ½ percent on middle market risk!

Apart from pricing erosion, competition for middle-market loans has emboldened borrowers, many of them poorly capitalized and thinly managed, to seek more relaxed covenants, fewer personal guarantees, and fewer ancillary obligations. For example, compensating demand balances, once quite common in commercial lending, are all but forgotten, even in the lower-middle market of, say, $10 million to $50 million in sales.

The competition comes not only from foreign and domestic banks. The upper-middle market of companies with, say, $50 million to $300 million in sales, has had much readier access to private-placement funds and even to public debt and equity markets through the investment banking community. For example, Drexel Burnham Lambert has opened a whole new world of debt and equity to smaller, less creditworthy companies through its high-yield (or junk) bonds, commercial paper, and so on. Other houses have also jumped on this profitable bandwagon that had been regarded as disreputable. Venture capital companies, insurance companies, pension funds, and other investors also became active in lending to and taking equity in middle-market companies.

In the end, risk-reward decisions must be made. Is the overcompetitive market forcing lenders to forgo payment for the risks they are taking?

VIII. Perceptions of Thrift Commitment

In the late 1960s and early 1970s, foreign banks began to enter the U.S. domestic corporate market. Many of them bid aggressively for corporate business and were rewarded with transactions. However, at the first sign of financial trouble, a few of these banks canceled credit facilities and gained a reputation for "cutting and running" that still sits poorly with some treasurers today. Some potential borrowers fear a similar reaction by the thrifts. They reason that if the thrift were to withdraw from their credit or the commercial banking business, they could be hurt, so why bother initiate a relationship? Bankers recruited to join the commercial banking units of the thrifts have had similar second thoughts about their own career prospects. Hence thrifts have had to pay more and provide better perks to retain the best people.

Account officers recruited by the thrifts are generally expected to bring with them business from former loyal clients. Once that business has been brought over, they may fear that it will be more difficult to forge new relationships unless the thrift's commitment to commercial banking remains firm. A corporate relationship officer can bring only a limited range of products to the client if he or she works for a savings institution. The commercial bank the officer used to work for could offer such services as foreign exchange, trade finance, foreign and domestic capital markets products of all sorts, a full range of corporate trust products, private banking for executives, and cross-border lending—more "arrows in the quiver."

IX. Participation in Structured Financings

For many thrifts, the focus of commercial banking has been the structure financing brought about in the mid-1980s by the acquisitions, leveraged buyouts, and corporate restructurings stemming from years of stock market undervaluation of major companies. The senior financing provided by commercial banks and thrifts has created substantial loan balances, analyzable credits, at good spreads with strong fees for the first time in years. Customers have been well-known major U.S. companies (even though usually radically reconfigured and highly leveraged; there are, after all, no free lunches).

Thrifts that have engaged in participations in these transactions have done remarkably well. Very few of the major structured financings have been problem credits. The senior positions have been well-insulated by junk (or subordinated) debt and equity (usually minimal). Thrift overhead is low in this type of transaction (low costs of business development, loan servicing, and so on). And some liquidity is developing. Participations of $5 million, $10 million, and $20 million in larger structured financing can be bought and sold in the trading rooms of Bankers Trust, Citibank, Security Pacific, and others.

However, many thrifts seem to rely too much on the quality of the agent or the primary bank group, deriving undue comfort from the presence of presumably savvy New York bankers in the credit. This kind of "me too" lending got a lot of regional commercial banks in trouble during the REIT loan crisis of the early 1970s and the problem loans to less developed countries during the 1980s. Today's buyers of bank loan participations are required to represent that they have done their own credit analysis and arrived at their own decisions.

Still, to the extent that these drawbacks can be avoided or overcome, structured financings could make good sense for the sophisticated thrift that wants to be in the commercial loan business. The future of this type of lending is uncertain at this time, but it appears that structured financings will continue and that senior bank debt will play a major role in these transactions.

X. Mezzanine Financing

To be adequately compensated for the risk of financing lower-middle-market companies, particularly new ones, many lenders are seeking equity and income "kickers" in their pricing structures. Thrifts, like commercial banks, are lending on this basis where they can. Cal Fed, Meritor, Glen Fed Capital, and Carteret are among the thrifts that have done mezzanine transactions within their commercial banking operations. Home Federal of San Diego has established a special mezzanine financing unit in downtown Los Angeles and is a major investor in a mezzanine fund (similar to the LBO and bridge loan funds set up during the past few years), which is designated to give thrifts entry into this type of lending.

XI. High-Yield Securities

Several thrifts have chosen to build substantial high-yield securities portfolios. Counted as commercial loans for regulatory purposes, these assets are often traded actively, which gives them liquidity as well as much higher yields than senior bank debt affords.

Often, they have equity kickers as well. Junk bonds, the more commonly used term fo these securities, reflects their subordinate status to senior bank, trade, and other debt. If cash flow coverage is weak, junior securities are at higher risk, and the investor must be rewarded for that risk.

To be comfortable with the higher risk, thrifts like Columbia Savings, Gibraltar Savings, and Far West Savings (all in Southern California) have hired teams of credit analysts to advise them on purchases of high-yield securities and (perhaps more important) to monitor the portfolio and make timely sell recommendations. These thrifts are constantly "in the market" and can make trading profits, as well as losses, in addition to earning interest on the bonds while owned.

Although this sort of operation is potentially very profitable and perfectly legal, it runs counter to the corporate culture in all but a very few thrifts. Even sophisticated thrifts with commercial banking operations have declined to enter this business.

XII. Fee-Based Services

Like commercial bank loans, banking services have been subjected to intense competition from other institutions. Concerning services, there is the additional problem that most thrifts are new to these businesses and must spend significant sums for systems and people to provide companies with basic cash management products. Thrifts entering the commercial banking arena have not tried to offer products such as trade finance and foreign exchange because the threshold cost is prohibitive. These are generally economy of scale activities that are better left to the likes of Citibank and Paribas. These services entail trading and country risk, which also run counter to the corporate cultures of thrifts.

To the extent that an S&L can develop the required standard banking services, it will offer demand accounts. But modern cash managment techniques are such that balances are kept as low as possible. It is difficult to obtain compensating balances for lending. Uses of certificates of deposit are apparently dictated by market considerations. Although corporate deposits can be a funding source for thrifts, their advantage over other funding sources should be negligible. Thus deposits do not seem like a blockbuster opportunity for thrift profit.

An increasingly important profit opportunity is the syndication of assets to other investors. So far, only a few thrifts have successfully "sold down" commercial banking assets. Home Federal Savings in San Diego and Meritor in Philadelphia are probably the most active in this. On these deals, the syndicator can retain part of the original front-end fee and even some of the spread over prime, LIBOR, or certificates of deposit. Special fees may be paid only to the agent.

Though there are great profit incentives for the syndicator, the activity requires considerable responsibility and commitment to the participants. One major thrift is putting increasing emphasis on sell-down more to spread risk than to increase yields. But the institution will not commit the staff or funds to create a syndications department or make other special provisions. The work therefore requires much line officer time, and some sell-downs simply do not get done.

XIII. Approaches to Commercial Banking: An Overview

Thrifts have been able to choose among the following approaches to successful commercial banking:

1. Large corporate market
   - Short-term strips at thin pricing; ⅛ percent to ¼ percent over cost of funds
   - Backup lines for commercial paper (pure gifts from the borrower that are typically part of an extensive relationship); fees on unused commitments, typically ⅜ percent
   - Participation (usually subparticipation below a $50 million commitment) in large structured financings such as LBOs, restructurings, and acquisitions; yields about 2 percent over cost of funds plus fees
2. Middle market
   - Loans and letters of credit (where a thrift's unenhanced letter of credit is acceptable) to companies being courted more intensively by commercial banks, investment banks, and others; yields usually 1.5 to 3 percent over cost of funds plus fees
   - Fee-based services, primarily cash management products
   - Syndication of loans (fee and spread retention, agency fees)
3. Mezzanine lending
   - Loans, often subordinated, with equity or other kickers, longer tenors; riskier but far more profitable, requiring much analysis and monitoring
   - Fee-based services and other relationship activity
4. High-yield securities
   - Subordinated debt, risky but profitable (excepting credit problems or market dislocation, these securities are often tradable, but "private" financings are not); requires heavy analysis, and draws regulatory criticism

XIV. A Case History

One of the early entrants into commercial banking was California Federal Savings & Loan Association, the principal subsidiary of Cal Fed, Inc. of Los Angeles. Like many thrifts, Cal Fed was badly hurt in the early 1980s by the rising cost of funds in relation to the fixed rates applicable to its real estate loan assets. Its senior management followed the legislation in Congress that led to the Garn-St. Germain Act. To reduce the asset-liability gap, they prepared not only to diversify Cal Fed's activity but also to take advantage of the unique steps a savings institution could legally take, for example, owning an insurance company.

Commercial banking was one of several diversification and profit opportunity businesses that Cal Fed entered. The others included a trust company (individual and corporate), a life insurance company, a real estate master limited partnership, and a thrift and loan (retail, higher risk lending). Some diversification moves (for example, a venture capital subsidiary were tried and abandoned when they failed to meet expectations.

Key to the early success of commercial banking at Cal Fed was the commitment made by the executive office: The president of the S&L subsidiary at that time was a former commercial banker. Its Commercial Banking Division was set up very soon after Garn-St. Germain was signed into law. Experienced bankers were hired at attractive salaries and given the resources needed to make the effort work.

Eventually, several regional offices for middle-market banking were set up. A department for large corporate banking was established. Operations and cash management systems were bought and installed. The investment was substantial. In just three years, commercial banking outstandings reached nearly $700 million, and the division's profitability was strong. Many successful relationships were forged with California and Florida middle-market companies. Up to 85 people worked in the division.

But beginning in late 1986, difficulties arose. They may have been caused by middle-market loan problems, reduced commitment from a reconfigured executive office, or questions about the risk-reward balance of middle-market banking. Fewer transactions were getting through the increasingly careful credit policy function. Two field offices were closed, several of the early account officers and department managers left, the level of outstandings languished, and morale sagged.

Despite heavy investment and early success, the future of commercial banking at Cal Fed is uncertain. The need for commercial banking as a gap reduction tool has all but disappeared. Secondary marketing of mortgages packaged into securities brings liquidity to Cal Fed's core business of single-family home mortgage lending. Adjustable mortgages, which account for more than 80 percent of Cal Fed's present volume, also help with gap management. The life insurance company is making good profits, as it has since its purchase in 1984. Perhaps the success of the other parts of the company has led Cal Fed's senior management to reduce its commitment to commercial banking, an industry that faces great uncertainty. Maintaining that effort may require more resources than it is willing to dedicate.

XV. The Future: Some Conclusions

Other entrants, like Home Federal in San Diego, have recognized the risk-reward problem and responded differently. Home Federal still maintains its middle-market effort although it has closed one of three field offices. However, it has a very successful group engaged in large corporate financings participation, taking very large (for an S&L) positions and syndicating them to other thrifts. Home Federal has moved into the mezzanine financing business. The thrift has not installed expensive cash management systems. Its overhead is relatively low, and its niches are carefully planned. Home Federal has carried out a strong "credit culture" commercial banking effort with minimal loan losses.

Under the commercial banking mandate given to the thrift industry five years ago by Garn-St. Germain, the more sophisticated thrifts entered the fray. But many of them found early on that commercial banking was in too much flux or did not mix with their traditional corporate cultures. Others pursued commercial banking and found that less ambitious approaches and niches have led to the greatest success.

If the successful niches are unacceptable, the appropriate choice for a thrift may be to abandon commercial banking, as many have done and some seem to be about to do. Diversifying the asset-liability structure and mix of business for a thrift is still a good idea. But commercial banking may not be the best or even a good solution. Those thrifts that continue to pursue mainstream commercial banking will doubtless experience credibility problems with customers as other thrifts withdraw. Capable staff members may also decide there is little future for them at a savings institution and leave. Therefore, we expect the following developments:

- There will be few new entrants into commercial banking except on a niche basis.
- More S&Ls will withdraw entirely from commercial banking as the competition heats up. If interstate banking ever comes, it should finish off all but the most profitable thrift and commercial banking operations.
- Stringent cost-saving measures will be imposed by S&Ls that stay in commercial banking to help yields keep pace with those in its other businesses.
- Mezzanine activity will become more popular so that yields can compete with real estate and other opportunities.

Interstate banking legislation at the state level may make thrifts with a decent commercial banking presence more attractive takeover targets for foreign and domestic money center banks since synergies with existing U.S. commercial banking operations may be possible. In any event, the thrifts' corporate culture will become more accustomed to this business.

The commercial banking business has frequently proved too volatile and too specialized to thrive in the thrift's corporate culture. Changes in the business and the competition have forced nicheing. Some thrifts are doing this successfully, some are still feeling their way, and some do not want to bother because core businesses have improved, and other tools are available for diversification and gap management. But overall, the experiment has been successful in that commercial banking gives the savings institution an additional diversification tool.

11

Developing a Niche Strategy

Roger V. Smith
President and CEO, Silicon Valley Bank

I. The Niche Market

Silicon Valley is 25 miles long, 20 miles wide, and located 35 miles south of San Francisco. Bordering on the north is Palo Alto (headquarters of Hewlett-Packard Company). San Jose is to the south, Cupertino (home of Apple Computer) to the west, and Fremont to the east. This small area is the home of the highest concentration of technology-based companies in the world.

Major corporations like Hewlett-Packard, Varian, Apple Computer, Intel, and National Semiconductor are headquartered in the Valley, and IBM and Lockheed have large operations there as well. Approximately 2,600 technology manufacturing companies, employing 250,000 people, are located in Silicon Valley.

The area is blessed with great weather and excellent schools such as Stanford University, Santa Clara University, and San Jose State University. The University of California at Berkeley is only 40 miles northeast. The area lends itself to the entrepreneurial spirit and technological innovation.

The explosion of technology companies concentrated in Silicon Valley is due primarily to the many venture capital firms headquartered in the area. Twenty venture capital firms are located in one office complex alone (at 3000 Sand Hill Road) in Menlo Park, and many others are based in Palo Alto and San Francisco.

Large law firms specializing in technology business are also in Palo Alto. All the local offices of the Big Eight accounting firms have specialized units working with technology companies.

With this solid concentration of technology business, the potential banking market is large. California banking is dominated by large chains, both domestic and foreign. There are also 350 independent banks in the state. Most of California's independent banks work with the business marketplace.

Bank of America is the leading technology bank in Silicon Valley. During the 1970s, the Bank established corporate lending groups in four offices to serve this market.

During a 1987 consolidation, all technology account officers were assigned to one office in Palo Alto. Instead of addressing all technology company prospects, as in the past, Bank of America seems to have now narrowed its focus and follows certain venture capitalists into selected companies.

Bank of the West (owned by Banque Nationale de Paris of France) has been number two in the Valley's technology marketplace. Its efforts are concentrated in the San Jose main office.

Union Bank (owned by Standard Charter of England) handles some technology lending, with varying degrees of effort in its regional offices.

The remaining major banks and independent banks in the Valley have policies that avoid the technology market. They are concerned about rapid uncontrolled growth and worried about short product life cycles. Basically, these banks lack knowledge of the specialized technology marketplace.

II. Our Approach

When we formed Silicon Valley Bank in 1983, we believed the technology marketplace was large and growing. Few banks were addressing this exciting market. Not one independent bank seemed to have the knowledge, much less the desire, to penetrate and service technology companies.

In planning the start-up phase of our bank, we had to do specific action items to establish our niche in the technology marketplace.

We had to create credibility quickly and to appear larger and stronger than we obviously were as a new company. We had to fit into, and be in constant communication with, the network of the Silicon Valley technology business community.

To show our commitment to technology banking, we located the Bank in an industrial area of north San Jose. Our office is right in the middle of Silicon Valley, in an office-industrial building that does not look like a typical bank.

We organized a founders group of 100 key business people to help us launch the Bank. They were divided into technology, commercial business, and real estate subgroups. Sixty of the 100 founders were heavily involved with technology companies. They became our technology founders group, and they, as well as the Commercial and Real Estate Founders' Groups, remain today. The founders' names and titles, as well as their company affiliations, were included in our prospectus when we raised our initial capitalization of $5 million.

We were unique in this market focus. With the special expertise of our founders, we were able to clearly show the markets we planned to address. The technology focus in particular helped us create exciting publicity.

From the outset, we believed wide press exposure could help us achieve credibility. It was helpful to have stories about the formation of the Bank in the local papers as well as the *San Francisco Chronicle* and *Time* magazine. Because of the cost, we decided to do very little advertising, and worked hard on publicity and editorial coverage.

Our bank opening had to feature something different since few people care about a ribbon-cutting ceremony. At our opening, we used clean-room suits which are worn in semiconductor production areas where a very clean environment is required. The all white suits have hoods so only the wearer's face shows. The suits were worn by three people: one of our founding directors, Pete N. McCloskey, Jr., a former U.S. congressman who had represented Silicon Valley for more than 10 years; Dave Titus, the Bank's vice president in charge of technology lending; and me, the Bank's president. We received excellent press. Photographs of the three of us were published in the *San Francisco Chronicle* and the *San Jose Business Journal*. A story and picture appeared in the San Jose Chamber of Commerce monthly newspaper. Four years later, we're still hearing comments about our opening.

To become profitable quickly, we decided to mass market the Bank. One-on-one lunches, dinners, and meetings would not do the job fast enough. We began with a big cocktail party at the Bank. Three hundred people attended. They were impressed by the people who were there, our location in an industrial area, and the office-like layout of our Bank.

We followed up with luncheons for prospects, referral sources, and clients representing six to ten different firms. These luncheons were held in the Bank, with discussions of the business activities of each guest, general topics of interest, and an update on the Bank's progress. In fact we continue to host these lunches monthly.

We held specialized luncheons, such as a "semiconductor lunch" with a senior vice president of Intel Corporation (a founder of the bank) leading the discussion. We had a "personal computer lunch" with an executive vice president of Apple Computer, leading the discussion (with, of course, apple pie for dessert).

In our market focus, we decided that we could not "bank" everyone, but we would take good care of those who become our selected customers. To emphasize this point to our customers and staff, from day one, we have referred to our customers as clients. All banks have customers, but Silicon Valley Bank has clients.

With only a few officers handling business development, we have maximized our referral sources. We call on venture capitalists, lawyers, and CPAs who emphasize technology companies in their work. Historically, 90 percent of our business has come from referrals from this group as well as from clients and friends.

To demonstrate our market knowledge and expertise in the technology market, we have been very active in trade associations. We have spoken at meetings of the American Electronic Association (the largest trade group) and the Electronic Association of California (which specializes in smaller technology companies). We have addressed their presidents' conference and breakfast meetings. We've been active in the Semiconductor Equipment and Materials Institute (SEMI) annual industry forecast dinner. We've also spoken at the Asian American Manufacturers Association (a group of Asian technology companies).

Additionally, we are active participants in meetings and seminars for entrepreneurs. We have spoken at Stanford University, Santa Clara University, and San Jose State University as well as many other groups that focus on starting and financing technology companies.

We decided to publish a newsletter to keep in touch with the marketplace. PG&E, American Express, Master Charge, Pacific Telephone, and others all have newsletters, but we wanted to do something different. At a brainstorming session, we created our "Did You Know?" letter (see Figure 1).

The "Did You Know?" letter is one page consisting of 16 headlines or, as we like to call them, 16 bullets, highlighting clients' activities and Bank news. We publish the letter monthly and mail to a list of more than 5,000 qualified names.

Our goal for the "Did You Know?" letter is to put it in the hands of decision-makers, give them some useful information they can read quickly, and make them think of our Bank.

"It is informative and doesn't take long to read," is the compliment our newsletter most often receives. We believe the readership is 95 percent of those who receive it. The letter is an inexpensive, easy way to get our message to our clients, referral sources, and prospects.

III. Our Results

Through these activities, we are recognized as a key player in the banking industry for technology firms. To emphasize what we do, we have created sayings and actions that distinguish us from our competitors.

1. "New Is Not Bad." We want to help new firms. In the early stages of our relationship, our help is offered mainly in the deposit area.
2. "Growth Is Good." We are not afraid of growth, but we want our clients to experience controlled growth.
3. "We Finance Growth in Assets, not Losses." We feel equity sources (the venture capital firms) should finance losses. Our Bank will then finance assets to allow the company to ship products and become profitable.

Adhering consistently to this market focus and our way of doing business, we have reached the number three spot in the technology banking marketplace in Silicon Valley.

We stay close to our clients and referral sources and work very hard to show the marketplace that we are a profitable, growing financial institution. Total assets at year end 1987 were $203 mm, with earnings of $1 mm. Our losses in banking technology companies have been minimal. Our rewards in deposits, loans, and fees have been very gratifying.

We firmly believe it's possible to penetrate a niche market even in competition with larger institutions. Focus, creativity, consistency, and hard work can capture market share.

Figure 1.

Silicon Valley Bank

"DID YOU KNOW?"
JULY '88

1. Silicon Valley Bancshares posted profits of $673,000 ($.63 per share) for the quarter ended June 30, 1988, an increase of 151% over last year. Total assets increased 26% to $237 million.

2. Silicon Valley Bancshares has completed a public offering of 430,000 shares of common stock at $14.00 per share, raising $6,020,000 in new capital.

3. SynOptics Communications, Inc., our client, has filed for an initial public offering of 1,500,000 shares. Morgan Stanley & Co., Inc. and Hambrecht & Quist, Inc. are co-managing the offering.

4. Our client Bell Microproducts, Inc., a distributor of microelectronic components and systems, received a new round of equity funding from an investor group led by Alpha Partners.

5. We are providing construction financing to our client The Mariani Group of Companies for a 7,030 square foot retail center in Cupertino.

6. Our client Medchoice Warehouse Club, a large medical supply discount store, opened their first outlet, an 18,000 square foot facility in Oakland.

7. Sherpa Corporation, our client, recently raised $2.6 million of new equity from Abingworth PLC, New Enterprise Associates, Tetraven Fund S.A., Century IV Partners, Commonwealth Venture Partners and Fostin Capital.

8. Our client Presentation Technologies introduced the Montage Film Recorder and has signed OEM agreements with Lasergraphics, Inc. and Raster Image Processing Systems to support this introduction.

9. Our client NeuroCare, Inc., developing facilities for post acute brain injured rehabilitation, closed their second round of financing from a group of investors led by 3i. Other investors included Grace Ventures, Inman & Bowman, Crosspoint Venture Partners, Robertson, Colman & Stephens, and Med Venture Associates.

10. Inova Microelectronics Corporation, our client, announced their first product—the industry's first monolithic 1-Megabit SRAM. Inova has also received $5 million of equity financing.

11. ASR, an affiliate of our client Sysorex, has introduced a new watch that is pre-programmed to give the time, date and direction of Mecca for 200 cities around the world.

12. Our client Norian Corporation, a bio-materials medical start-up, raised its first round of venture capital. The investor group included Technology Venture Investors and Sutter Hill Ventures.

13. Our client Equity Engineering, a full service securities broker-dealer, merged with Lloyd M. Ebert & Assoc. The merger more than doubles Equity Engineering's size.

14. Our client Cygnus Research recently obtained a $9.5 million venture funding which included Alan Patricof Associates, Inc., Matrix Partners, Technology Venture Investors, Fairfield Venture Partners, Grace Ventures, Interwest Partners, Merrill, Pickard, Anderson & Eyre, and Elf Technologies Inc.

15. Novellus Systems, Inc., our client, has filed for an initial public offering of 1,500,000 shares of common stock, which is being managed by Bear, Stearns & Co., Hambrecht & Quist, Inc., and Needham & Co., Inc.

■ **Palo Alto Offices:** Two Palo Alto Square, Suite 110, Palo Alto, CA 94306 . . . . . . (415) 493-9001

  755 Page Mill Road, Suite A-130, Palo Alto, CA 94304 . . . . . (415) 493-1600

■ **Santa Clara Office:** 3000 Lakeside Drive, Santa Clara, CA 95054 . . . . (408) 980-0766

■ **San Jose Office:** 2262 North First Street, San Jose, CA 95131 . . . . (408) 435-9500

12

Marketing Thrifts:
Escaping the Gap Trap

Charlotte A. Chamberlain
Executive Vice President and
Director of Strategic Planning,
Glendale Federal S&L Association

James C. Lam
Vice President and Manager of the
Strategic Risk Management Group,
Glendale Federal S&L Association

Thrift stock prices revolve largely around market perceptions of how robust core earnings are relative to fluctuations in interest rates. Over the past ten years, financial deregulation has dramatically revised the market's view of thrifts as *interest rate plays*. It is well known that the ability of thrifts to originate variable rate mortgages, diversify into commercial loans, and engage in hedging transactions has reduced the sensitivity of their core earnings to change in interest rates.

However, the measurement of this change in rate sensitivity is still imprecise. Over 90 percent of thrift managements still use the risk measurement required by regulators as the basis for risk management within their own firms. They are in good company because a large majority of stock analysts, as well as the regulators themselves, also rely on the same measurement of risk to determine changes in earnings relative to interest rate fluctuations.

In this chapter, we will focus on two basic aspects of risk management. First, gap ratios, the most widely used measurement of risk exposure for thrifts, are far too imprecise for the formation of risk strategies for management. Furthermore, while these measurements show accurately the firm's direction of risk management over time, they are far too imprecise for differentiating in a meaningful way among institutions. Second, it is very important that better measures of risk management be adopted by management, analysts, and regulators because of the weight that risk management strategies have on shareholder returns, market valuation, and regulatory compliance.

I. Thrift Stock Valuation

Thrift stocks are selling at bargain-basement prices, relative to both their earnings and book values. At the end of September 1988, the average publicly held thrift stock traded at approximately 6.9 times earnings, representing only 57 percent of the market (S&P 500) price–earnings ratio of 12.1. In other words, investors were indifferent to $0.57 of earnings per share of an average stock, or $1.00 of earnings per share on a thrift stock. By historical standards, these relative prices for thrifts are at normal levels. Between 1979 and 1987, the average price–earnings ratio for a thrift stock was 54 percent of the market's multiple.

Thrift stocks are also trading at a discount to book values. At the end of September 1988, the average thrift stock was selling at a 35 percent discount of its book value.

These market valuations suggest that thrift stocks are relatively undervalued, particularly the select stocks of profitable, strongly capitalized and well-managed institutions. Further evidence can be found in the premium acquisition prices offered for thrift institutions in 1988. The average acquisition price was 16.6 times earnings and 45 percent above tangible book value.

Thrift managers are asking why their stocks are selling at such discounts to other equities, particularly after so many thrift institutions have successfully completed major balance sheet restructuring strategies initiated years ago to reduce rate risk. The answer may be that investors are still concerned with interest rate risk as well as recent thrift failures and the well-publicized insolvency of the Federal Savings and Loan Insurance Corporation (FSLIC). It appears that the paramount management (and marketing) issue confronting thrifts today is one of risk management. After all, the market perspective on an investment's risk-adjusted return is a major force behind the marketability of that investment. Therefore, it is in a thrift's self-interest to ensure that accurate measurements of rate risk are computed internally by management, and externally by analysts and regulators.

II. Risk Measurement

In 1983 the Federal Home Loan Bank Board (FHLBB) changed reporting requirements for member institutions. The new Quarterly FHLBB Report includes a schedule H for presenting breakdowns of the volume of repricing assets versus liabilities by various time periods. In addition, a separate line item is included for reporting hedging activities such as futures positions and interest rate swaps. (Unfortunately, the report also includes scheduled items, so it is not a reliable benchmark for failing institutions.)

Schedule H is the basis for computing the one-year gap, the most widely used measurement of risk for thrift institutions. Table 1 shows a simplified example that will suffice to show the risk measurement concept embedded in a one-year gap or the gap for any arbitrary period.

Table 1. Simple Gap Example.

	Initial Balance	Maturity/Repricing				
	Sun	**Mon**	**Tues**	**Wed**	**Thu**	**Fri**
Assets	30			10	10	10
Liabilities	30	10	10	10		
Gap	0	(10)	(10)	0	10	10
Impact on net interest margin when rates are						
Rising		−	−	Neutral	+	+
Falling		+	+	Neutral	−	−

This example shows a thrift customer with $30 of both assets and liabilities at the beginning of the week. On each day of the week, $10 of assets and/or liabilities comes up for repricing or replacement. This person's income is simply:

Income = $30 × (rate spread between assets and liabilities)

On Monday and Tuesday, this person's income would be adversely affected by a rise in interest rates because on each day $10 more of liabilities than assets are repriced. Similarly, on Thursday and Friday, this person's income would be adversely affected by falling interest rates because $10 more in assets than liabilities are repriced. Only on Wednesday, when $10 of both assets and liabilities are repriced, is the person indifferent to rate movements. As shown in this example, this person has a negative gap of $10 on Monday and Tuesday and a positive gap of the same amount on Thursday and Friday.

The allure of gap as a risk measurement device is apparent even in this example because the expected change in income due to a change in interest rates is simply:

Change in income = Gap × (change in interest rates)

Gap measurement for financial institutions is conceptually no different from the above example. The only wrinkle is that mortgages are stochastic financial instruments and, therefore, the maturities of these assets must be estimated from assumed prepayment rates.

Duration and simulation are two measurements of risk that are used less frequently. Like gap, duration is a scalar measurement of risk. However, duration measures the change in the net worth or market value of a firm relative to changes in interest rates. For ongoing financial institutions, the concept of duration is somewhat less meaningful than gap because duration looks at the changes in the liquidation value of a firm's balance sheet relative to changes in rates rather than changes in its expected ongoing earnings stream. For the same reasons that most thrift managements adamantly oppose proposals for market-to-market reporting, the duration concept is inappropriate for management decisions.

Figure 1. Overview of the Risk Management Process.

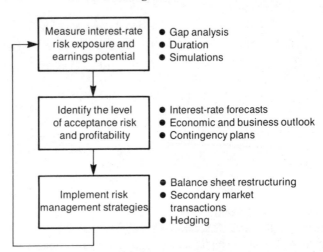

Of these three measures, income simulation is the most complex but also the most meaningful. This measurement superimposes the firm's business plan and contingency plans on its existing balance sheet and repricing schedules as shown in Schedule H of the FHLB Quarterly Report. It is the only measurement tool among the three that does not assume that management is brain-dead. Because both duration and gap are scalar, management is assumed to make no difference in the outcome of income-relative-to-rate changes. Simulation, on the other hand, combines a numerical representation of management's plan and contingencies with the embedded rate risk and spread of the existing balance sheet.

III. Risk Management

While Wall Street is invaluable in advising on hedging strategies, it is essential that management first develop analytical tools to assess the risk-earnings tradeoffs that are embedded in its balance sheet and business plans. Typically, hedging on an asset-by-asset or liability-by-liability basis will result in overhedging the institution, because the natural hedges inherent in its ongoing business will be missed unless a company-wide assessment of the risk is made.

Figure 1 shows an iterative process for establishing and monitoring an ongoing risk management program.

The first step is measuring the tradeoff that the firm already has between interest rate risk and operating earnings. Though simulation typically gives management a much more focused and detailed picture of the tradeoff, the essential element is the requirement that management uses some analytical tool that permits concentration on the tradeoff rather than on the risk alone.

The second step requires management to articulate its objective for the future risk–earnings tradeoff for the company. In other words, it is not sufficient to say that the risk management goal is to reduce the one-year gap to, say, 15 percent of assets. Management must also agree to the estimate of the expected level of operating earnings that such a gap implies, or it must revise its business plan strategies. Neither gap nor duration analysis can readily reflect changes in the business plan that are not embedded in the balance sheet. Thus, management is pretty well locked into the status quo of the initial earnings risk tradeoff that these measurements show. Simulation, however, can readily incorporate changes in the business plan and will show the projected new results consistent with revised strategies.

Once management has agreed to the earnings-versus-risk targets that are acceptable, specific strategies for hedging the firm's activities should be considered. In designing these hedging programs, gap analysis and duration will typically show the correct direction of the risk position for the firm. But using either of these measures as a basis for deciding the level of hedging activities will generally result in overhedging; i.e., using too many futures, options, or swaps to obtain the desired level of risk.

IV. Hiding Behind the Gap

Overhedging based on gap or duration measures can result for several reasons. One of the most important is the time span of the repricing periods that are used. In Table 2, two tabulations of repricing characteristics are shown for the same thrift. The only difference between the two is that the top table shows the repricing mismatches based only on the existing maturity schedule, while the bottom table includes the reinvestment and rollover of all financial assets and liabilities. (These examples focus on gap analysis, but analogous arguments can also be made for duration analysis.)

Both tabulations show the institution with $100 million of assets, $95 million of liabilities and $5 million of net worth. However, the static gap shows a 25 percent negative six-month and one-year gap, while the dynamic gap indicates that the association is completely matched. Since the assets and liabilities are the same in both reports for the same firm, the results differ because the reporting conventions differ.

In the case of a six-month or one-year gap (as in the static gap), no matter how many times the actual assets or liabilities are repriced during either time frame, for reporting purposes each is assumed to be repriced only once. However, with the monthly time period in the dynamic gap, the assets and liabilities with inherent maturities or repricings of less than six months are shown to be repriced once in each monthly time frame. Therefore, on this dynamic gap basis the association is completely matched. It follows that any hedges devised to hedge this institution's 25 percent negative static gap would clearly be excessive.

The FHLBB would not grant this institution "maturity matching credit" on net worth for growth purposes even though the association has virtually no interest rate risk exposure! Finally, it is likely that stock analysts would regard this institution as having far less stable core earnings than is actually the case.

Table 2. Two Tabulations of Repricing Characteristics.

The Static Gap[a]

	Init. Bal.	Months											
		1	2	3	4	5	6	7	8	9	10	11	12
Assets													
Fed. funds	10	10											
Var. inv.	30	30											
Var. loans	30	5	5	5	5	5	5						
Fixed loans	30												
Total	100	45	5	5	5	5	5	0	0	0	0	0	0
Liabilities													
MMDA	20	20											
1-mo. CDs	15	15											
6-mo. CDs	60	10	10	10	10	10	10						
Net worth	5												
Total	100	45	10	10	10	10	10	0	0	0	0	0	0
Gap		0	(5)	(5)	(5)	(5)	(5)	0	0	0	0	0	0
Cumulative gap		0	(5)	(10)	(15)	(20)	(25)	(25)	(25)	(25)	(25)	(25)	(25)

a. The static gap shows an asset-based exposure of 25 percent in the six-month and one-year gaps. Only the first repricing of assets and liabilities is represented.

The Dynamic Gap[b]

	Init. Bal.	Months											
		1	2	3	4	5	6	7	8	9	10	11	12
Assets													
Fed. funds	10	10	10	10	10	10	10	10	10	10	10	10	10
Var. inv.	30	30	30	30	30	30	30	30	30	30	30	30	30
Var. loans	30	5	5	5	5	5	5	5	5	5	5	5	5
Fixed loans	30												
Total	100	45	45	45	45	45	45	45	45	45	45	45	45
Liabilities													
MMDA	20	20	20	20	20	20	20	20	20	20	20	20	20
1-mo. CDs	15	15	15	15	15	15	15	15	15	15	15	15	15
6-mo. CDs	60	10	10	10	10	10	10	10	10	10	10	10	10
Net worth	5												
Total	100	45	45	45	45	45	45	45	45	45	45	45	45
Gap		0	0	0	0	0	0	0	0	0	0	0	0
Cumulative gap		0	0	0	0	0	0	0	0	0	0	0	0

b. The dynamic gap shows perfect matching. All assets and liabilities are assumed to rollover in the same account. For example, fed funds will reprice 12 times in the first year, and 6-month CDs maturing in month 1 will rollover into 6-month CDs maturing in month 7.

Duration and gap measures have other serious flaws that mar their accuracy in reflecting the risk position of a firm. Among these flaws are:

- Lack of synchronization between market rate changes and product rates
- Rotations in the yield curve (i.e., interest rate movements) are rarely the same for all maturities along the yield curve
- Rate caps on adjustable mortgages
- Spread changes between market rates and product rates

V. Appearances Can Be Deceiving

The preceding example showed that thrift management can be misled by using only gap reports for risk management strategies. External analysts can also be misled in their comparisons of earnings sensitivity among thrifts. Table 3 illustrates how two thrifts can have the same six-month and one-year gaps while their sensitivities to interest rate changes differ. In this example, both Thrift A and Thrift B have a six-month gap of −$20 and a one-year gap of −$15, representing 20 percent and 15 percent of assets, respectively.

The one-year gap implies that if interest rates increase one percent, next year's earnings at both thrifts would decline 15 percent. However, when a simulation model is used to measure each thrift's earnings sensitivity, a considerable difference emerges. Given a one percent rise in market rates, Thrift A's earnings decline by 5.4 percent while Thrift B's earnings fall 3.1 percent. Table 4 summarizes the comparison between gap and simulation estimates.

This example highlights two major weaknesses of gap analysis. First, gap provides an inaccurate estimate of earnings sensitivity. In the example, gap overestimated the earnings sensitivity of each thrift by significant amounts (see the differences in Table 4). Second, gap is far too imprecise to differentiate the rate risk exposures among institutions.

In this example, gap would lead an analyst to conclude that the two thrifts have the same degree of rate risk. But Thrift A's exposure to rising rates is considerably higher than that of Thrift B. The differential between the rate risks of these two institutions results from differences in their asset composition. Thrift B has a higher proportion of consumer and commercial loans that are repriced monthly, thereby increasing the repricing sensitivity of its assets.

VI. Trends in Risk Exposure Among 11th District Thrifts

The Eleventh District of the Federal Home Loan Bank System includes almost every savings and loan and savings bank in the states of California, Arizona, and Nevada. These institutions have more than 20 percent of the assets of all members of the entire nationwide FHLB system. Because California-state chartered institutions were allowed to offer adjustable-rate mortgages (ARMs) in the early 1970s, borrowers adapted to these mortgages well ahead of the rest of the country. As a result, these institutions have been able to restructure their balance sheets more rapidly than thrifts in other areas. Figure 2 shows that even with this head start,

Table 3. Comparison of Two Thrifts with the Same Gap but Different Rate Risk.

Thrift A

| | | Maturity/Repricing Schedule | | |
	Initial	Within 6 Months	6 Months to 1 Year	Over 1 Year
Assets				
Adjustable mortgages	35	20	15	0
Fixed mortgages and securities	40	10	5	25
Consumer loans	5	5	0	0
Commercial loans	5	5	0	0
Other assets	15	0	0	15
Total	100	40	20	40
Liabilities				
Time deposits	45	30	10	5
Passbook and NOW accounts	15	0	0	15
Money market accounts	25	25	0	0
Other borrowings	10	5	5	0
Equity	5	0	0	5
Total	100	60	15	25
Gap		(20)	5	15
Cumulative gap		(20)	(15)	0

Thrift B

| | | Maturity/Repricing Schedule | | |
	Initial	Within 6 Months	6 Months to 1 Year	Over 1 Year
Assets				
Adjustable mortgages	20	5	15	0
Fixed mortgages and securities	35	5	5	25
Consumer loans	20	20	0	0
Commercial loans	10	10	0	0
Other assets	15	0	0	15
Total	100	40	20	40
Liabilities				
Time deposits	45	30	10	5
Passbook and NOW accounts	15	0	0	15
Money market accounts	25	25	0	0
Other borrowings	10	5	5	0
Equity	5	0	0	5
Total	100	60	15	25
Gap		(20)	5	15
Cumulative gap		(20)	(15)	0

Table 4. Comparison Between Gap and Simulation Estimates.

	Thrift A (percent)	Thrift B (percent)
One-year gap per assets	15.0	15.0
Earnings sensitivity derived from gap	15.0	15.0
Earnings sensitivity measured by simulations	5.4	3.1
Difference	9.6	11.9

Note: A computer model was used to simulate the earnings of each thrift under two interest rate scenarios: (1) flat rates and (2) with rates shifted upward by 1 percent. Earnings sensitivity is measured by the change in earnings divided by the earnings of the flat-rates scenario.

Figure 2. One-Year Hedged Gap for the 11th District.

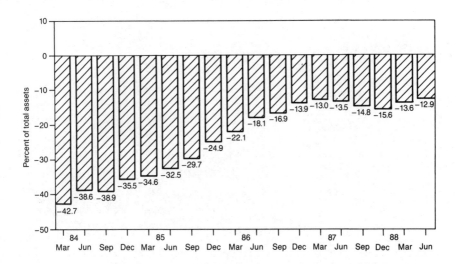

11th District thrifts as a group were still viewed as very risk-sensitive as late as March 1984, when they had an average gap of −42.7 percent. Since then, this risk position has improved steadily to the latest reporting level of −12.9 percent. Still, this is high compared with the low single-digit gaps of most regional banks.

Figure 3. Financial Asset Mix.

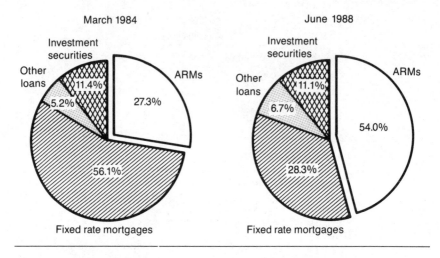

Figure 4. Financial Liability Mix.

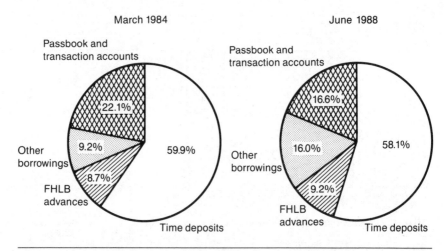

As Figures 3 and 4 show, this improvement has come largely from improvements on the asset side of the ledger. Eleventh District thrifts have been more successful in shortening the maturities of their assets than in lengthening the maturities of their liabilities. Since March 1984, adjustable rate mortgages have increased from 27 to 54 percent of all assets. As a result, in March 1984, 34 percent of all financial assets were scheduled to reprice within one year. By June 1988, this proportion had increased to 62 percent.

Table 5. Simulation of an Increase of 100 Basis Points in Rates for the 11th District.

| | For the Year Ending June 1989 | | | |
Asset Size	NII As % of Assets (1)	Impact of 100 bp Chg in C.O.F. (2)	% Change in NII After 100 bp Chg (2)÷(1)×100	Rate Risk Coverage Ratio (1)÷(2)
$0–$100 million	1.81	(.25)	(14)	7.2
$100 million–$500 million	1.70	(.26)	(15)	6.5
$500 million–$3 billion	1.64	(.26)	(16)	6.3
Over $3 billion	2.15	(.21)	(10)	10.2
The 11th District	2.03	(.21)	(10)	9.7

Restructuring on the liability side has been less successful, with daily access accounts (passbook and transaction accounts) declining from 22 to 17 percent. Over the same period, the percentage of financial liabilities repriced within one year remained the same at 77 percent.

VII. Is Gap the Whole Story?

Using simulation will also show how much income for 11th District thrifts is expected to change for an increase of 100 basis points in rates. It was assumed the overall mix of assets and liabilities would remain the same as at the end of June 1988 but net asset growth would be 8 percent for the year. Table 5 summarizes the results of this simulation.

Even looking at thrifts on a highly aggregated basis, interest rate sensitivity measured with simulation tools is much lower than gap analysis would indicate. In this case, gap shows that 11th District thrifts have a 13 percent risk exposure. But taking into account the timing differences in repricing, standard prepayment expectations, and spread relationships, the risk exposure is only 10 percent; a noteworthy difference. The table also shows that there are significant variations among the various asset-size classes of thrifts as well.

VIII. Conclusions

The *sizzle* in the marketing of thrift institutions is their earnings sensitivity. Robust core earnings whet the appetites of investors more than any diversification strategy. Unfortunately, however, thrifts have much more sizzle than is readily apparent from looking at the most popular measurement of earnings sensitivity, gap ratios. This chapter has shown that the simple scalar measurements of risk exposure for thrifts, gap and duration, typically understate the stability of thrift core earnings to volatile interest rates. Therefore, using these tools as the basis for establishing a risk management program within the firm or for differentiating risk between firms generally produces flawed results. In risk management, using the six-month or one-year gap as a basis for hedging generally will result in putting on too many hedges. Using the one-year gap for comparing the interest sensitivity between thrifts is misleading without knowing more detail on the actual repricing characteristics of their balance sheets. This is particularly important since this measurement is used by the institutions themselves in marketing their stocks and by stock analysts in making recommendations for the purchase of thrift stocks. Since earnings leverage depends on net worth requirements, it is also regrettable that any regulators rely on gap ratios in the granting of credits for growth. It is hoped that all three groups—thrifts, analysts, and regulators—will adopt the more comprehensive tool of simulation to more precisely measure risk trends over time and between firms. The alternative is unappealing to all three groups. If gap ratios continue to be the basis for judging the marketing sizzle of thrifts, it is unlikely that the appetites of investors will ever be as hearty for thrifts as they are for regional banks.

13

Developing a Marketing Strategy for a Large Regional Bank

Marshall C. Tyndall
Executive Vice President, Texas Commerce Bancshares, Inc.

Introduction

Each marketing challenge is governed by the unique circumstances of its environment as measured by the economy, the competition, and industry regulation.

The time spans more than a decade beginning in the early 1970s, and the place is Texas. During the 1950s, 1960s, and 1970s, Texas led the nation in overall economic growth. Bank deposits in the state increased almost twice as fast as in the nation as a whole. From 1973 to 1983, dollar values of construction contracts, retail sales, personal income, and bank deposits more than tripled (see Table 1). Employment increased by more than two thirds, and the state's population grew by 40 percent.

Texas banking is centered in the state's two largest cities: Dallas and Houston. Even so, at the beginning of the 1980s, only 21 percent of the state's deposits were concentrated in the five largest banks, which were located in those cities. Four states had bank deposit totals larger than that of Texas, and the concentration of deposits among the five largest banks in those states ranged from 38 percent in Pennsylvania to 78 percent in California. The number of banks in Texas far surpassed the number in any other state.

Texas's legislative restrictions prohibited branch banking, and meaningful multiple locations of any kind were not feasible until the Bank Holding Company Act of 1956 was amended in 1970. The 1970 amendments enabled Texas banks to form multibank holding companies and begin to penetrate the array of markets across

Table 1. FDIC-Insured Deposits

	Texas[a]		United States[b]	
Date	Banks	Total Deposits ($ millions)	Banks	Total Deposits ($ millions)
1970	1,183	$26,343	13,511	$480,711
1974	1,306	$42,516	14,228	$744,138
1975	1,336	$47,282	14,384	$777,860
1976	1,357	$57,486	14,411	$992,032
1980	1,467	$97,476	14,430	$1,481,161
1984	1,789	$136,170	14,797	$1,686,805
1985	1,907	$147,836	14,776	$1,829,486
1986	1,962	$152,357	14,801	$2,002,757
1986 (2Q)	1,872	$150,586	13,946	$1,929,023

a. Texas percent of change 1974–1984: 220.3 percent; annual rate of change: 22.03 percent.
b. U.S. percent of change 1974–1984: 126.7 percent; annual rate of change: 12.67 percent.
Sources: Federal Deposit Insurance Corporation, *Bank Operating Statistics, 1970–1980*, (Washington, D.C.: Government Printing Office) and *Data Book— Operating Banks and Branches, Summary of Deposits in all Commercial and Mutual Savings Banks*, Volume 16 (Washington, D.C.: Government Printing Office, 1984–86).

the state. Texas banks finally had legislative freedom to capitalize on the opportunities presented by the state's growing economy.

II. Keys to Marketing Success

The six keys to marketing success that we discuss are related to the activities of Texas Commerce Bancshares, Inc., which traces its history to 1886 in Houston, Texas.

The institution formed a multibank holding company in 1971, completed its first mergers in 1972, and grew to 70 member banks by 1985. Total assets increased from $3 billion in 1973 to $20 billion in 1983 (see Table 2). For the decade 1973–1983, Texas Commerce ranked first among the nation's 25 largest banking organizations in asset growth, earnings per share growth, and return on assets (see Figure 1).

Set Geographic Priorities for Expansion

In a regional setting where there are opportunities for geographic expansion, the first step is to systematically evaluate and prioritize the markets according to the organization's overall strategy. As Texas Commerce moved into its geographic expansion phase, the chosen strategy was to grow into a balanced statewide banking organization with a strong presence in the six major Texas markets: Houston, Dallas, Fort Worth, San Antonio, Austin, and El Paso. As Table 3 shows, these six markets encompassed 55 percent of the state's population in 1970.

Table 2. Texas Commerce Bancshares, 1973–1983.

Year	Assets ($ billions)	Rank[a]
1973	$2.828	44
1974	3.684	33
1975	4.524	26
1976	5.196	27
1977	6.643	24
1978	8.027	24
1979	8.260	24
1980	11.286	21
1981	14.512	21
1982	17.217	19
1983	19.499	20

a. Position of Texas Commerce in the nation's banks by total assets.
Source: Walter L. Buenger and Joseph A. Pratt, *But Also Good Business, Texas Commerce Banks and the Financing of Houston and Texas, 1886–1986*, (College Station, Tex: Texas A&M Press, 1986), p. 298. (Data compiled from *Moody's Bank and Finance Manual, Fortune*, and *Business Week*.)

A merger and acquisition committee was established to review market evaluations and merger opportunities. First, the economic viability of each standard metropolitan statistical area (SMSA) in Texas was examined and ranked by size. The SMSAs were evaluated by the regulatory atmosphere governing the probability of merger approval for each key bank in a market. Nineteen SMSAs were identified initially, and the six major markets were assigned the highest priority.

The committee regularly considered new priorities in the top five markets where Texas Commerce had no banks. Each bank in each market was analyzed to determine the current possibility of a merger, and an action plan was assigned to each institution. Finally, the committee reviewed markets where Texas Commerce already had member banks, and locations were pinpointed for potential expansion through merger or the establishment of a new bank.

After more than a decade, this disciplined review gave Texas Commerce representation in 17 markets throughout the state. The markets with a Texas Commerce presence accounted for 72 percent of the state's population and 82 percent of its population growth in the 1980s.

Proper planning can improve your chances for success, but it cannot guarantee success. The unpredictable winds that arise during a storm of mergers and acquisitions can drive you away from a carefully planned path. Remember, the negotiating table does have two sides.

Figure 1. Performance Comparisons, 1974–1983.

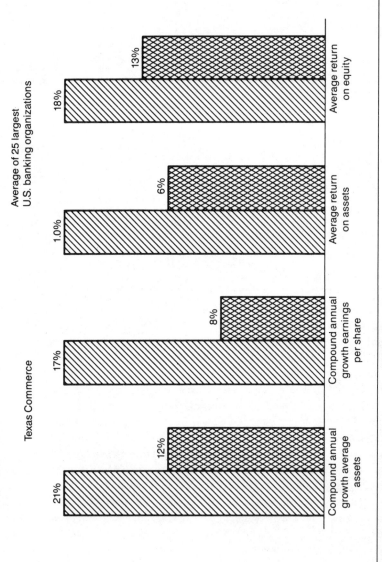

Source: Texas Commerce Bancshares, Inc., Financial Planning Department.

Table 3. Population.

	1970	1980	1984	1985	1986	Percent Change			Annual Percent Population Change		
						1970–1980	1980–1984	1980–1986	1980–1982	1982–1984	1980–1985
Houston CMSA	2,169.1	3,099.9	3,591.3	3,623.3	3,634.1	42.9	15.0	17.2	5.3	2.0	3.3
Dallas/Ft. Worth CMSA	2,351.6	2,930.5	3,379.2	3,511.6	3,655.3	24.6	14.2	25.0	3.2	3.8	3.8
San Antonio	888.2	1,072.1	1,205.3	1,235.7	1,276.4	20.7	10.9	19.1	2.6	3.1	2.9
Austin	360.5	536.7	650.4	695.5	726.4	48.9	20.3	35.3	3.9	5.7	5.6
El Paso	359.3	479.9	538.1	545.0	561.5	33.6	9.7	17.0	2.3	3.3	6.5
Texas	11,198.7	14,225.5	16,083.0	16,370.0	16,682.0	27.0	13.1	17.3	3.7	2.7	3.0

Source: U.S. Bureau of the Census, *State and Metropolitan Area Date Book* (Washington, D.C.: Government Printing Office, 1986), *Provisional Estimates of the Population of Counties* (Washington, D.C.: Government Printing Office, 1986), and *Metropolitan Statistical Areas by Population Rank* (Washington, D.C.: Government Printing Office, 1986); and Texas State Data Center, *Update 1987—The Continued Slowdown in Texas Population Growth* (Austin, Tex.: Texas State Data Center, 1987).

The Texas Commerce policy was to concentrate on merger opportunities that would not dilute the value of current shareholders and pass on the rest. Further, a strong sense of independence is a Texas attribute; several Texas banks felt strongly about retaining their independence. Largely because of these two factors, Texas Commerce came away with only a 3 percent share of the market in Dallas, Fort Worth, and San Antonio. Expanding market penetration in these cities is still one of the greatest challenges facing the organization.

Build Credibility in New Markets

The second step in an expansion program is establishing credibility in the new markets. The banking business is based on confidence and credibility. Entering a new market can be a challenging task even when you do so via a merger.

All of us are judged by the company we keep, and this holds true for banks as well. Texas Commerce established market credibility through its directors. In a multibank holding company, each member bank is a wholly owned subsidiary with its own board of directors. Men and women in each market who were known and respected as community leaders were invited to serve on member bank boards.

The strategy was to make that board of directors a very visible entity in the market. Print advertising was used extensively with photographs of directors displayed prominently. The strategy was also implemented at the parent company. Among the directors of Texas Commerce Bancshares were business leaders and public figures such as former President Gerald R. Ford, former First Lady Mrs. Lyndon B. Johnson, and former Congresswoman Barbara Jordan (who made her mark during the Watergate hearings). These well-known directors were active participants, with nearly 100 percent attendance at board meetings and important involvement in board committees. For example, President Ford chaired the key International Strategy Committee.

The number of directors throughout all the Texas Commerce member banks exceeded 1,100. Because they came from all sections of the state and represented many different businesses, their association with one another became a tangible benefit. To enhance that advantage, a *Directors Directory* was published periodically, including photos of all directors, cross-referenced by member bank, company affiliation, and type of business. Thus a Texas Commerce director in San Antonio who needed a business contact in El Paso could refer to his or her directory for the name of a fellow director. Being a Texas Commerce director became much like being a member of a special club.

Bank directors offer more than credibility, more than the traditional guidance and diligence expected from those who sit on boards. Directors can be a primary source of referrals. Their broad base of associations can help sell the bank to identified prospects. Communication is the key that unlocks this valuable resource, and the bank has the responsibility for initiating the communication.

Directors need to be well informed to feel comfortable when acting on behalf of the bank. Between board meetings, Texas Commerce Bancshares Chairman and Chief Executive Officer Ben Love and member bank CEOs write frequently to all directors about matters of importance to the organization. Member banks regularly review top new business prospects with directors. Action plans, competition, and key decisionmakers are included in the reviews that gave directors the facts to make their support of Texas Commerce comfortable and productive. Many member banks review their new business under consideration and business declined to help directors understand fully the kind of banking business that can be accommodated. The objective is to give the directors the comfort that will encourage their taking an active role on behalf of the bank.

A directors' marketing committee can serve as an effective prospect-screening vehicle. Working through a prospect list with this kind of group serves two purposes. First, the directors' knowledge of the market assists the bankers in prioritizing prospects. Second, the appropriate assistance from individual directors can be identified and committed on the spot.

Position Services to Target Customer Base

The third step in creating a successful marketing program is to decide what kind of bank you want to be. To try to be all things to all people and do them all successfully is very difficult.

In 11 out of 14 years, during the 1970s and early 1980s, Texas led the nation in growth of bank deposits. Moreover, the ratio of demand deposits to total deposits in Texas as a whole was high compared with those of money center banks and other major regional banks (see Figure 2). In a mature market, the consumer becomes the principal provider of funds. But in Texas, the significant expansion of existing companies and the influx of new businesses fueled the growth in the state's economy and the growth in bank deposits.

The ability to gain a large volume of new business dictated that Texas Commerce should be oriented primarily toward business customers, with convenience of location the main consumer thrust. Resources, including advertising dollars, were allocated accordingly.

Enhance Salesmanship

The fourth step in organizing for marketing success is selling to get the business. Commercial banking business is sold face to face. Banking products have to be sold, which means bankers must be salespeople. There are two schools of thought about selling. One requires the salesperson to solicit the business and then introduce the prospect to a credit officer. The second school of thought, which has gained advocates in recent years, requires the banker to be skilled in both selling and lending. It assigns the banker the responsibility for getting the business and keeping it.

Texas Commerce followed the second school of thought, believing the selling process (1) requires a knowledgeable discussion of specific financing alternatives and (2) begins in earnest after the first business is booked. Existing customers remain the source of most new loans, deposits, and fees each year.

Today's banker needs an ever-increasing knowledge of new products that reach beyond the traditional credit skills. Even in companies with annual sales volume between $1 million and $50 million, cash management, trust, and capital markets

Figure 2. Source of Funds of Texas Commerce, 1969–1984[a].

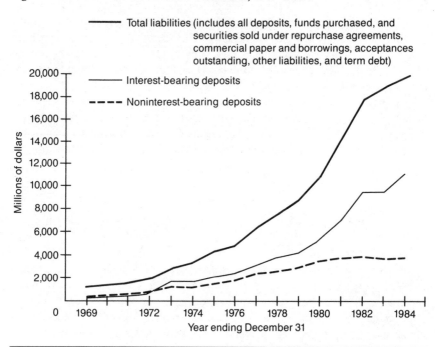

a. Texas Commerce Bank before 1971; Texas Commerce Bancshares from 1971 forward.
Source: Texas Commerce Bancshares, Inc., Financial Planning Department.

products can make the difference between winning and losing a piece of business. True, there are specialists in these product areas, but the relationship banker must lead in selling them because that banker is on the frontline, actually making the contacts with the customer.

New business is measured in loans, deposits, fees, relationships gained, and services sold. But the sales process can take a long time in banking. Therefore, business in the pipeline must be monitored. One way to do that is to monitor the activity that initiates the flow into the pipeline, namely, business development calls on clients and prospective clients. The format of a business development call must be clearly defined. Using a form like that shown in Figure 3, the purpose of the call, the business discussed, and the specific follow-up required must be reported.

At Texas Commerce, a valid business development call is made outside the bank at the client's or prospective client's place of business. Customer calls and prospect calls should be projected annually and monitored monthly by management against a projected monthly average number of calls per officer. This form of tracking is used to monitor activity in the marketplace rather than officer activity per se. Only one call is recorded for each visit; if two bankers make the call, each records one-half call.

Figure 3. BDS Call Report.

___ REQUEST BDS COOR
STATUS FOR OFFICER
CIRCLED BELOW

CO NAME:
STREET:
P.O. BOX:
CITY: ST: ZIP: ___ CUSTOMER
PHONE: ___ PROSPECT
D&B #:   AMT
CALL DATE: ___ / ___ / ___   BLUE
                                                          OFF BOOK
PERSON(S) CONTACTED & TITLE   CALLING OFFICER(S) & BANK/LOC   INIT CRED

CALL PURPOSE: _____

BUSINESS DISCUSSED: _____

SERVICES DISCUSSED ON CALL: (CIRCLE)

COMMERCIAL   PERSONAL

LENDING	DDA	DISBUR	SWAPS	LOAN	TRUST
L/C	CD	CONCEN	PR PLCMTS	DDA	VISA/MC
EXPT FIN	BROK	MERCHANT	___	MMKT	___
FOR EXCHG	LOCKBOX	CORRSP BK	___	CD	___
CORP TRUST	TEXCOMM	TAXABLE INV	___	BROK	___
INST TRUST	ACCT REC	TAX-FREE INV	___	IRA	___

OFF
INIT   DATE

PURPOSE OF NEXT CALL(S) & DATE(S):
___ ___ / ___ / ___
___ ___ / ___ / ___

OTHER ACTION REQUIRED:
___ ___ / ___ / ___
___ ___ / ___ / ___

COPIES TO: _____
(ATTACH PAGES 2 & 3 OF CALL REPORT FOR BRIEFING MEMO UPDATE)

Source: Texas Commerce Bancshares, Inc. Marketing Information Division, "Business Development Call Tracking System," May 1986, p. 11.

The quality of business development calls can be monitored by line management through a review of written call reports and in weekly new-business meetings where calls made and calls to be made are discussed and action plans evaluated. At Texas Commerce, the number of calls increased from 66,316 in 1981, for an average of 12 calls per calling officer each month, to 116,095 in 1984, for an average of 17 calls per calling officer each month.

Providing focus for the business development effort is another marketing challenge. An undirected new-business call can be a costly waste of time. Focus must come from management. A tool used successfully at Texas Commerce is the *Top 50 Report*, which lists a member bank's best sources of potential new business from either prospects or present customers. The report is taken from account officer information. It defines the new business opportunity by company, quantifies the estimated new business potential, and sets forth a short but specific action plan. This tool enables a line manager to monitor the business in the pipeline and, by applying probabilities of success, to determine if the identified opportunities are sufficient to meet budgeted objectives. The line manager uses the *Top 50 Report* to evaluate the account officer's specific strategy for getting the business and to ensure the most effective allocation of resources.

Coordinating the calling effort is particularly critical when multiple member banks or line units are calling across city or state geographic areas. At Texas Commerce, the coordination is achieved through the creation of a computerized Business Development System that retains a file of more than 460,000 companies. Primary and secondary Business Development Coordinators are assigned to the companies. When a banker prepares to call on a company in, say, Austin, he or she can access that company's file on a computer screen, determine whether it is a present customer or a designated prospect, and identify the related Business Development Coordinators (see Figure 4). A telephone call to the coordinator(s) keeps the bank from stepping on its own toes by duplicating efforts and, very likely, makes the call more effective.

The Business Development System also focuses efforts by permitting selection of companies to call on by type, size, and location of business or a myriad of other criteria. Competitive banks are also noted in the file so that customers of a particular competitor bank can be identified when a blitz against that target segment is launched.

Focus in business development is one of the greatest marketing challenges. Focus clarifies the objectives of the task. It ensures that the business development team will call on prospects with an enhanced probability of success and a resulting return to the bank that will meet targeted objectives. Focus motivates the business development team and means management is communicating a clear business development assignment instead of leaving each unit to the struggle of finding its own way.

Provide Targeted Advertising Support

The fifth step in developing a regional coordinated marketing effort is the creation of advertising that directly supports the business developing effort. Advertising philosophies are highly subjective; virtually every person has his or her own

Figure 4. Primary BDS Company Inquiry Screen.

```
PAGE 1 OF 1                  TCBK BUSINESS DEVELOPMENT SYSTEM      OPT
ACTION     NEXT TRAN           DATE 86/08/21   TIME  10:53:28   TERM T001100
************************************************************************
CO SNM    _____   __                     D&B#      __ __ ___
CO NAME   _____        SIC CODE  ___  ___  ___
STREET    _____        BUSINESS  _____
MAILING   _____        YR ESTAB  ____
CITY      _____ ST __ ZIP _____ ___   YR SALES  _____  (000)
CONTACT   _____        #EMP TOT  _____ HERE _____
PHONE     __ ___ - ____   TITLE _____        ULT D&B#  __ __ ___
TCBK REL  ___  CR _  DEP _  CM _  TR _  INV _  CHEM REL  ____

TCBK BUSINESS DEVELOPMENT COORDINATOR             COMPETITOR INFORMATION
COOR1  _____  BK1  _____
BK LOC1 _____  BK2  _____
PH   __ ___ - ____   TIMS # _ ___ ___    OTHER TCBK OFFICERS
COOR2  _____  CM   _____
BK LOC2 _____  TR   _____
COMMENTS: _____
          _____
          _____
=========================================================================
PRESS TO VIEW ADD'L COMMENTS          PRESS PF2 FOR ADD'L D&B INFO
```

■ Enhanced version of current BDS primary screen.
■ Additions include three SIC codes, line of business description, employees "here," Chemical Bank
  prospect/customer relationship, and specialized TCBK cash management/trust officers.
Source: Texas Commerce Bancshares, Inc., Marketing Information Division, "Business Development
Call Tracking System," May 1987, p. 43.

approach. We feel there are two principles of successful advertising. First, work very hard to differentiate your bank from your competitors'; this identity can be the foundation of your communication program. Second, present a consistent message and creative concept. Of course, this does not mean you should be boring or run dated and ineffective advertising. It does mean we tend to watch our own advertising more closely than anyone else does, and we tire of it much sooner than anyone else. The classic advertising campaigns have freshened their creative approach as needed, but their basic concept has remained consistent. The more often you change your public image, the more difficult it is for the public to understand who you are and what you do.

In 1976, Texas Commerce conducted research that showed our people to be our chief differentiating advantage over the competition. The competitor bank was perceived to be a good bank by virtue of its size, whereas Texas Commerce's strength was attributed directly to the quality of service provided by its people.

During this same period, we increased our emphasis on making business development calls at our customer's or prospect's place of business. The advertising campaign, designed to support the call program, was built around the concept of showing Texas Commerce bankers with customers at their places of business, at construction sites, on oil rigs and ranches, and in steel plants and machine shops. This concept supported the externally perceived differentiation from competition while it served internally to motivate and support the aggressive business development call program. Directed at the target market of large and small businesses, the concept and direction of this campaign remained consistent for more than a decade.

The communications medium must complement the creative effort. Because Texas Commerce's creative strategy called for bankers to virtually sell themselves, in effect, through their actions in the advertising, the medium had to show their personalities. Television was the medium chosen because it affords the greatest flexibility of sight, sound, and movement. In each Texas Commerce market, we produced TV spots that used local bankers and customers. The spots greatly increased the visibility of the calling officers in the marketplace, thereby increasing their productivity. The advertising program supported the business development call program by broadening positive awareness of Texas Commerce and its bankers.

In a targeted advertising program, the media buy is as important as the creative effort. Our first priority was to identify the segment that influences business banking decisions. For media buying, the target segment included males with household incomes of at least $35,000. We concentrated on news, sports, and selective prime-time programs. Each prime-time show and movie was painstakingly screened.

The advertising results were subjectively and objectively measured. Because the advertising was designed to support the business development call program by broadening positive awareness of Texas Commerce and its bankers, subjective responses from the bankers making business development calls were considered. The advertising was favorably mentioned by customers and prospects in more than half the business development calls made.

An objective evaluation was obtained through regular primary research studies. Three measurements in the research were particularly useful in determining how effectively the advertising achieved its defined objective: advertising awareness, specific message recall, and scores against predetermined value statements such as "good bank for business" and "good bank for individuals." For this last measurement, we compared the scores of those familiar with Texas Commerce advertising with the scores of those who were not. The same measures were applied to competitive advertising.

Research showed that results of the targeted market advertising campaign were consistent for more than a decade. Texas Commerce advertising awareness levels ranged between 65 and 70 percent, far outstripping competitors even though they spent similar amounts for advertising. Figure 5 shows accurate message recall within the target market reached levels that were four times greater than those the competition achieved. Measurement against predetermined value statements showed people who had seen the Texas Commerce advertising came away with a better impression of the bank in relation to important image variables. The difference was statistically significant.

Although advertising must be targeted against primary market segments, it is also necessary to monitor its effect on non-targeted segments. Here, the target segment included those who influenced business banking decisions for large and small businesses, meaning persons in the higher socioeconomic market. At the same time, it was important to avoid positioning Texas Commerce negatively with

Figure 5. Accurate Message Recall, Target Market.

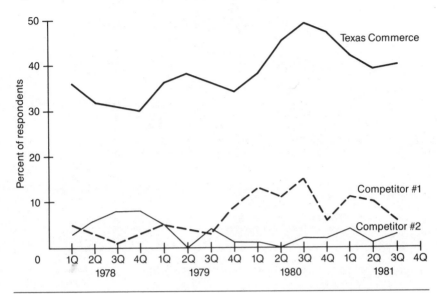

Source: Texas Commerce Bancshares, Inc. Marketing Research Section, advertising market monitor reports, 1978–81.

the general consumer market. When research compared Texas Commerce with its primary competitors, who devoted most of their advertising dollars to consumer messages, at worst there was no statistically significant difference in the value measurement of a "good bank for individuals," and in some years, Texas Commerce outscored its competition (see Table 4). As Figure 6 shows, awareness of Texas Commerce advertising and accurate message recall levels within the general consumer market segment consistently exceeded those of competitor banks by 25 to 50 percent.

The Texas Commerce advertising campaign was unusual because actual bank officers were rarely shown in high-quality television production. Using your own people on television was usually associated with the used-car dealers until Lee Iacocca legitimized the concept. Use of television for commercial banking was also uncommon. The more frequent approach was to use broadcast, the retail medium, for consumer business and reserve the more targeted print medium for commercial advertising. Finally, the campaign's decade of consistency was unusual and paid off measurably in the marketplace.

A market awareness effort is incomplete without the coordination of a consistent corporate identity program that is as much a part of a bank's public image as its advertising. It is integral to the advertising campaign because if it is lacking or poorly done, your ad could be anybody's ad. Corporate identity goes beyond advertising. It is the specific identity on your signs that directs customers and

Table 4. Good Bank for Individuals.

	Houston Area			Statewide
	1978	1981	1984	1987
Texas Commerce	31%	26%	23%	34%
Competitor #1	22	26	12	29
Competitor #2	22	13	12	36

Sources: Texas Commerce Bancshares, Marketing Research Section, advertising market monitor reports, 1978–1984; Creative Consumer Research, "Executive Summary Retail Advertising Monitor—Texas Commerce Bank," November 1987.

Figure 6. Accurate Message Recall, Total Sample.

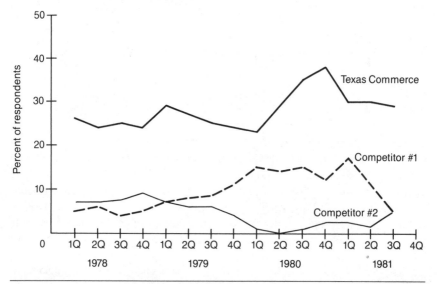

Source: Texas Commerce Bancshares, Inc., Marketing Research Section, advertising market monitor reports, 1978–81.

potential customers to your bank or branch. It makes a statement about your corporate personality. It is the glue that holds your market awareness program together.

In the mid-1960s, a logo was developed for Texas Commerce that was a variation of the Texas flag and incorporated the bank's name in the field of the flag. Many who saw it would swear that it was the Texas flag. The similarity of the state flag gave the logo unusually strong recognition value. Use of the bank's name as part of the logo linked the recognition immediately and unquestionably to Texas Commerce. The red, white, and blue coloring gave the logo a vibrancy and an enhanced visibility. Its visual strength was associated with the strength and aggressive image of the Texas Commerce organization. In 1982, an independent market survey placed the recognition of the Texas Commerce logo at nearly three times that of the closest-ranking competitor.

The rectangular shape of the flag logo was readily adapted to sign requirements for geographic expansion. The original Times Roman typeface was changed to Helvetica Medium in the mid-1970s to improve readability, and the logo became the sign.

The use of the logo was controlled and centralized so that wherever you went in Texas, you saw the same Texas Commerce image, and awareness of the bank was reinforced. As mergers with other banks were completed, possible changes of name were carefully reviewed for retention of value within the market. However, the adoption of the Texas Commerce logo, which could accommodate the merged bank's existing name, was expedited to achieve the desired continuity awareness.

Create the Right Marketing Attitude

The most important key to a successful marketing program is the right marketing attitude. An organization's marketing attitude originates at the top. The chief executive officer is truly the chief marketing officer in a marketing-oriented organization. The right marketing attitude breeds a positive sales-oriented atmosphere. It fosters teamwork, with the objective of working together to build the business rather than concentrating on "turf fighting." It encourages people to be involved and visible in the marketplace, which in turn, builds a positive public awareness of the bank and its bankers.

III. Conclusion

Flexibility, the ability to change as the market changes, is critical to marketing success. The Texas market has changed. In 1985, the U.S. rotary rig count declined by 28 percent, and Texas no longer led the major states in the country in growth of bank deposits (see Figure 7). During 1986, bank deposits in Texas actually declined, unemployment increased, and the state fell below the national level in new businesses incorporated.

Even in this difficult economic environment, the commercial middle market is still the primary contributor to our earnings, but new business is now derived mainly from expansion of our share of the existing market rather than from overall market growth.

On May 1, 1987, Texas Commerce merged with Chemical Bank in New York to create the nation's fourth largest banking organization. This long-range strategic decision has short-range business development implications as well. In a market beset by problems in its financial institutions, the continued strength and stability of Texas Commerce combined with an enhanced array of services provides a positive position of differentiation that we can sell aggressively to the commercial middle-market segment. New business calls in 1988 are projected to exceed 106,000 compared to 83,000 calls in 1987.

The consumer market has taken on a new look. In 1986, the Texas State Legislature passed enabling legislation that opened the way for countywide branch

Figure 7. Rotary Rig Count in Texas, The Southwest (Tex., Okla., La.) and the United States, 1973–1987.

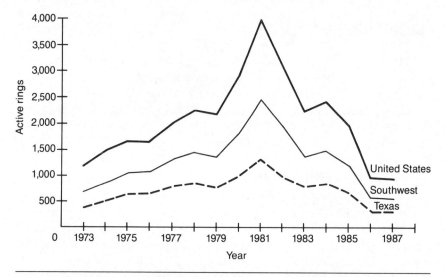

Source: Hughes Tool Company, Houston, Tex., "Rotary Rigs Running by States."

banking, which was established when the voters approved a constitutional amendment in November of that year. Texas Commerce moved quickly in 1987 to become the first major Texas banking organization to implement the branch banking in the state's six largest markets. The number of new accounts increased by an average of 25 to 35 percent.

Changes in the Texas economic environment and in Texas laws have dictated a change in Texas Commerce's basic market strategy. Today, the marketing challenge is to bring the consumer business into a closer balance with the commercial business without damaging the bank's strong commercial position.

For more than a decade, the keys to marketing success for Texas Commerce were (1) selective geographic expansion, (2) establishment of credibility in new markets, (3) effective market positioning, (4) enhanced salesmanship to get the business, (5) consistent targeted advertising support, and (6) development of the right marketing attitude. But even these keys to marketing success lose their luster without a good measure of flexibility. Flexibility is adapting to change—for change is the only thing that is certain.

14

Starting a Bank in London:
The Nomura Experience

Andreas R. Prindl
Managing Director, Nomura Bank International plc

I. Introduction

Nomura International Finance plc opened as a licensed deposit taker in London on November 3, 1986. It had taken a long time to obtain the license, and the process raised issues, particularly of supervision and reciprocity, which were discussed at high levels of the Japanese and British governments.

The parent company, The Nomura Securities Co., Limited, is the largest Japanese securities house (also the largest financial house of any kind when market capitalization is used as the measure), but it had little banking experience, few trained bankers, and no foreign exchange dealers. Further, the role of commercial wholesale banking had been changing drastically in the latter half of the 1980s under pressure of the international debt crisis, rising costs, disintermediation, and the decline of house bank relationships. The typical strategies of the large international banks were to profit from securitization and move into investment banking. Nomura's move into commercial banking was both countercyclic and eye-catching.

In this chapter, we focus on the issues involved in this undertaking as well as how the bank was started and structured in its first year of operation.

II. Rationale for Banking Operation

The parent company had moved into banking many years before Nomura International Finance was established. Nomura Europe NV in Amsterdam had received a full banking license in 1972, when it functioned as Nomura's European headquarters. It built up a loan book of some $400 million, mainly in the form of syndicated loans in which it participated as co-manager. When the headquarters function was moved to London in 1980, the banking part remained in Amsterdam with a small staff of Japanese officers and Dutch clerks. Although its total assets reached about $1 billion by 1985, Nomura Europe NV never developed full banking services. For example, it rarely dealt in foreign exchange or off-balance-sheet products because the bank had no professional dealers in those areas. The decline of the syndicated loan market and the difficulties of competing with the large Japanese bank branches in Europe caused Nomura Europe NV to rely increasingly on the securities business in The Netherlands during the latter 1980s.

Nomura was also part owner of a London consortium bank, Associated Japanese Bank (International) Ltd. (AJB). Started in 1970, AJB was owned in equal shares (25 percent each) by Nomura, Mitsui Bank, Sanwa Bank, and Dai-Ichi Kangyo Bank. AJB acted as a traditional consortium bank at a time when its owners had either much smaller or no banking activities in London. Concentrating on syndicated loans, AJB faced the problems of rescheduling payments that confronted other banks.

Nomura was interested in commercial banking for several reasons. Despite its dominance in many areas of Japanese finance, Nomura depends heavily on securities transactions, usually involving a Japanese purchaser or issuer. It accounts for one third of the Japanese primary and secondary bond market, more than 20 percent of the equity market, and as Japanese capital outflows have increased, as much as one third of outwards portfolio investment (that is, overseas portfolio investment from Japan). But Nomura remains a securities house. Even its underwriting prowess, which brought it to the number one position in the Eurobond league tables in 1987, is mainly Japanese-oriented and does not constitute a real diversification.

Diversification is a key strategy for Nomura in the 1980s. Witness its purchase of 50 percent of the New York real estate advisory firm Eastdil and its joint partnership with Babcock and Brown in the big-ticket leasing area. Banking is an obvious area for Nomura's diversification since it complements the firm's securities business and offers many areas of profitable synergy. Further, Nomura's most important rivals are not so much the other Japanese securities house (Daiwa, Nikko, Yamaichi) but the large global banks such as Deutsche Bank or those in the process of formation (Morgan Guaranty, Citicorp, and others). Many observers believe by the turn of the century only a few giant financial "supermarkets" will cover the range of financial services. Deutsche Bank, Morgan Guaranty, Citicorp, Union Bank of Switzerland, Credit Suisse, and Swiss Bank Corporation will be among the winners.

Nomura, because of its size, capital, research abilities, placing power, and leading position in the largest creditor nation, should certainly be in the top group. But without a banking base, and particularly without foreign exchange capabilities, funding expertise, and credit analysis, it could be at a competitive disadvantage.

In Japan, Nomura cannot offer banking services or own a bank, owing to the restrictions of Article 65 of the Securities Exchange Law, which is adapted from the U.S. Glass-Steagall Act. New York, where Nomura has been represented since 1927, has similar restrictions.

III. London As Location

London was considered the best location for the new Nomura banking venture. London is the cockpit of international finance. Its magnificent infrastructure of banking, insurance, and commodity markets is unrivaled in Europe. The city also has a tradition of welcoming and offering freedom of access to foreign institutions that wish to participate in its financial markets. Regulation of the banking section is intelligent and flexible, and securities regulation has been rather loose until recently. Exchange control was abolished in 1979.

Not only is the regulatory and structural side attractive, but London also has a large pool of trained labor, both managerial and clerical, in the financial sector. English is the language of world finance. Although demand for good banking space has outstripped supply, causing very high rentals, and the telephone system is mediocre, London has generally good communications. For all these reasons, it is the prime location. Indeed, one cannot function in international banking without a London base.

IV. Difficulties in Obtaining a License

In Nomura's case, obtaining a banking license was neither straightforward nor rapid. The parent company had made some quiet approaches to the Bank of England before 1979, the year the U.K. Banking Act came into effect; that act revised the rules of bank establishment. Before the Banking Act, it was left to the Banking Supervision Department of the Bank of England to decide, case by case, whether new banking applicants would be allowed to engage in banking. The Bank of England evaluated them on such criteria as the quality and experience of their management, their proposed business and income streams, and minimization of risks.

Of particular concern for Nomura was the potential for mixing securities and banking risks if the license were to be granted to the main London securities and underwriting vehicle, Nomura International Ltd. (NIL). This question had not been resolved before the 1979 Banking Act was passed. For the first time in U.K. history, the new act required that a U.K.-based bank that is owned by a foreign financial institution must be regulated by the legal and competent authority in that institution's home country.

This posed a real problem for Nomura and the Japanese Ministry of Finance (MOF). The Nomura parent is supervised by its legal authority, the Securities Bureau of the Ministry of Finance. The competent authority for banking, however, is the Banking Bureau of MOF, which also protects the interests of Japanese commercial banks. A Nomura bank, even in London, would pose direct competition to Japanese banks, and the Banking Bureau had no motivation for undertaking such supervision. Thus Nomura had no direct way of meeting the U.K. regulatory requirements.

Further, the U.K. authorities were not ecstatic about receiving yet another Japanese entrant into London banking. In the mid-1980s, about 25 Japanese houses were authorized to offer banking services in the United Kindgom. Many more representative offices and several securities firms were also present. This was perceived as *overrepresentation* although it reflected the unusually large number of powerful financial houses in Japan. The British government and, frequently, the City of London were critical of this phenomenon.

Exacerbating the situation was the reluctance of the Tokyo authorities to allow more U.K. financial houses to enter the Japanese market with securities branches or as members of the Tokyo Stock Exchange. Thus *reciprocity* became a big issue. It was clear that Nomura was unlikely to get a banking license in the United Kingdom if, for example, County Bank or Warburgs was unable to conduct a securities business in Japan, where only a few British houses were active.

These problems were finally resolved in early 1986. The Bank of England worked out an agreement with the Japanese Ministry of Finance whereby both its Securities Bureau and Banking Bureau would take joint responsibility for supervising Nomura's new bank in London. Three British or British-related firms became members of the Tokyo Stock Exchange. Barclays obtained a trust banking license. County Bank and several other merchant banks received the securities licenses in Tokyo that they had sought. In May 1986, Nomura was invited to submit an application, which was approved in September of that year.

V. Initial Projections

At the time of application, only I and my very capable executive assistant staffed Nomura International Finance. Two senior Japanese were seconded from Tokyo, one as deputy managing director and the other as general manager of administration. We agreed on the bank's services, its projected balance sheets and income statement for three years, its structure, and staffing. Our plans were rather limited at first, projecting only modest balance sheet growth (and profits), with London Interbank Mean Rate (LIMEAN) or even London Interbank Offered Rate (LIBOR) funding. As Figure 1 shows, the structure was traditional.

The figure is self-explanatory except, perhaps, for the investment banking area. Some of this was a gleam in our eye. The blank box in investment banking area is eventually intended to encompass advisory services. Asset management developed from a transfer of an existing department within the sister company, Nomura International Limited, whose "Chinese Wall"[1] problems made it advisable to place such a function in a nonsecurities company. That team came to NIF already fully constituted and profitable.

On the general banking side, we did not wish to go into term lending or to compete with Japanese banks in general for Japanese clients where the spread was miniscule.

Figure 1. Structure in 1986 of Nomura International Finance.

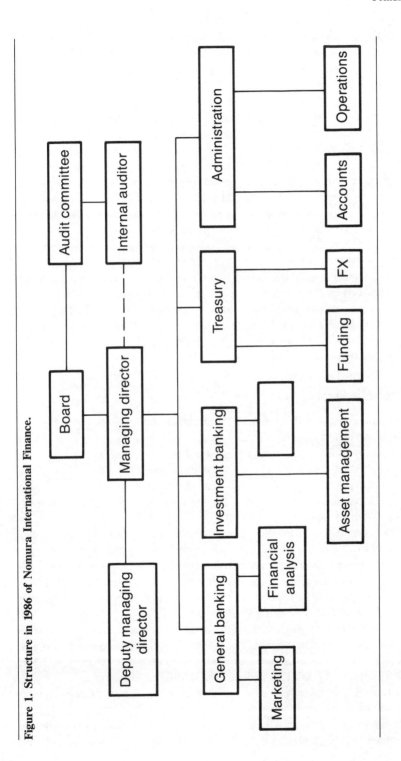

Banking spreads were (and are) a problem. Corporate and acceptable-risk foreign loans have spreads over LIBOR that scarcely cover the administrative costs but involve a risk weighting for capital adequacy purposes that is five times greater than transactions with banks.

Indeed, capital adequacy has been one of our greatest problems, ironic as that may seem for a subsidiary of Nomura, whose market capitalization is some $60 billion. U.K. banks are regulated on the basis of their capital. Loan and position limits and balance sheet leverage all derive from ratios or multiples of underlying capital. NIF started with quite a large capital injection of £50 million. Nevertheless, that limited our maximum loan to one corporate customer to £12.5 million and total balance sheet assets to around £1 billion. Because of the "connected lending constraint," NIF could lend only an amount equal to its capital to members of the Nomura Group (the parent or its foreign subsidiaries).

Therefore, treasury products became our primary focus. Foreign exchange, the largest international financial market, offered profit potential to a group that handled such a large volume of international flows. Competition is fierce in this area, which accounts for earnings of several hundred million dollars annually in each of the top foreign exchange banks. Interest-rate-driven products such as swaps, futures, and options offered another clear niche because of their off-balance-sheet nature. Highly qualified foreign exchange and specialized personnel were readily available although at rather high costs.

VI. First Findings

Many of our projections proved to be lower than results. For example, funding flooded in and at attractively low cost. Indeed, NIF could and does fund itself at lower cost than its parent does. In retrospect, this is not surprising. Nomura International Finance is a new counterparty in the interbank market, backed by an AAA-rated parent. Many traditional counterparties have weakened balance sheets due to their loans to less developed countries or other debtors, or may themselves have been downgraded. Many banks have undoubtedly reached their borrowing limits. Virtually no Nomura paper is available in international markets. The parent company has rarely issued bonds and issues no CDs at all. It has been only a marginal borrower in the interbank area through the Amsterdam subsidiary. Thus NIF had no trouble in obtaining lines, selling our CDs, or issuing a $150 million straight subordinated five-year bond in April, which added £25 million to the calculation of our capital base in Bank of England terms.

NIF has been liability-driven from the start, which has enabled us to achieve fast growth and reasonable profitability. Treasury deals have become the crux of our operation, accounting for more than 90 percent of assets, when deployment of capital is included, and slightly more in profit contribution.

Good banking assets, as expected, remain hard to find. The top group of potential customers are basically nonborrowers although we have set up several "hot lines," treasury lines for very short-term lending at what are, effectively, interbank rates for the blue-chip multinationals. Nomura International Finance was offered and has accepted various secondary market transactions from other banks that wished to reduce their balance sheets or credit concentrations. This built up a useful short-term, low-risk portfolio but with the drawback of lack of direct contact with the ultimate customer.

Corporate contact is critical if you still believe, as we do, that the way to build a business is through long-term customer relationships and problem solving, rather than through price-cutting, shelf registration, and the like.

We started with a small General Banking Department team. An important part of their job has been to set up the credit control framework of the bank, reviewing and authorizing lines through the Credit Committee. Fortunately, they can draw on the numerous relationships already developed by Nomura in Europe, as well as on dozens of marketing and sales people in Nomura International or the European offices. Japanese companies have unbeatable internal communications, cohesion, and support, which NIF has used to its advantage in marketing. Our colleagues speak daily with Tokyo and know intimately company policy, strategy, and its customers. A treasury marketing team also has been built up, and it has succeeded in fostering relationships with many of the multinationals that are called every day.

It has been harder to develop consistently profitable foreign exchange business. Very good traders have joined us. Their profit potential depends on the ability to develop (a) a steady flow of customer business, (b) internal transactions generated by the group, and (c) better or quicker market information. As a first step, we started by taking positions: small movements in and out of currencies and some intergroup dealing. Our longer-term strategy is to become a market maker in certain currencies, a task that entails larger start-up expense and a long buildup period.

Asset management has been more successful and has developed with more relationships to the rest of the bank than we had anticipated. Because of the Japanese connection or the interest in the Tokyo stock and bond markets, a variety of new accounts have come in, and funds under management are increasing steadily. The internal synergy is clearly present, with the General Banking Department for marketing and with the Treasury Department for analysis of market trends.

VII. NIF after a Year

Our fiscal year closed on September 30, 1987, 11 months after opening. The balance sheet reached £1.068 billion by that date (around $1.750 billion), as Table 1 shows.

The operating income for the fiscal year reached £2.3 million; after deduction of the U.K. stamp duty (1 percent of the initial capital injection) and income tax, net profits were £1.2 million.

More important for the longer term are the banking expertise and other capabilities that Nomura International Finance has developed.

For the first time, the Nomura Group has become a market maker in the foreign exchange market, particularly for the yen. It can handle foreign exchange transactions of the Group (except for the parent itself because of Japanese regulations) and offer competitive quotes to Nomura customers. It now deals widely in the

Table 1. Nomura International Finance plc, Balance Sheet as of September 30, 1987 (in billions).

Assets		Liabilities	
CDs	26	Deposits	299
Gilts	22	CDs issued	55
FRNs	30	Interbank	561
TDs	860		
		Other	10
Loans and advances	123		925
Other	7		
	1068	Capital	51
		Bonds issued	92
			1068

money markets, including off-balance-sheet areas of swaps, futures, options, and arbitrage. Swaps may prove very valuable for the underwriting activities of the Group since many of the deals Nomura underwrites depend on favorable swaps. NIF's liability management methods may also be useful for other members of the Group that are beginning to borrow to finance their securities activities, such as bond investment. Some securities transactions are enhanced by a link to credit extension. Indeed, there is more potential for synergy to be explored.

NIF has now changed its name to Nomura Bank International plc (NBI) because provisions of the Banking Act have been changed: all U.K. institutions meeting minimal size and activity requirements are now designated as banks. An expected increase in capital, which is important in our planning, and further bond issues should allow Nomura Bank International to better handle the sizable financial transactions of all kinds generated by the Group.

VIII. Conclusion

NBI grew at a faster rate than any of us expected, mainly due to its liability-driven nature. The reasons for its immediate market acceptance certainly included the following:

- NBI was an attractive new counterparty in the interbank market and for corporate depositers at a time when many banks' credit standing was being downgraded or lines were full up. Although not guaranteed by The Nomura Securities Co., Ltd., NBI was seen as having the same AAA credit rating as its parent, due to the nature of Japanse support of subsidiaries and the comfort letter submitted to the Bank of England.
- NBI attracted a lot of attention before and at its opening since it was the subject of serious bilateral discussions between the U.K. and Japanese governments about access of foreign financial institutions in London and Tokyo. The agreement to let Nomura undertake banking operations in London was a significant event and widely publicized.

- Some counterparties also extended large lines to us and gave us significant business as a way to get closer to the Nomura Group. Visible ties with the new bank would be reported to and valued by Tokyo.
- The treasury staff of NBI came from large international banks, such as Citibank, Chase, and Midland, with widespread knowledge of and contacts with international markets and market players. They had the ability to set up and control a relatively large-scale dealing and trading operation. And most important, perhaps they already thought like a large institution: even at inception, our psychology was one of feeling strong, part of the Nomura Group, and unhampered by past horrors like Latin American debt.

This feeling of Nomura's strengths was and remains our marketing thrust. We can draw on Nomura's reputation, its capital power, its research. Nomura's marketing ability—with 5500 male and 2500 female salespeople in Japan—is legendary. These are augmented by some 2000 personnel stationed outside Japan. Using some part of this structure to make people knowledgeable about NBI and its products was very important.

Similarly, our marketing concentration was on yen-based or securities-related products and toward existing Nomura customers. One would likely not open a bank in 1987 or give it £50 million in capital without having such strengths to draw on or without a long-term plan of diversifying securities income. We found that marketing products and developing trading books related to Nomura's core business was the best—possibly the only—way to start off in such poor banking markets. Indeed, this was our main conclusion: dealing from strength in times of disintermediation and capital adequacy problems gave significant impetus to a new entrant. We had no other good way to become a recognizable participant in international markets but were delighted by the rapid acceptance of NBI and its product line, coming from Japan's and Nomura's own position in international finance today.

IX. Notes

1. "Chinese Wall" is a term that means to keep competitive secrets within departments of the same firm.

15

The Start-up Experience with a Debt Swap Business

J. Hallam Dawson
Chairman, IDI Associates

IDI Associates was formed in early 1987 to sponsor and manage debt swap funds in Latin America for commercial banks. Its first such fund, IDI Mexico Fund I, is directed toward Mexico.

In its brief history, IDI has had to make three marketing decisions:

1. How to market IDI to sources of venture capital
2. How to market the funds sponsored by IDI to prospective bank participants
3. How to market the funds to potential investee companies

In this chapter, we focus on the marketing of the funds, specifically IDI Mexico Fund I, to prospective bank participants.

I. The Background

The events that created the opportunity for IDI go back for more than 20 years although the analysis leading to its formation began in 1986.

Until the mid-1960s, the banking industry was still in the blissful ignorance of the regulated state. It was all rather cozy. Banks had product exclusivity, they had geographic protection, and they had benevolent regulators who permitted comfortable spreads. Banks were regarded by themselves and by others as institutions rather than real businesses. Bank stocks were not listed on the exchanges and generally did not publish profit and loss statements. Return on assets, return on equity, earnings per share, price–earnings ratio, and so on were not considered important concepts for a bank. Size was the principal criterion for comparing banks.

All that began to change in the latter half of the 1960s. Led by several progressive innovators, banks started becoming real businesses, vying to drive up the earnings per share and the stock price. Impressive compound rates of growth in earnings per share were targeted. The easiest way to achieve this growth was to increase leverage. Earlier capital ratios were now considered too conservative. In fact, some banks argued that they didn't need any capital at all. Additional leverage was piled on. The regulators didn't object, and neither did the stock market. We entered the go-go era of banking.

Against that backdrop, an evolution was occurring in international banking. In the early 1960s, international banking was a mainstream activity in only a handful of U.S. banks. For most, it was very much a peripheral area. International banking revolved around international trade, involving letters of credit, collections, payments, remittances, foreign exchange, and correspondent banking. By the mid-1960s, the transformation of international banking had begun. A growing number of banks considered moving abroad to serve the international needs of their domestic customers, but not many thought very carefully about what their customers needed and what they could realistically supply. Nevertheless, pins were gleefully stuck on maps, and new installations were heralded in annual reports.

As the U.S. banking industry began seeking expanded leverage through loan growth, international banking began to take on a new allure. It was perceived as an area where a lot of loan volume could be generated with very little overhead. These loans had little to do with following customers overseas, which was the original justification for an international thrust.

The pricing of international loans was never very attractive, but the contribution at the margin through expanded leverage accomplished what many bank managements desired at the time: growth, increased earnings per share, and a reputation for being aggressive. The economic dislocations caused by the OPEC oil price increases created marvelous opportunities for loan growth. Banks were even permitted a bow for their economic statesmanship in handling the recycling that occurred and that did, indeed, cushion some of the shocks. A "feeding frenzy" of lending materialized. This was the heyday of the jumbo syndicated loan.

Much of this lending activity involved the developing world, particularly Latin America. Problems were surfacing with these developing country loans, but few recognized them. The market adjustment of the mid-1970s has been so impressive that many felt the markets would simply adjust again. But we failed to foresee two events: (1) the extraordinarily high real interest rates caused by U.S. monetary policy as it moved to fight inflation beginning in 1980 and (2) the deep, prolonged recession triggered by this policy a year later (the deepest, longest downturn since the Great Depression). The impact on the developing world was devastating. Beginning with the Mexican crisis of 1982, developing-country debt has been a continuing problem of major importance.

It became apparent that the problem was serious and involved long-term solvency, not short-term liquidity. Further, there was no single, big solution for this debt problem. Austerity alone would not solve it. Growth was needed. But this growth had to be driven by investment, and domestic investment in most debtor countries was inadequate because domestic savings rates and capital markets were inadequate. Foreign investment was necessary, but incentives were needed to attract it.

One of the options discussed and implemented was the debt–equity swap. This technique induces foreign investment by permitting debtholders to convert their debt into equity. Chile adopted such a program in 1985, and Mexico followed with its own program in the summer of 1986.

II. The Concept

By 1986, as the enormousness of the developing-country debt problem began to sink in, banks began to feel uncomfortable with their limited options. Continuing to hold the debt was associated with a meaningful credit risk. Moreover, the lender banks were exposed to periodic new money requirements, further renegotiations, and increasingly unattractive terms and conditions. The renegotiation process itself caused a lot of psychological wear and tear on all concerned. On the other hand, the option of selling the debt in the secondary market, at least in any significant amounts, produced losses of such magnitude that few had the stomach for this alternative.

As the debt–equity swap became an option in some countries, and other innovative approaches to the developing-country debt problem were being devised, some of the largest banks in the United States and other countries gained expertise in the field. Worldwide, 400 to 500 banks had lender exposure to Latin America. To most of them, it seemed unlikely and imprudent to consider direct participation in debt–equity swaps and other innovative techniques no matter how useful these approaches might be in dealing with the debt problem. These new techniques are highly complex, change constantly, and require specialized skills. These specialized skills come only from concentration, and only a few banks can afford it.

Therefore, IDI developed the concept of permitting more banks to participate in these innovative techniques through a pooled-fund approach in which IDI would provide the required specialized expertise.

III. The Analysis

We began by visiting with banks that we considered potential participants in a fund. Initial responses to our concept were encouraging. Yes, they agreed with us that the developing-country debt problem was very serious and long term. Yes, they agreed it was time for some innovations in dealing with this problem. Yes, they were unsatisfied with their current options of holding the debt or selling it. Yes, they agreed that new techniques such as debt–equity swaps offered promise. Yes, they were unlikely to have the expertise to engage in these activities directly. Yes, they would be happy to have a serious look at the kind of fund that we were considering.

The next step was to continue our exploration in a potential target country to determine the host government's attitude toward the debt–equity swap technique and our approach to it. Mexico was selected for this purpose. Through friends of long standing, we arranged a series of fruitful discussions with several government units, including the Ministry of Finance, the Central Bank, and the Foreign Investment Commission.

There was a clear consensus. The program was viewed positively, provided that the inflationary effect could be controlled and the investments met the government criteria. It was agreed that the inflationary effect could be controlled by limiting the program to a certain monthly volume of swaps. A case-by-case approval process would enable the government to approve only those proposals that met its criteria. The process should also guard against the political embarrassment that would be associated with any sham swaps, intended only to "round-trip" money out of Mexico. Government officials were disappointed by the heavy use of the program by multinational companies, who bought debt at a big discount in the secondary market. This "profit-making" irked some officials. Thus our fund concept was particularly appealing because it required banks to contribute their own debt.

Next, we evaluated investment opportunities. In a series of meetings with Mexican companies, we concluded that attractive investment opportunities were available in Mexico largely because of the undervalued peso and the trade liberalization put in place by the current administration. Overall, we were encouraged that a fund like ours would be well received by prospective investees.

During our discussions, it became apparent that the investing could not be done from a distance but had to be done in the host country by people completely familiar with its markets.

We considered current and potential competition. At that time, multinational companies buying debt in the secondary market were by far the greatest users of debt–equity swap programs. Direct swaps by banks using their own debt generally were confined to a few situations associated in some way with the financial services sector. No funds of the sort that we contemplated had been launched although several had been under discussion. For example, the IFC had been considering a Mexican fund for some time but was not near to closing anything. Several U.S. investment banks and Mexican financial institutions were discussing a link to offer a Mexican "junk bond" fund, probably to private individuals.

If our fund concept were to prove viable, many institutions would be in a position to act as sponsors, among them large commercial banks. However, the banks' ability to participate might be affected by their role in syndicating many of the developing-country loans and by potential conflicts of interest as they dealt with their own portfolios.

Clearly several complex issues had to be resolved before a fund could go forward successfully. For example, there were accounting issues such as loss recognition and "contamination" of remaining debt. Regulatory issues affected the permissible range of bank activities. Legal issues raised possibilities of constraints. There were also the ever-present tax considerations. Because these issues had to be dealt with country by country, it was decided early on that the fund should be directed primarily to U.S. banks, with all the issue resolution effort devoted to the U.S.

perspective. It was apparent that we would be pioneering the resolution of some of these issues.

Having decided to concentrate on U.S. banks, we reviewed more than 150 U.S.-chartered institutions that were creditors of the Mexican government. We decided our target market probably ranged from banks just below the eight or ten largest to banks with public sector exposure in the target country of only $5 million and $10 million. Within that range, the most desirable bank participants would be those that

1. Were well regarded by peers, regulators, and the stock market
2. Had an ongoing interest (and a customer base with an ongoing interest) in the target country
3. Were in good standing in the target country
4. Represented desirable geographic diversification in the United States

Obviously, we needed a "lead bank" that would work intensively with us early in the game, performing extensive due diligence and announcing its commitment in principle to participate before the general marketing effort began. Such a lead bank should probably be a "superregional" of very high quality.

Equally obvious, *credibility* was the key to success in marketing ourselves, first to potential lead banks and then to other participants in the fund. No one had a track record with debt swaps, then a new concept. There were no established models or patterns; we were sailing in unchartered waters.

We had to build credibility for our people, concept, structure, and investment criteria. IDI's key people had to be well known within banking circles, with reputations for ability and integrity and the backgrounds and experience necessary for the task. IDI's concept had to appeal to banks by offering them something useful. Our structure had to respond to the accounting, regulatory, legal, and tax issues as well as provide an effective mechanism for carrying out the mission. Finally, IDI's investment criteria had to meet the bank's objectives and appear both reasonable and achievable.

Ideally, the marketing approach to establish this credibility had to be made at two levels: (1) primarily at the international level because a lack of enthusiastic support at that point would probably be fatal and (2) secondarily at a senior level in the bank to remove potential impediments to approval and reduce any perceptions of risk among the international people in making a recommendation in a sensitive area.

Finally, we focused on the strategic issues of defining the business, the range of services to be provided, and the markets to be served. The keys to our strategy were concentration on Latin America and the desire to assist banks in dealing with their problems in the region. We wanted to build a business that did these things systematically over time; we were not just promoting a series of deals. Although we started with debt–equity swaps and other types of debt swaps, our focus was broader. We did not want to depend exclusively on specific government programs that might come and go. We would represent the interests of the banks that participated in our funds, but our investment activities should also benefit the host countries.

IV. The Implementation

The results of our exploration persuaded us to launch IDI. We concluded that a pooled-fund concept employing specialized new techniques like the debt–equity swap would appeal to a broad range of banks—from those just below the eight or ten largest in the United States to those with any significant exposure in the target country. We believed such an approach would appeal to the host country.

Mexico was selected as the target country for the first fund because it had one of the largest foreign debts of any country, and its debt–equity swap program was well defined and functioning. There were attractive economic opportunities in Mexico for the investment ideas we had in mind. The experience and interest of IDI's principals also pointed to Mexico as a starting point. In short, we thought we had a good idea, at the right time, with the appropriate people, and that Mexico was the place to start.

We double-checked with several U.S banks to confirm that Mexico would be high on their list of countries suited to such an activity. Additional visits in the Mexican public sector convinced us that our initial reading of their reactions was correct. Another round of visits to potential investee companies corroborated our earlier findings. We also checked again on potential competitive efforts from the IFC and the U.S. investment banks.

Next, we arranged for an "on the ground" investment capability in Mexico. We had anticipated that the burst of entrepreneurial activity in Mexico's financial services sector, fueled perhaps by the earlier nationalization of the banks, would produce a firm particularly well suited to the activity we envisioned. Unfortunately, this did not prove to be so. Some extremely talented people were doing some very interesting things, but we could not find the right match-up and decided we would have to build our own capability from scratch.

Happily, Luis de la Fuente, a senior officer at a major Mexican company whom I had known for many years, became available at that time and joined IDI. Besides his impressive array of basic business skills and knowledge of the Mexican economy, he brought with him a large, devoted following among many banks, both in the United States and around the world.

At this point, we debated whether to launch IDI with our personal resources or to seek outside investors. We decided to do the latter. Though our own resources might have been adequate, we thought outside investors would provide a good oversight discipline for us as well as a valuable source of advice and counsel. The right kind of investor group would also enhance our credibility. To our great satisfaction, a distinguished group of individual investors was put together, and $500,000 was raised to finance our startup.

We then began resolving the key issues mentioned earlier. By this time, the accounting questions of contamination of debt had been largely resolved, but there were still wide differences of opinion in the accounting profession about loss recognition. Many believed a write-down to secondary market values (then approximately 60 percent of face value) was required on entry into a fund like ours. In the face of such an accounting opinion, few if any, banks would have been prepared to participate. But after a disappointing experience with one Big Eight firm, another took an aggressive but well-reasoned view that permitted us to move ahead.

Our law firm devised a limited partnership approach that would permit U.S. bank holding companies to participate in our fund up to 25 percent without prior approval of the Federal Reserve Board. We found no other legal impediments. The tax questions were important and complex, particularly regarding the new foreign tax credit provisions of the Tax Reform Act of 1986, but they appeared manageable if everything else worked.

We prepared a draft confidential offering memorandum for the fund and discussed it with a short list of potential lead banks. Each bank that heard our presentation responded favorably, but as is usual in such a situation, there was a great reluctance to lead the way. Fortunately, we were able to reach agreement with First Wachovia Corporation, a bank that was virtually a prototype of the superregional that we had in mind for the fund. They did their due diligence carefully, but once it was completed, they had the courage of their convictions. They were assisted in this by their long relationship with our Mexican partner, Luis de la Fuente, and by other contacts with IDI principals and investors.

With the First Wachovia commitment in hand, the confidential offering memorandum was completed, and a marketing effort was undertaken with some three dozen U.S. banks. During this marketing period, several developments significantly affected our efforts.

First, the Mexican government (encouraged by some of the large U.S. banks) decided to differentiate between banks that had contributed their "fair share" in the latest Mexican debt restructuring, which had just been completed, and those that had not. The banks termed this "blacklisting," but the Mexican government insisted that it had simply wanted to reward its friends. In any event, the result was that the blacklisted banks found their paper "tainted" and unacceptable for the debt–equity swap program. This significantly reduced the number of target banks available to us although over time we found a way to resolve this issue.

Citicorp's dramatic decision to substantially increase its loan loss reserve to accommodate its developing-country loan exposure also affected our program. Virtually all U.S. banks followed the Citicorp lead. Once the reserves were established, the accounting issues became less problematic because the accounting firms felt more comfortable, and the banks felt more flexible.

The secondary market value of the debt continued to decline. Eventually, some banks took further loan loss provisions, and some actually wrote off a major part of its exposure. Late in 1987, the Mexican government advanced a proposal, developed with Morgan, that allowed Mexico to take advantage of secondary market discounts and decrease its debt levels. All this reinforced the conclusion that the government's debt could not be paid according to its terms, and other approaches must be found. Those other approaches are the focus of IDI.

A gradual development that surprised us was the interest shown by banks that were initially considered either too large or marginal at best for our fund. These larger banks felt that though they might be able to do swaps directly, they respected our specialized expertise and believed we could do better deals together than they could do alone. This fit well with IDI's concept that the fund was pleased to cooperate with partner banks on deals they produced from their customer bases. Recognizing that this is a new and specialized activity, the larger banks also welcomed another informed viewpoint on such deals.

Our marketing efforts with the banks confirmed that the default option for them was doing nothing. "No" was the easy answer. One was unlikely to be criticized for doing what most were doing, namely, nothing. It took a lot of effort and far more time than we had expected to overcome this natural tendency. Many of the banks that declined to participate in IDI Mexico Fund I said they would like to be in IDI Mexico Fund II. Of course, there were good reasons for a bank to take a lot of time to decide on participation in the Fund. The concept was new, the issues were complex, and the first fund was only a modest step. IDI could not solve a major part of anyone's problem. We could only experiment, point to some new directions, and serve as a catalyst. Control was an issue for some banks, as was the Fund's strategic fit with their future international plans.

Eventually, we secured commitments in principle from First Wachovia and three other banks to participate for $10 million each in IDI Mexico Fund I. At that point (October 1987), the Mexican government suspended its debt–equity swap program. As we go to press, the suspension continues. There are differences of opinion about it in the government, and there is the possibility that the program might be held hostage to Mexico's negotiations with its banks, including the Morgan-led plan.

Several of the banks who had committed to the Fund felt it advisable to delay closing the Fund until the suspension was lifted, and we honored their wishes. In the meantime, we have adjusted our concept to (1) permit the Fund to operate deal by deal and (2) shift our investment emphasis to deals that do not require a formal program. Happily, we have been successful in both. Our first deal should close in March 1988, with others advancing rapidly. Still, the original concept is better, and we hope to return to it soon.

V. The Outlook

We are very positive about the outlook for IDI. Part of this optimism reflects the results achieved so far, which include (1) establishing a reputation as a leader and innovator in the field of new solutions to the Latin American debt problems of banks, (2) attracting the interest and support of an impressive group of banks as participants in the Fund, and (3) getting the Fund's investment activities off to a promising start.

The magnitude of the Latin American debt problem and its very long-term nature also give rise to optimism about our future. A miniscule market share translates into much opportunity over many years. The potential among non-U.S. banks is still to be tapped. Moreover, other types of funds can be sponsored in Mexico, including FICORCA relending funds. IDI's activities also can be expanded to other countries. Such expansion must be carefully controlled because the investment side of the fund is very country specific, and expertise must be provided in each new market.

Finally, IDI may well find opportunities extending beyond fund management. A broader range of services could be offered to banks to assist them in Latin America. Also, the financial services industry in Latin America has much growth and transformation ahead of it. If IDI has the skills to do a fine job of investing in these countries, it should be able to build on that expertise to pursue other financial services opportunities, including investment banking, venture capital, and mutual funds.

Although IDI is optimistic about its future, we recognize that there are many uncertainties and potential problems. Principal among them is the possibility of unsatisfactory investment performance. Moreover, the markets IDI intends to operate in will certainly not be orderly or stable. Indeed, IDI will have to deal with an environment of constant change. The debt–equity swap programs themselves are fragile and may be altered significantly or eliminated altogether. They are politically sensitive and encounter some academic opposition. In some sectors, the debt–equity swaps are perceived as too attractive to foreign investors.

Another danger arises from the fact that debt–equity swaps are becoming "fashionable." As the history of the banking industry illustrates, the stampede that follows the rise of a new fashion sometimes destroys opportunities for all.

The critical factors for future success will differ from those required in the past. At first, the key was successfully marketing the fund to commercial banks, with our credibility a major factor. In the future, the critical success factors will be investment performance, marketing to potential investee companies, and displaying the flexibility and agility needed to deal with the rapidly changing environment in Latin America.

VI. A Critique

Hindsight, of course, is wonderful and enables one to see things much more clearly. It is useful to review what we did right and what we did wrong in launching IDI.

We were right about

1. The desirability of raising venture capital
2. The frustration that lender banks felt with the hold and sell options
3. The uneasiness that many banks felt about undertaking debt–equity swaps on their own
4. The limited partnership fund approach to structuring the product
5. The targeting of the fund to U.S. banks
6. The investment criteria selected, including the emphasis on divestiture
7. The need to establish our own investment capability in Mexico
8. Mexico as the initial country

We were wrong about

1. The proportion of banks that were seriously interested and then signed commitments in principle to participate in the fund (It was low, reflecting a natural hesitation to be out in front on innovations like this.)
2. The effort required to convert written commitments in principle to signed closing documents (It was more time consuming than we anticipated.)

3. The time required overall from start to closing (We underestimated badly here.)
4. The assumption of continuity in the Mexican debt–equity swap program (There was more change and uncertainty than we had bargained for.)
5. The interest among banks at the upper end of our target range (We were more appealing than we anticipated.)

Besides being right about some things and wrong about others, we were lucky about some things and unlucky about others. We were lucky in finding a lead bank with the courage and conviction of First Wachovia. They have been a constant source of support and encouragement. The availability of Luis de la Fuente to spearhead our activities in Mexico was a major piece of good luck. And we were lucky to have found the impressive and helpful group of investors who funded our startup.

Our timing was also lucky. The debt–equity swap mechanism was novel and untried when we began our deliberations, but subsequent events made it virtually a household word.

Finally, we were lucky in having some independent variables work in our favor, particularly the loan loss reserve creation triggered by Citicorp (which made banks and their auditors more flexible), the decline in the secondary market prices of the debt (which highlighted the need to do something different), and the Morgan-led plan (which confirmed that the debt was not worth anywhere near its face value).

There was some bad luck as well. The blacklisting that occurred midway through our marketing effort eliminated many banks. Even though a way was found to resolve the issue, some banks were annoyed or alienated beyond the point of wanting to do anything in the debt–equity swap area in Mexico.

Our worst luck was with the Mexican debt–equity swap program itself. A brief suspension of the program early on was annoying. But more serious was the suspension in late October 1987. Rumors abound about if, when, and on what terms the progam will reopen. IDI Mexico Fund I cannot close in the form originally contemplated until the situation has been clarified.

Overall, we found the launching of IDI stimulating and enjoyable. The marketing of the first fund to the commercial banks was both physically and emotionally demanding. But the rewards of entrepreneurial activity were driven home. God did not intend for all of us to work in big companies.

16

Private Banking:
A Market, a Product, a Label, or a Business?

John W. Heilshorn
Principal, Avenir Group Inc.
Retired Executive Vice President, Citibank N.A.

I. Introduction

Private banking was a new idea to many U.S. bankers when it was announced by Citibank in the early 1970s. In fewer than 20 years, this market, product, new business, or what might be termed a brand or label, has achieved much visibility in the industry. Its prominence as a new bank marketing initiative has been matched in recent years only by consumer banking and merchant banking.

Private banking has become a main-tent attraction at bankers' conferences nationwide. Personal career promotions into private banking have made the "People to Watch" column in *Fortune* magazine. If success can be judged solely by counting the number of banking and Wall Street houses proudly advertising their private banking talent before the readers of national and local magazines and newspapers, private banking has been a real winner.

Obviously, these are only superficial indicators of success. The critical question is, Has private banking been successful in the marketplace? Is the customer achieving his or her objectives by buying the services of a private bank or banker? The companion question to success in the marketplace is, Has private banking been a success for the bank's stockholders; has it been profitable?

To measure it, you must define it. How do you define private banking? Is it a product, a market, a label, or a new brand name for an old product? Is it a business? One could probably argue it is all the above. There are as many variations as there are banks and financial service competitors advertising their particular brand of private banking.

Private banking at Citibank was one of the important by-products of a 1969 decision to reorganize the bank opposite customer market segments. The critical issues facing Citibank in the late 1960s, were not significantly different from those confronting many banks today:

- Heated competition for the customer's business was coming from conventional as well as nonconventional competitors.
- Banking institutions needed to improve their profitability substantially to compete for new capital in the debt and equity markets. They simply could not automatically translate market growth into improved profitability without reorienting the organization structure around the customer.
- The velocity of change in the marketplace mandated an organization focus on the customer.
- The customer's changing needs required a creative, flexible decision-making structure positioned as close to the customer as possible.
- To compete successfully, the structure had to be a catalyst to anticipating the customer's needs, expediting decisions, and delivering a quality service.

II. Identifying the Private Banking Customer

At that time, Citibank defined the private banking customer as the "high net worth market": families and individuals who had millions of dollars in assets. They were the traditional market of the old line trust departments. The conventional off-the-shelf trust department product lines included

- The custody business: safekeeping negotiable instruments and cutting coupons
- Investment management: directing and managing assets
- The trust and estate business: distributing and investing family assets prudently for the next generations

Before the reorganization at Citibank, these wealthy customers obtained their custody, investment, and trust services from the Citibank trust department. They kept their time deposits and checking accounts at a Citibank branch. If they had any credit needs, they had to go through another door of the bank to negotiate the terms of a loan.

To describe our reorganization objective, we cited as an example the experience of one of our very bright investment officers whose customer had just sold his business. The customer's objective was to diversify his assets, but he was unable to sell the control stock he had received from the buyer. It took the investment officer a week or more to find a banker in the same bank who would lend the trust department customer the money necessary to diversify his asset base. An example of customer service? No. An example of protecting turf? Yes. Clearly, the customer wasn't doing business with the bank or the institution; he was doing business with individual departments that had specific product responsibilities. We made it difficult, if not impossible, for the customer to cross from one department to another.

The objective of Citibank's private banking was to organize around the customer the product lines dictated by his or her needs. We sought to eliminate the turf barriers that impede customer service execution. In the old organization, the managers of the banking and trust and investment product lines each reported separately to the bank's chief executive officer. It was a product-driven organization. The new organization brought the responsibility and accountability for managing these products two organization levels below the chairman: a Private Banking Department within the Investment Management Group of Citibank.

The high net worth segment of the Citibank client base was the initial focus of the private banking business, but it soon became clear that our definition of the private banking market was too narrow. The experience of our bright investment officer had given us an insight into a different category of high net worth persons: persons who got there the hard way, who earned their wealth in their own lifetimes, in their own business careers, who qualified for high net worth status, not as birthrights, but as entrepreneurs. Over time, the market segment of private banking at Citibank extended to athletes whose earning power peaked in the first five years of their careers, as distinct from the peak reached in the later years by the typical entrepreneurial businessperson. Managing and investing the income flows of these subsegments of the private banking market added an exciting new dimension to investment management. The investment objectives of the beneficiaries of "inherited wealth" are most often dramatically different from those of the high net worth entrepreneur. The entrepreneurial customers, for example, typically have a different risk tolerance. The investment product designed for one market segment will not fit the other.

Had we stayed with the conventional-wisdom definition of private banking, that is, catering to inherited wealth, Citibank would have lost its position in the fastest growing, largest segment of the market. It is generally recognized that today, more than two thirds of the wealthy persons in the United States have not been the beneficiaries of inherited wealth. They have built their wealth in their own lifetimes, usually around a business or profession. You can't succeed in both high net worth market segments with the same talent base and the same product lines.

This was the definition of the private banking market within the framework of Citibank's reorganization in the late 1960s. Was it invented in 1969 by Citibank? Of course not. Students of banking history can argue persuasively that only the name was changed: The private banking function dates back to the early history of the merchant bankers in Europe and America. Most banks, including Citibank, can trace their lineage to wealthy merchants who founded their banks to service the financial transactions of their families and business activities. Citibank may have applied the name private banking to the business of serving the wealthy in the United States, but the function of supplying a customer with a product array and an execution capability he or she needs is "Marketing 101" to successful businesspeople in any industry.

III. Profitability of Private Banking

So, the first measure of success of private banking is the degree to which it has served the market. Has it "created" a customer? If it has successfully fulfilled

188 / Private Banking

that mission, the bank stockholder has been the winner, and usually, private banking has contributed to the growth of bank profitability.

The bottom line was critical to Citibank and to the trust industry in general. At the time of Citibank's reorganization, the trust business was its least profitable product segment. Bankers had not established a rationale, or yardstick, for measuring return on investment in the trust business. But even by the inadequate measure Citibank used at the time, the trust business was not meeting the corporate objective for return on equity. The profit and loss statement was driven by a "fee for service" business proposition with fees often regulated and profit margins thin to nonexistent.

Since most trust departments had little or no information about their costs, they didn't have a frame of reference for identifying profitable customers or pricing their services. Therefore, most trust departments couldn't manage the revenue line of their P&L.

Since most trust departments bought their products other parts of their bank, they typically had little or no control over their production costs. Unable to manage revenues and lacking control over their costs, the trust departments had no control over their profitability.

The private banking charter at Citibank, with responsibility for all products the wealthy customer needed, brought to the business a substantial bottom-line enhancement in the form of interest differential earnings. The private banker's balance sheet at Citibank included deposits and loans. Our profitability was further enhanced with the addition of the international high net worth customer base to our business charter. This market segment brought to Citibank at that time a major and rapidly growing dollar deposit base.

Citibank's domestic and overseas private banking earnings grew substantially as the customer base expanded. Private banking was a success in both market response and profitability. It became a very successful business. It was not just a market, a product, a brand, or a label.

IV. Reorganizing for Private Banking

Many of the problems and opportunities encountered along the way took us over territory that is no doubt familiar to most businesspeople and to private bank managers in particular.

Any new marketing initiative that doesn't have the enthusiastic support and drive of the chief executive officer is in trouble at the outset. We were the beneficiaries of Citibank's newly appointed chairman, Walter B. Wriston, who was the industry leader in identifying antiquated regulation, profitability improvement, and capital generation as the most serious problems facing the industry. The external issue was deregulation. The internal issue was profitability. The strategy for achieving higher profits was simple: Organize our businesses around the customer, not the product.

We believed strongly that the business manager with customer segment responsibility should have all the tools he or she needed to be responsible and accountable for achieving market share leadership and profitability. This resulted in decentralizing to the business managers all the functions needed to manage the revenues and costs of the customer group they were responsible for. The creation of the private banking business was one part of a major, corporatewide reorganization.

This level of CEO support for private banking at Citibank was unique in the industry. During this period, I was chairman of the Trust Management Committee of the American Bankers' Association. The greatest overall frustration at that time was the inability of trust departments to get the attention of the banks' chief executive officers. In fact, we conducted a survey of CEO attitudes toward the trust business. Did they see the business as a standalone profit generator, or was it a secondary product line that subsidized other more important parts of the bank? What were their expectations concerning future profit growth?

The responses we received were not encouraging. It came as no surprise at the time that trust department managers had difficulty getting the attention of their CEOs or getting on their agendas for any decision. Few trust department champions were among the CEOs of American banking. There was a lack of conviction about profitability. There was little confidence in the profit growth potential of trust departments. At that time, private banking was considered high risk and organizationally disruptive. There was only limited confidence in a profitable outcome for the trust business. The ABA Trust Management Committee concluded at the time that unless management of the trust departments could make a better case for future profitability of the business, they could not expect to make major inroads in the battle ahead for high net worth market share. And they would continue to operate at a disadvantage internally. They were likely to have a low relative priority for people, capital, and the operating support needed to sharpen their competitive positions.

Private banking called for a new set of priorities. In the analogy I used then, and continue to use today, bankers and other financial institutions competing for the business of the private banking customer make the customer assemble the parts of a private banking service on an almost do-it-yourself basis. It's as ridiculous as telling a car buyer that if he wants an automobile, he must buy *all* the parts and assemble them himself. A whole series of internal policy issues must be resolved in favor of the customer if we're going to take our customers to the showroom, so to speak, instead of to the parts department. You can't get from here to there without a CEO who understands the marketing proposition and is prepared to make the tradeoffs and take the internal risks of organizing in favor of the customer.

Even with the support of the CEO for this business proposition, we spent a lot of time on turf issues, and it took years to resolve some of them. Private banking clients were usually highly profitable accounts at the branches: Who should get the P&L credit for the customer's deposits if the customer has been doing business with a branch as a depositer? This question and the related P&L issues wasted much of the shareholders' money. We lost some customers to the competition. The burden of proof was on the private banking business manager, who had to convince his or her colleagues that both Citibank and the customer would be ahead if the customer were served by private banking experts instead of branch generalists. This was not always easy to do in an organization that was rapidly adjusting to a new bottom-line performance measurement system.

As everyone who has lived in a large organization knows, the CEO's support does not always guarantee the end of turf issues. The private bankers had to make this sale to their Citibank colleagues every day.

We faced additional turf issues as the market segment served by private banking shifted from the inherited wealth customer to the successful, wealthy entrepreneur. For the latter customer, it was critical to bring skilled lending officers into the private banking operation. We had to make the case that the private banking client was highly profitable to the institution, but these customers could be a high credit risk to the institution if private banking didn't have the lending officer skills required in this business.

Citibank's reorganization into market segment profit centers compounded some of these turf issues. Driving the profit-center-business-manager culture into an organization works best where the decentralized business managers operate more or less independently of one another. It is much easier to implement this business proposition if the business managers have clearly defined markets with little or no customer or product overlap.

At the outset, private banking needed the services of the branch system and the operating support of some banking product lines. This interdependency was further complicated when the private banking marketing charter was extended to the wealthy entrepreneurs. Accounting solutions such as matrix accounting systems and double counting were tried and failed. For obvious reasons, these conflicts rarely surfaced at the chairman's office, and they were allowed to fester at the operating level. We should have resolved them earlier in the implementation of the reorganization, before structure and behavior patterns became established. We made some progress in the turf issues but not enough.

On the other side of the coin, what experienced corporate lending officer would leave the corporate bank to join the old-style trust department? But not long after the private banking concept was launched, we began to build a reputation as an exciting place for corporate lending officers. Corporate lending itself began to lose some of its glamour as profit margins shrank. The corporate lending function began to look more like a commodity than a custom-designed credit product. The loan to the entrepreneur was perceived as being more demanding in structure and price. Eventually, private banking attracted the talent it needed, not only at Citibank but also at the other institutions that offer credit as a main-line private banking product.

V. Some Lessons Learned

The question always arises: What would you have done differently? What didn't work out as planned? To this day, it is my sense that at the customer level, most private banking initiatives are still in the automobile parts department, not in the showroom. There is little evidence that private banking has produced the generalists who are comfortable in bringing the customer to the showroom floor. Assembling the products two levels below the chairman is not enough. Theodore Leavitt's classic article, "Marketing Myopia," challenges readers even today to consider what American railroads could have done if they had defined their business as transportation rather than the carriage of goods and people over the rails. Using Leavitt's railroad analogy, the private banker today is aware of the airline and truck alternatives to rails. But does he or she see the airlines and trucking companies as competition or part of a solution to the customer's transportation needs? Does the customer want space in a railroad car, or does he or she want transportation from point A to point B? Private bankers still sell more space on railroad cars than solutions to transportation problems.

The agenda of private banking seminars is dominated by the credit product. This is probably appropriate for the age of infinited leverage, the LBO, and so on. But if leverage does not produce the market multiples that predated October 19, what then? Is the next generation of product skills ready for the post October 19, 1987, period. Will it be a retrained lender, a retrained investment officer, or business as usual? Who is the quarterback making the decision on how to stay ahead of the dramatically changing customer needs—what some people today say will be a whole new ballgame? It's the same customer, but has October 19 changed his or her attitude toward risk both as a borrower and an investor? Are private bankers focusing on the customer's new needs or on selling yesterday's products?

The major thrust of Citibank's 1969 reorganization was to significantly increase the corporation's sensitivity to the importance of the customer and build businesses around customer segments to ensure delivery of a level of service that would differentiate Citibank from its old and new competitors. Although the strategy was successful in the marketplace and in terms of shareholders' profitability, the focus on customers developed more slowly than we expected. Frankly, we underestimated the extent of the culture change we had to make. The private banking charter mandated a change from product delivery to definition of customer needs and creative assembly of multiple products to satisfy these needs. This was not a minor shift in staff responses. It required extensive training, bringing people's skills in new products up to the levels they had in their former single-product-line jobs. We underestimated the training required by this marketing proposition.

As the private banking seminar agendas attest, we are investing heavily in product training, but to use the earlier analogies, have we trained private bankers adequately for private banking? Are they looking at the parts department or the automobile showroom? How do they define their business—as a railroad or the transportation business?

In the early days of private banking at Citibank, we incorrectly assumed that every junior investment officer would see a loan opportunity in the sale of an entrepreneur's business. We overinvested in product skills experience and underinvested in private banking training—meaning the assembly of parts or the interconnection of the available forms of transportation. This issue of multiple product training is still being debated. Can an insurance salesman sell new investment products? Can a banker sell securities and insurance products? If they can't, private banking is nothing more than a new label for a parts department.

If we can't teach private banking to private bankers, we're admitting that, with all of our expertise, we cannot understand the issues and alternatives our customers face every day in managing their financial affairs. If we can't train private banking generalists, we're admitting that we're incapable of understanding the complexity of the customer's financial management problems and opportunities. If these statements are true, we can be certain that new competitors will see the opportunity. Is it an issue of culture as well as product knowledge? Are our institutions incapable of changing a culture bias that favors yesterday's product and yesterday's way of doing business? At Citibank, we brought the organization responsibility for the products the customer needs two levels below the chairman—that was progress, but it wasn't good enough. Bankers design and manufacture their "services" in the customer's office by listening to the customer's needs in the customer's office. Private bankers also need the skills, training, and motivation to assemble the parts, to manufacture solutions to customer needs in the customer's office.

Finally, we did not place enough emphasis on "selling" itself as a critical success variable in the marketing equation. This was a more serious problem in the private bank than in some of the other groups where selling had become recognized earlier as "acceptable behavior" for the traditional banker. In most banks, the trust department was the last to convert from a "telephone answering service" to a proactive sales organization.

One of the best examples of the cultural revolution under way was our early experience with compensation systems. We found that the best of the young breed of private banker and investment specialists we were recruiting came from nonbank competitors, whose compensation systems tracked performance. Our professionals had been brought up in an environment where salaries, annual merit increases, and benefits were almost a ritual based on the calendar rather than individual performance. In fact, many of our experienced professional people were uncomfortable in taking performance risks. In other words, we faced a "generation gap" in compensation systems as well. This problem was compounded by institutional resistance to changing the more traditional patterns of compensation. There were serious reservations about altering what had been a successful institutionalized approach to the structure of compensation systems.

We learned through these experiences that reorienting a business to a nontraditional direction requires management to identify and realistically face up to the critical success variable of the "new business." If there is much discomfort breaking some of the institution's conventions in entering a new business, you may not be able to compete. There is usually enough risk in any new business venture without adding institutional roadblocks along the way.

Some banks and financial institutions will continue to prosper with a product focus. But by any measure, the growth prospects are far greater if you start with the customer, satisfy his or her access to the products needed, and organize a business dedicated to delivering superior service. Private banking is not just a market. It's not just a product. It's not a brand or label. It's a new business.

17

Information for Marketing Decisionmaking

Kathryn Britney*
Vice President, Chase Manhattan Bank

I. Introduction

Obtaining information useful for marketing decisionmaking involves four steps: (1) problem definition, (2) data gathering, (3) analysis, and (4) interpretation. Like many aspects of business, these steps are easier to define than to implement. In this chapter, we point out some of the unique opportunities and problems associated with this process in the financial services industry.

II. Problem Definition

The first step in determining the required information is to specify the problem or decision. For example, the management of a bank asked its research staff to determine whether current customers were satisfied with the bank's quality of service. When asked to describe the decisions this information would be used for, management said it would be used to develop a service marketing strategy to attract more customers. However, the information requested was not what was needed to make decisions about how to attract new customers, even if the bank had wanted to make "quality service" its competitive advantage.

To make decisions about how to attract new customers, management needed information about the consumers' decisionmaking process, particularly the relative

---

*This chapter represents the views of the author and not of Chase Manhattan Bank. For reasons of privacy, some names and identifying details have been changed.

importance of service among other attributes consumers consider when choosing a bank for the total market. A large segment of the market might value rate or convenience higher than quality service. Different segments of the market might focus on different aspects of banking service (for example, check-clearing time versus teller-line wait) as the services considered important when choosing a bank. Finally, it is necessary to understand not only how satisfied the bank's own customers are with the current delivery of important services but also how satisfied the competitive banks' customers are so that gaps between customer needs and current service levels can be identified for the total market or the segment being targeted.

The original research request to examine only the service satisfaction levels of the firm's own customers would have failed to provide the information needed for management's real problem.

- It would not have examined the relative importance of attributes other than service (rate, convenience, and so on) in the consumer's choice process.
- It would not have examined the service needs and perceptions of current non-customers (the group new customers must be attracted from).

The original research request would have been directionally more correct if management had said it wanted to determine whether it was living up to the service expectations of its current customers. Even then, what was the decision to be made? Assuming all the firm's customers were probably not perfectly satisfied, the decision was whether to improve the service (for example, add more tellers to reduce customer line wait time) because the cost of lost client business due to the service shortfall is greater than the cost of bank programs to improve the service. Today, many financial service firms address the question of identifying current service shortfalls by surveying their current customers and obtaining satisfaction ratings for the firm and different aspects of their service. But few firms obtain the information needed for good resource decisionmaking in this area, namely, estimates of the opportunity cost of imperfect service.

For example, one bank that focused on service as an important aspect of its strategy measured its success by annually surveying a random sample of its customers to determine the proportion satisfied with the bank. But what was the cost of dissatisfaction? Respondents might indicate dissatisfaction in a survey, but considering the consumer inertia in the financial services market and the probability that competition forced the bank and its key competitors to offer similar service levels, were dissatisfied customers taking their business elsewhere? How much business was being lost because of dissatisfaction with the bank's current level of service?

The answers to these questions were needed to provide management with some benchmarks for assessing the level of resources that could *profitably* be allocated to this aspect of the firm's marketing strategy.

By linking the customers' internal balance data with the survey data, it was possible to determine whether the survey answers of dissatisfaction correlated with loss of business at the bank and by how much. The estimated opportunity cost, in terms of lower balances and profit (projected to the total customer base), turned out to be substantially lower than this bank's management had expected.

The importance, difficulty, and frustrations of the problem definition stage are probably best described by these three maxims from Edmund Berkeley's *Notebook on Common Sense*[1]:

- A vast amount of time and effort is wasted in solving the wrong problems.
- *Half* the work of producing an answer that is correct is in phrasing the correct problem.
- The correct expression of a problem may be markedly different from the first half dozen efforts to express it.

After defining the decision(s) to be made, it is necessary to determine what information will add value. Information derives its value from its potential to permit switching of decisions by resolving uncertainties or creating new or better alternatives. At this stage, it is often useful to develop a flowchart or decision tree that maps the key assumptions driving the decision. The role of research then becomes clearer: finding information that sheds light on some or all of these crucial assumptions.

If there is no structure to provide focus for the information needed, there is a reasonable chance that useless data will be collected while some necessary data will not be. Both the market expertise of the line manager making the decision and the research expertise of the researcher are needed to develop a clear understanding of the problem and the role, if any, that research can play in providing information that will affect decisionmaking.

III. Data Gathering

The Value of Internal Data

The most popular traditional data-gathering techniques for marketing research studies are surveys and small-group discussions that focus on a series of topics introduced by a discussion leader. These are called focus groups. But in the financial services industry, the firm's internal data about the behavior of its customers and sales forces constitute one of the best information sources.

Surveys and focus groups are useful for gathering information about customers' awareness of and attitudes toward different products and vendors. They can also provide very useful insights into clients' wants, needs, and decision-making processes. However, these data become more powerful when they are linked to the buying behavior that they stimulate, as in the earlier banking example where customer survey dissatisfaction data were linked to actual balance behavior at the bank.

Because of respondents' poor memories, and sometimes biased answers, surveys have never been an accurate source of data about customers' buying behavior in terms of quantity or timing. This problem is more acute in financial services, where it is more difficult to remember balance data and trading data than it is to remember how many boxes of Jell-O were bought in the past six months.

For example, in the bank service survey discussed earlier, respondents were asked whether the amount of business they had done with the bank over the past

Table 1. Self-Reported versus Actual Balance Data.

Satisfaction Segment[a]	Percent Increased Balances in Past Two Years According to		Reported-Actual Difference
	Survey	Actual[b]	
Satisfied/Satisfied	29	41	−12
Increased Satisfaction	32	48	−16
Decreased Satisfaction	21	44	−23
Dissatisfied/Dissatisfied	14	59	−45

a. Segments were defined by the customers' overall satisfaction ratings for the bank at two points in time two years apart.
b. The percent of respondents whose average monthly balances increased by at least 50 percent from the beginning period to the ending period two years later according to internal records.

two years had increased, decreased, or stayed the same. As Table 1 shows, if survey responses had been the source of information, the percentage of customers whose balances at the bank had increased by more than 50 percent over the two-year period would have been substantially underestimated for all segments and biased for some segments. These underestimates would have been grossly misleading with respect to the relationship between customers' satisfaction ratings and their actual buying (banking) behavior.

In monitoring a marketing strategy, we want to estimate both the direction and magnitude of its effectiveness. Both the survey and internal data provided a valid indicator of direction; that is, both indicated that service dissatisfaction was related to *some* loss in business. However, *only* the firm's internal balance data accurately estimated the magnitude of the effect of service dissatisfaction in terms of lost revenues and profits. The latter is the information that managment needs to make good strategic (resource allocation) decisions.

The packaged-goods industry has spent millions of dollars on diary panel data and scanner data to acquire more accurate consumer behavior data. The financial services industry has the ability to obtain some of this valuable information by building and analyzing a customer database that reflects purchase behavior at the firm. Financial services firms are sitting on an information gold mine; they just need to develop the tools to get the information out. In the Appendix, we discuss some of the key issues in building this capability.

Determining the Sample

Many executives believe sampling is a technical, statistical area that should be left to the researcher. However, the most important issue in choosing a sample is whether the people selected for the research represent those who really matter to the success of the strategy being researched. Common sense is a good guide in this area.

For example, many marketing research surveys are aimed at understanding current customers' reactions to existing services (satisfaction studies) or current customers' reactions to proposed new programs (pricing studies). The typical method is to select a random sample of names of customers from the firm's customer database. But since most of a financial service business's revenues and profits are derived from only a few of its customers, this random sample produces a study that focuses on the attitudes and responses of the small-revenue customer.

For example, analysis of one retail bank's customer database indicated that 5 percent of its customers accounted for 45 percent of its revenues, and 20 percent of its customers accounted for 74 percent of its revenues. Put another way, the loss of 1 of its high-value customers would be equivalent to losing 28 of its smaller customers. However, the customer satisfaction survey was based on a random sample (1,000 customers) of the total customer base. This meant only 50 out of the 1,000 customers in the sample represented the high-value customers who accounted for 45 percent of current revenues.

In practical effect, these studies based on random samples of the total customer base are measuring the satisfaction or reactions of the small, relatively unprofitable customers. If the characteristics, attitudes, and reactions of small-value and high-value customers do not differ, the information obtained in these studies is useful for decisionmaking. But if these segments do differ significantly, this method will not reveal the differences and will incorrectly ascribe the small-value customers' reactions to the high-value customers.

Some researchers try to address this problem by increasing the size of the random sample. Then, based on consumers' recollections of the business they did with the firm in the past year, the respondents who report high balances are segregated. This is an inefficient way to do the study. For a sample of 300 high-revenue customers (the top 5 percent), 5,700 low-revenue customers would also be interviewed.

More important, there is a high probability that the results of this type of analysis would be incorrect because (as we discussed earlier) the self-reported revenue or balance data collected in surveys from respondents are inaccurate. As a result, a portion of the supposedly "high-value customer sample" consists of incorrectly classified small-value customers. This reduces the possibility of identifying significant differences between the two segments.

These studies should be based on a stratified sample of the firm's high-, medium-, and small-value customers. To do this, the researcher must first analyze customers' revenues or profits with the firm for the past six months or year using the firm's internal customer database to determine the cutoff values that define high-, medium-, and small-revenue or profit customers. With this information, random samples of high-, medium-, and small-value customers can be drawn from the database and surveyed (for example, 300 in each segment). Analysis of the survey results *by segment* will give management the full customer-base picture, not only the reactions of the small-value customer.

A random sample of total current customers is appropriate when examining reaction to a new product and there is no reason to believe it would be specifically targeted to the current high-value customer. For example, in the banking industry, current high-value customers tend to be older and have high deposit balances at an institution. They would probably not be the primary target market for a new credit product.

To summarize, the 5-50 and 20-80 rules frequently operate for customers whether or not we recognize them. To the extent that we do not recognize them and we focus on the "average" customer in our strategic thinking and marketing research, we are focusing on the small-profit-contributor segment.

One way of presenting this fallacy is to relate a response given by a student when asked to define an average and describe its limitations. He said an average was like taking two shots in duck-hunting. The first shot went a foot above the duck, and the second shot went a foot below the duck. On "average," the duck was dead. But the problem was that the duck kept flying. How many of our strategic decisions are based on data from customer samples that represent "flying dead ducks"?

Another sampling problem particularly prevalent in the financial services industry is that the types of people one needs to interview (for example, active stock investors, and home equity borrowers) are difficult and, therefore, expensive to find. Thus some studies ask the right questions of the wrong people because it is easier (and cheaper) to find them.

For example, a bank was trying to obtain information on how customers chose a bank for their checking account business. Its purpose was to develop a strategy that would attract a greater share of the checking account opener market. Should the survey be based on a sample of customers who had recently opened a checking account at the bank or a sample of those who had recently opened a checking account at any bank in the trading area? Many executives would choose the first approach because it is substantially cheaper since the sample of checking account openers can be identified from the bank's internal records. The problem is that a study based on a sample of the bank's own openers will offer no information about many consumers who selected competitors' offerings, which is what the decisionmaker must know to evaluate the bank's current strategy. But the correct approach (selecting a sample of all recent checking account openers in the trading area) will cost four to five times as much as the customer-only study because of the great expense of locating the (low-incidence) people needed for it.

In summary, it is better not to do the research at all than to base decisions on information gathered from people other than those you are trying to market to and influence. The major issue of the representativeness of the proposed sample for the decision to be made simply requires common sense and should be monitored by the decisionmaker.

Limitations

In general, today's marketing research techniques are better able to provide useful information for decisionmaking about strategies for existing financial services than for ideas about new financial services. The traditional approach to measuring the appeal of products or services that have not yet been introduced in the market is a technique called concept testing. People in the target market are given a verbal description of the new product or service and are asked whether they would purchase it. The problems with this research approach for most financial services and products are twofold.

1. Because of the complexity of many new financial products (zero coupon bonds, adjustable-rate CDs, and so on) the interviewees do not understand the products being described to them. Therefore, their answers do not necessarily indicate what they would do if they had time to study these products or received advice from an influencer such as their broker.

2. We do not have any valid way of estimating real purchase behavior based on respondents' answers about whether they intend to buy the new product. Even in the traditional packaged-goods research world, there is evidence that intention-to-buy responses do not translate into reasonable estimates of buying behavior. In the financial services world, the problem is complicated because many respondents do not understand clearly the benefits and risks of the product concept being tested. Thus their answers about buying intentions are even more suspect and unreliable for decisionmaking. Some researchers believe they can overcome this problem by using concept tests to at least rank-order several different concepts. But there is no evidence that the errors in the intention-to-buy measures are consistent from concept to concept. Therefore, using this technique to rank-order the market acceptability of different new financial services is incorrect and may provide misleading information for decisionmaking.

This does not mean one should never do marketing research on new product and service ideas. Research can often provide diagnostic information about potential buyers' understanding and reaction to the new product that will be extremely helpful in designing effective introduction strategies.

But it is important to recognize that the state of the art in measurement will probably be unable to provide a valid estimate of the size of the market for the new product. Decisionmakers are best advised to use their marketing research budgets for satisfying other, more solvable information needs like building an internal data analysis capability to monitor buyer behavior after a new product has been introduced. At this stage, studies examining buyers' characteristics or why people with similar characteristics are not buying the product can often provide valuable insights to improve the current strategy or suggest why a new product should be dropped.

IV. Analysis

Ideally, management has postulated some hypotheses during the problem definition stage. So the first step in the analysis is to test these hypotheses, which means looking for particular patterns in the data. But this is just the beginning. A good analyst will test the a priori hypotheses and look for meaningful patterns in the data that might suggest hypotheses about consumer behavior not indicated by management.

Two common problems in the analysis stage are underanalysis and failure to separate the "signal" from the "noise."

Underanalysis of data results in reports that are merely descriptive, not interpretive. These reports tell management that X percent of the people said this, and Y percent said that, but they don't pull the data together and explain how these findings apply to the decision under consideration.

Underanalysis can also result in erroneous interpretations of data. For example, a survey of investors done by a brokerage firm indicated that the average satisfaction rating for its brokers was (statistically) significantly lower than for its competitors' brokers although there was no supporting evidence to explain the disparity. Based on this information, top management put considerable pressure on sales management and the sales force to develop programs that would raise their satisfaction ratings to the competitive average.

Some time later, further analysis of the data revealed that the broker-satisfaction scores were positively correlated with customer size. Higher-revenue customers, who received more of the brokers' time and attention, gave them higher satisfaction ratings than did smaller-revenue customers. For some methodological reason, the sample of investors from the firm underrepresented the high-revenue investor group. Therefore, the lower *average* satisfaction rating for the firm's brokers represented a sampling bias and not the truth.

For similar-size customers, the customer satisfaction scores were similar for the firm's brokers and competitors' brokers, and with corrected samples, the averages were the same. This information mistake caused management to waste considerable resources trying to solve a nonexistent problem.

The second issue in data analysis is separating the signal from the noise. When an interesting finding results from data analysis based on a sample, one should ask, Does the empirical finding represent a sampling accident? Statistical testing addresses this issue.

For example, in a survey of mutual fund owners, the average age of those who had bought their fund through a salesperson was 51 years. The average age of those who had bought their (no-load or low-load) fund directly from the sponsor was 54 years. Is the observed difference caused only by sampling error, or are the two populations really different with respect to age? If the difference could be caused by sampling fluctuations, it makes little sense to spend additional time on the result or to base decisions on it. If the result is not caused by sampling variations, there is reason to consider it further.

Statistical significance testing should be used as a screening process by which the researcher decides whether an empirical result should be considered further. However, it is not an end in itself. Many results are statistically significant but not usable or meaningful for decisionmaking. In our mutual fund example, even if the average age of the mutual fund owner who buys from a sales force is statistically significantly lower than the average age of the direct-purchase mutual fund owner, there is still considerable overlap in the age distributions of the two buyer segments. Thus age is not a useful criterion for targeting one segment versus the other.

Figure 1. Revenue Concentration for Brokerage Firm's Retail Customers.

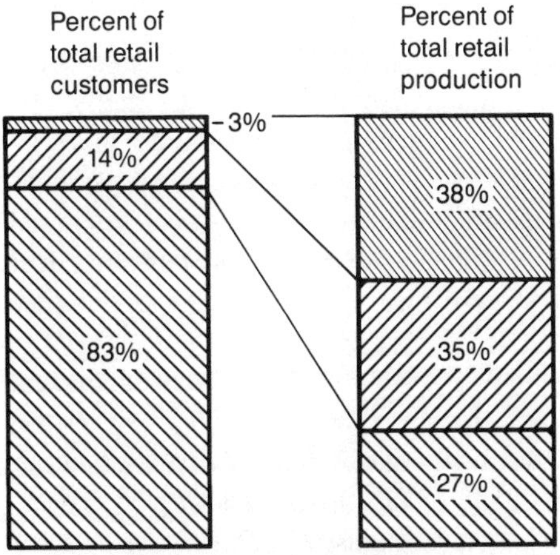

Percent of total retail customers	Percent of total retail production	Average indexed to "low"		
		Revenue per customer	Orders per customer	Order size
14% (—3%)	38%	36	20	4
83%	35%	6	5	2
	27%	1	1	1

Finally, no amount of statistical testing will detect biases. Most biases are not removed or diminished simply by increasing the size of the sample. Since there are many potential sources of bias (the questionnaire, the sampling, the interviewer, nonresponse) throughout the research process, statistical significance testing should not be used as the sole standard of differences between populations. Judgment and supporting analyses should be used continually to validate conclusions.

V. Interpretation

Once the analysis is completed, the value of the information lies in the way it is used for decisionmaking. For example, analysis of the internal customer database for a retail brokerage firm indicated that 3 percent of the customers accounted for almost 40 percent of the revenues (see Figure 1). The question was, So what?

Sometimes the high-value customers are also high-volume customers. Analysis of the internal data verified that this was so. Although the average order size for the high-value customer segment was four times the order size of the small customer, the driving force behind the high-revenue segment was the frequency it traded with (20 times the small customer average in a year). Once again we asked, So what?

Since errors and back-office problems usually happen randomly, the probability that these high-value customers would have a problem was substantially higher than for the smaller customers because of the former group's significantly higher trading frequency. The loss of one high-value customer was equivalent to losing the business of 36 smaller customers. The high-value customer was substantially more likely to encounter a problem in a given year.

This finding was validated in a survey in which customers indicated the frequency of problems at the firm in the past six months. The high-revenue customers reported more problems. However, the frequency of problems reported was not as great as one would have expected on the basis of probability theory because the broker probably monitored the transactions of these key customers carefully and caught some of the errors before they reached the customer.

This understanding of customer behavior has led to "priority service" and "key customer" programs in some banks and brokerage firms. Essentially, they recognize that some of their best customers for repeat-purchase products and services are getting more than the firm's average rate of errors because of high transaction volumes. Although it is usually unprofitable to process business separately for these high-value customers, they could be identified in the firm's customer database and, at least, be given priority by the customer service staff resolving their problems.

Not all high-volume customers are high-revenue or high-profit customers, and some high-revenue customers can be relatively unprofitable if they have excessively high volumes of small order sizes. This is exactly the kind of information management can obtain by having researchers analyze the firm's customer database.

In the full-service brokerage and insurance industries, the broker or agent is often the customer. Once again, analysis of the firm's internal sales force database yields concentration statistics. In a study of agents at an insurance firm, 25 percent were found to account for almost 70 percent of new premium revenues in a typical year. In a retail brokerage firm, the results were less skewed, with 20 percent of the brokers accounting for 50 percent of the revenues. For both firms, about 60 percent of the sales force accounted for about 90 percent of the revenues.

The implication of these findings is not simply to fire the 40 percent of the sales force that accounts for only 10 percent of the revenues. Instead, through further analysis of the database, much can be learned about the high producers versus the low producers to help management identify unprofitable producers and monitor programs aimed at increasing their productivity.

In one such study, a brokerage firm found that for each individual product (for example, options, muni bonds, tax shelters) except equities, about 20 percent of the brokers who sold the product accounted for 80 percent of the revenues in that product. They also found that the brokers in this top 20 percent for a product were not in the top 20 percent for any other product. This led to the strategic position that the firm's cross-selling goals might be achieved most effectively through team selling or referrals instead of expecting one broker to be able to sell all types of products.

Another important analysis using internal customer data is estimating the revenue or profit impact of current strategies. One example is the customer dissatisfaction research that we discussed earlier.

Another example is a study done by a brokerage firm to estimate the incremental revenue generated by a new product it had introduced. The product had been rolled out relatively randomly to half the states in the United States. The product was designed to attract more active investors. If it did, one would expect that the productivity of brokers in the half of the country where the new service was available would be higher than that of brokers in areas where the service had not yet been introduced.

There is a learning curve that affects the average level of broker productivity for the first ten years of experience, and it is necessary to consider this when measuring changes in productivity (see Figure 2). At the end of two years, the percentage change in the brokers' productivity in the new-product test offices was compared with the change for the brokers in the nontest offices. As Figure 3 shows, the new service appeared to have increased productivity by 10 percent for relatively inexperienced brokers (those registered fewer than five years) but had no significant effect on the productivity of the more experienced brokers in the sales force.

In retrospect, these results made sense because this new service was a good prospecting tool and so had more impact on the portion of the sales force that was building its client base. On the other hand, since the new service was improving the productivity of only a portion of the sales force, the incremental revenues thereby generated were smaller than anticipated. Depending on management's objectives concerning breakeven and profits, this might suggest a need to scale down the original aggressive strategy for rolling out the product nationally to something less ambitious and less costly.

To summarize, it is often difficult to be objective when interpreting information and answering the question, So what? To the extent that the role of the information in the decision has been clearly defined in the problem definition stage, objective interpretations within the limits of the data are more likely.

But in the financial services industry, many studies are undertaken as "fishing expeditions" to find a basis for understanding the customer or sales force. Here, it is important that biases do not enter into interpretations of the findings, particularly by drawing conclusions beyond the scope of the data.

VI. Conclusion

The task of obtaining information for marketing decisionmaking presents two overriding challenges.

1. Focusing limited information resources on situations where the value of the information is greater than the cost of obtaining it.
2. Providing management with "correct" information that is interpreted correctly.

The successful completion of these two tasks is interrelated. Since there will always be more requests for information than resources allocated to collect and analyze data, managers and researchers must try to assess the value of the information for its intended decision *before* the research is undertaken. If resources are wasted on obtaining information for less valuable situations, they will not be adequately available for more difficult but more valuable studies.

For example, some firms continue to do annual tactical tracking studies that do not given management any new information and, at the same time, use up research resources that prevent major, expensive strategic studies of the marketplace. Worse yet, because adequate resources are not available to do a study correctly, expense-cutting measures may be taken (for example, modifying the sample) that could produce incorrect information for decisionmaking.

Figure 2. Broker Production versus Experience.

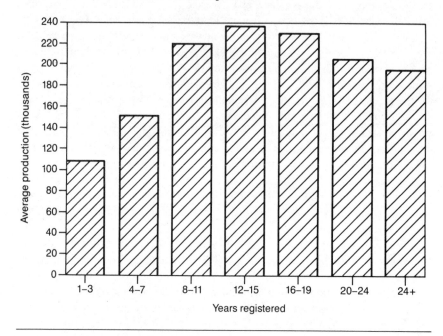

Figure 3. Incremental Broker Productivity.

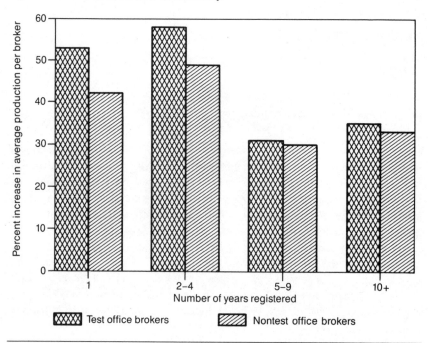

Figure 4. Information Workplan.

Form to be completed by decisionmaker requesting research *before* a study is designed by the research staff. After an appropriate study has been designed and its cost estimated, an assessment of the expected value of the information compared with its cost should be made to determine whether the study is worth executing.

1. Decision Background
   - What is the marketing decision to be made?
   - What are your alternative courses of action?

2. Role of Information
   - What are your hypotheses about the consumer that would affect this decision (or the alternative course of action you would choose)?
   - Which of these hypotheses or assumptions are to be examined in this research?

3. Action Standards
   - What, if any, of the research results will be used to select the best alternative?

4. Value of Information Requested
   - What are the risks if this decision is incorrect?
   - What is the expected value of this information for making a correct decision?

5. Timing
   - By what date do you need the results for decisionmaking?

One way to focus management on the need to define the problem and assess the potential value of information needed to address it is to require an "information workplan" *before* any research is undertaken. Figure 4 gives an example of an information workplan.

In this chapter, we have emphasized some of the key factors in the data-collection, analysis, and interpretation stages of the research process that will yield "correct" information for decisionmaking. Since the final objective of many consumer studies is to understand which marketing strategies affect consumers' buying behavior, internal data that accurately measures consumers' buying behavior is a powerful information tool for the financial services industry. To take advantage of this unique opportunity, management must build not only a customer database but also the systems and staff needed to analyze it for strategic decisionmaking.

Appendix
Building a Customer Information System

I. The Database

In most financial institutions, data are collected by "account" number on different operating systems. The most difficult (and expensive) part of developing a customer database is bringing together the account data from the different operating systems in the firm and matching the account records so that the resulting record indicates the total business being done with the institution by the customer. If the customer is an individual, the account matching is usually done on social security number

Figure 5. Different MIS Needs for Different Decisions.

Decision Type	Scope of Data Needed	Analysis Needed	Timing Needed	Measurement Accuracy Needed	Relative Cost/Risk If Decision Is Wrong
Strategic	Broad	Complex	Monthly or Yearly	Ballpark Estimates	High
Tactical					
Operational	Narrow	Simple	Instant	Precise	Low

or tax identification number. If the customer is the household, the account matching is based on similar account name and address data. To the extent that the institution (particularly banks) link accounts for legal or pricing purposes, this information is also used to try to identify all the accounts associated with a customer.

After developing the capability to turn account data into customer data, the following questions arise about the content and maintenance of the database:

1. Which data elements should be retained (account open dates, transaction data, financial data)?
2. For what periods (daily data for the past three months, monthly data for the past five years)?
3. How frequently should the database be updated (daily, monthly)?

The answers to these questions depend on the *primary* purpose of the database, that is, its use for operational, tactical or strategic decisions. These three types of decisions require differing information systems in terms of scope of data, analysis, timing, and measurement accuracy (see Figure 5).

For example, in a bank, many customer service representatives and account managers need information for operational decisions such as determining whether a customer has the balances required for a particular product price. Here, the scope of data needed is narrow (for example, balance data for the current period), no analysis is needed (except possibly to add some balances), the information probably has to be retrieved quickly (the customer is probably waiting for an answer on the telephone), and the data has to be accurate (for example, the current daily balance).

At the other extreme, a few managers need information for strategic decisions such as the following: What businesses should we be in and with what level of resources? Is our strategy achieving its goals and if not, why not?

To address these strategic issues, one must be able to do complex analyses that measure relationships and trends in a broad array of data for a relatively long time period (usually the past three to five years). However, the most recent daily data are not needed, and the focus is on estimating general relationships rather than obtaining precise measures.

Clearly, the requirements in terms of customer database content and frequency of updating vary substantially for strategic versus operational decisionmaking. In this chapter, we focused on developing a database for strategic decisions. This usually involves a wide array of financial data (balances, prices or commissions charged), transaction data (number of monthly transactions, average monthly order size), and product or account opening and closing dates. However, monthly (versus daily) updating of the database is usually sufficient.

II. Analyzing the Customer Database

In many financial service firms the customer database exists, but there are major barriers to achieving the next step, analysis of the data. Most customer databases are designed for data retrieval, not analysis. As a result, you have to be an Einstein of programming or have worked in the corporate systems group for five years to extract data from the database in any other form than the standard screens that have been set up for data retrieval. Moreover, the customer records and resulting databases are huge and therefore slow and expensive to manipulate when doing statistical analyses. And because large data sets are usually involved, the firm's mainframe computers are needed to provide the capacity to manipulate the data. The problem is that the research group usually has low priority for use of these computers (versus processing the firm's business). Therefore, many of their programs are bumped, delayed, or lost.

One way to break through these barriers is to do the following:

1. Pay a programming genius to develop generic extract programs for getting the data out of the central customer database and into a form that is ready for input into statistical packages. When you do some of the analyses discussed in this chapter, you will find a pattern in the types of customer data needed. Therefore, it is possible to design a list of variables that will facilitate 60 to 70 percent of all strategic studies. A standardized program can be developed to extract these variables readily from the central customer database.
2. Use stratified samples for most of the studies using internal data. You must be able to manipulate a few variables from the total customer base to understand the concentration statistics and draw the appropriate stratified samples for each study. Once these key statistics are known, detailed behavioral analyses can be done, using the full record of data for the stratified sample of customers.
3. Develop a separate processing environment (for example, a minicomputer) for doing the analyses. Working with samples then becomes very important.
4. Use statistical packages (like SAS) and analysts accustomed to doing behavioral data analyses (for example, those who have analyzed panel data for packaged goods.)

In most firms, it is difficult to obtain the processing and manpower resources needed to develop this flexible, analytical capability because the yardstick for determining whose information needs will be satisfied is usually the number of people in the firm who will use the system. The number of people making operational decisions based on information from the consumer database is considerably larger than the number involved with strategic decisionmaking. Therefore, the focus has been on data retrieval and servicing the needs of the operational decisionmaking users. When management realizes that the costs and risks associated with incorrect strategic decisions are far greater than those for incorrect operational decisions, the differing needs of the strategic decisionmaking users of the database will be appropriately serviced.

III. Notes

1. Edmund C. Berkeley, ed., *Common Sense, Elementary and Advanced*, vol. 2, no. 7B (Newtonville, Mass.: Berkeley Enterprises, Inc., 1972), p. 6.

18

Strategic and Organizational Considerations in Developing New Financial Service Products

Philip A. Dover
Associate Professor of Business Administration and Director of the
International M.B.A. Program, Babson College

I. Introduction

The development of new products and services can be rewarding and, often, necessary to maintain a healthy organization. But though there may be rich reward for innovation, the introduction of new products is also risky.

Reviewing several studies on new product failure rates, Merle Crawford concluded that about 20 to 25 percent of industrial products and 30 to 35 percent of consumer products fail.[1] Further, the life cycle of successful products is shortening as technological changes render products obsolete at an ever-faster rate. New product development is also a costly business. Successful products have to return their own development costs and contribute to the costs of other products that failed or did not even reach the marketplace.

Banks and other financial institutions face an environment that more and more requires the search for new products. Among the initiating factors are rapidly expanding technological developments, a trend toward deregulation that both broadens and intensifies competitive activity, and social changes that have raised the level of consumer knowledge and sophistication, leading to heightened product expectations. Problems and opportunities for new product innovation will be illustrated mainly from recent developments in in-home computerized banking.

Technological advances offer a solution and create additional problems for financial institutions seeking product or service innovations. In a recent research study carried out by consultants Arthur Anderson for the European Banking Association, 97 percent of the respondents believed that technology will be important in maintaining or increasing competitive advantage. But the report also indicated that banks must think more strategically about technology in view of the amount of investment required for new technology and its central place in bank operations: "When the level of technology was low, banks could change direction rapidly. Now the level of technology is such that rapid changes of direction are not possible, so they must take a much more long-term view."[2]

There is a paradox here. The technology-induced shortening of product life cycles implies that companies should take a flexible, adaptive approach to innovation. For instance, the development of competitive screen-based and voice-based systems of delivering in-home banking services offers an example of the heightened risk of investing in emerging technologies. The recent commercialization of voice-based systems, requiring only the attachment of a tonepad device to a conventional telephone, is thought to overcome such screen-based system problems as high equipment costs, complex usage instructions, and lengthy transaction time. Major U.S. banks like Citibank and Chemical Bank have invested heavily in screen-based systems and are now wondering about the wisdom of their choice.

Pressures to create innovative products cause another major problem for financial institutions. The variety of influences on market demand and the changing characteristics of the competitive environment have greatly complicated the prediction of new product adoption patterns. Therefore, it has become very difficult to make accurate forecasts of demand. A 1986 Bank Marketing Association survey revealed that nearly one third of bank customers in the United States use automated teller machines (ATMs), and nearly everybody knows what they are.[3] These penetration figures may sound impressive, but when ATMs were introduced to the retail market in the early 1970s, most consumers were expected to make some use of the machines within five years.

Similarly, initial expectations about the potential for home banking in North America were vastly overstated. Early survey research suggested that 50 to 70 percent of the U.S. population would ultimately subscribe to a home banking service, creating a $7 billion industry. Actual experience suggests that the household sector market potential is nowhere near that figure.[4]

In this chapter, we examine procedural and organizational approaches that financial institutions can use to improve their new product development performance. We do not intend a comprehensive step-by-step description of management of the innovation stages. (That subject is well covered in sources noted at the end of the chapter.[5]) Rather, we discuss the concerns that we believe management must address to achieve success in any new product program.

II. Strategic Considerations in Developing New Products

It is increasingly clear that the management of financial services firms must adopt a more strategic focus, particularly a longer-term view of technology requirements.

As the Arthur Anderson study noted, "Most bank managements are good at short-term decisions but technology is now much more a long-term issue." There are three key steps in adopting a strategic perspective on the new product development process: (1) undertaking situation assessments, (2) determining strategic focus, and (3) establishing strategic goals.

Undertaking Situation Assessments

The first and most critical requirement for new financial product planning is an accurate understanding of the organization's current situation. A situation assessment entails "the systematic analysis of past, present, and future data to identify trends, forces, and conditions with the potential to influence the performance of the business and the choice of appropriate strategies."[6]

The relevant data encompass both the external environment and the internal resources and capabilities. Questions can be classified under the headings of the four C's:

1. Climate: trends in the industry and specific markets, impact of regulatory and technological changes
2. Customer: need and behavior analysis by market segment
3. Competitor: identification of present and potential competitors and how they compete
4. Company: self-assessment of resources and competences

The analysis of climate, customers, and competitors leads to an evaluation of market opportunity. The analysis of the company itself aims to determine whether the organization is equipped to seize the opportunity.

Without a doubt, the situation assessment is the most time-consuming and frustrating phase of new product planning. Data can be incomplete, unreliable, hard to find, and even harder to interpret. It is a major challenge to piece together a comprehensive picture of opportunities in the prospective business environment in the face of inherent uncertainty. Unfortunately, many companies fail to do a thorough job at this stage. This is a serious deficiency since out of this analysis comes the identification of markets that offer the widest scope for innovation by the organization. Techniques for determining market attractiveness are beyond the range of this article,[7] but several financial organizations have succeeded in redefining their market boundaries following systematic market analysis.

Perhaps the most dramatic investment sector foray into the depository institutions market has been the cash management account (CMA). Introduced originally by Merrill Lynch, the CMA is really nothing more than a computer-driven repackaging of existing financial services that is more banking oriented than investment oriented.

Cash balances of brokerage clients are automatically deposited into a money fund that is underwritten and managed by the investment banker. All customer securities (stocks, bonds, and so on) left with the broker are added to the money fund holdings to create an asset base, against which the investor or depositer can write checks or offset purchases made with a credit card issued by a cooperating bank. At an account level, the result is a comprehensive personal financial management account, far superior to any single retail service ever introduced.

At a competitive level, the result is a bank-broker organization with a repertoire of financial services well suited to the banking and investment needs of its chosen market. Merrill Lynch and others identified and seized the opportunity to consolidate many financial activities for the affluent, busy executive seeking efficiency in his or her resource management.

Situation assessment must be a *dynamic* process. Market evolution has to be monitored continuously. After carefully tracking some key factors, the Nottingham Building Society (NBS), a small regional organization, became the first financial institution in the United Kingdom to introduce in-home banking. Since the U.K. banking industry was both mature and increasingly competitive, the clear differentiation of services was becoming more problematic. Continuous environmental scanning suggested that technology developed outside the banking industry would have an increasing internal effect. Specifically, improvements in computerization would enable financial institutions to bring many of their services directly into the home. Although the potential benefits of in-home banking were generally accepted, most banks and building societies took a traditional, conservative, wait-and-see approach to this service. Such caution allowed NBS to make a preemptive move into this market.

Finally, urgent attention must be paid to improving the quality of management information used in new product deliberations. The Arthur Anderson study notes that "83 percent agreed that product profitability systems would be vital to a bank's survival over the next 10 years and almost as many—79 percent—said the same about customer profitability." Financial institutions can still do much to improve data collection and the management of decision support systems.

Determining Strategic Focus

Although product innovation must be considered the lifeblood of any organization, the direction for new product development must be carefully selected. A company must establish whether there is an effective fit between the product, company, and market for the new idea. Does the situation assessment indicate both a potential market demand for a product and a particular "distinctive competence" for the interested company? What distinguishes its mode of doing business, its resources, or its management and employee value systems from those of competitors in the market?

For example, a regional New England bank entered the personal banking market (the provision of goods and services to high net worth persons) in an affluent area of Boston. Despite clear market potential for the product, the regional bank failed because of its image as an established community institution serving a predominantly blue-collar clientele. Similarly, large British banks have been reluctant to introduce commercial in-home banking programs. Although they believe there is good market demand, the innovation poses a potential competitive threat to their extensive branch network systems and substantial investments in bricks and mortar.

Timing is a further strategic consideration in new product planning. The term, *strategic window,* has been used to indicate that there are often only limited periods when the fit between the key requirements of a market and the particular competences of a company competing in that market is optimal.

Investment in product or service line development has to be timed to coincide with periods when a strategic window is expected to be open, that is, when a close fit exists. In-home banking has been extremely successful in France, where it is a component of Minitel, a national videotext network. Minitel is operated by the French Posts and Telecoms Ministry (PTT), which provides the basic equipment (a screen and keyboard attachment for the telephone) free to subscribers. Initially, Minitel introduced simple services (automated telephone services), adding more complex services (home banking) as subscribers' computer knowledge and confidence expanded. They waited until the time was right!

Establishing Strategic Goals

A company must be clear about its reasons for developing new products and how this process contributes to overall corporate strategy. Corporate strategies and objectives provide a framework within which new product strategies are chosen and goals and objectives are set. Alternative product strategies have their own financial requirements, risks, and rewards. These provide the basis for goal formation, which gives specific guidance to the functions and people involved in the new product process. Goals also provide a basis for evaluating and controlling these activities.

However, a financial institution must do considerable homework before establishing new product goals. Look again at the example of home banking. Banks have tended to look at home banking projects in terms of return on investment (net profit divided by the cost of investment). The problem is that this standard profitability equation does not apply well to most home banking projects because it fails to consider the many tactical and strategic benefits involved, most of them quantifiable.

Such benefits include increased market share, account consolidation, and cross-selling opportunities. Productivity gains are an important quantifiable consideration since home banking projects displace other costs and frequently use excess systems capacity. Such benefits need to be balanced against aspects of the investment that are more difficult to measure, namely, soft costs such as nonallocated overhead or software development or the value of other projects that have to be delayed to make room for the home banking project.[8]

After the goals and measures of performance are established, the organization must consider alternative means of achieving these goals. One of the basic strategic decisions is whether to be reactive or proactive.

A reactive product strategy deals with the initiating pressures as they arise. The approach is to wait until the competition introduces a product and emulate it if it is successful. A proactive strategy explicitly allocates resources to identify and seize opportunities and preempt possible adverse events. This is done by being first on the market with a product that competitors find difficult to match. An organization must recognize the factors that make each strategy appropriate (for example, market size and trends, technology access, financial and human resources, and competitive position) and react accordingly.[9]

It is now generally accepted, in North America at least, that home banking projects attract 15 or more percent of their customers from other financial institutions. Moreover, these new customers tend to be upscale persons who consolidate their account relationships with the sponsoring bank. This implies that financial institutions have to develop defensive as well as offensive new product strategies. Often, they may be forced into investing in home banking to hold on to market share.

III. Organizational Concerns in Developing New Products

Organizing the product development effort and effective product management are two challenging tasks that cut across many departmental lines. If there is no organizational unit with specific responsibility for managing new products, few innovations will result. A good formal organization is important, but the informal, unstructured aspects of an organization really determine how well the process is implemented. Here are a few ideas that might improve prospects for successful cooperation in new product development.

The Role of the Product Champion

As financial service innovations diverge increasingly from the base technologies traditionally applied to the industry, bank executives have recognized the need to redefine their institutions' business strategy. But they have hesitated to initiate change for fear of causing "organizational disruptions." In such a situation, a product champion can be an important catalyst.

A product champion has been described as "an individual who plays a key role in selling an idea to management, maintaining management's interest in the project and bearing the risks associated with the development of a new venture."[10] As a key manager throughout the innovation process, the product champion must be able to assume multiple roles. During the management of a new product, a product champion must serve as stimulator (start the process of idea generation), initiator (translate the idea into a plan of action), and legitimizer (have the social power to sanction the idea).

The product champion is usually someone who has sound *technical* understanding of the new product and can assess realistically its limitations and advantages. This ability to evaluate the future of the new product is often based primarily on technical intuitiveness with very little supporting data.

To facilitate development of a suitable marketing strategy, the product champion must also be able to realistically appraise the new product's *market* potential. Most significant, the product champion must have the drive to get the work done and decisions made as well as the political astuteness to identify power centers and communicate successfully with others at different levels within the organization.

However, unbridled enthusiasm for the new product should be avoided. Too often, product champions become blind to the market deficiencies of their "brain-child," with ego-involvement supplanting rational decision-making. It is harder to terminate the development of a new product on which much time, expense, and emotional energy have been invested than to simply move ahead with product introduction in the hope that market resistance can be overcome by clever marketing and consumer education.

Unquestionably, the successful development of the Nottingham Building Society's home banking program depended greatly on the guidance and direction of a product champion (in this case, the general manager). He had technical as well as market competence and commanded the respect of the management team. Moreover, his perceived knowledge and commitment led the nonexecutive board of directors to allocate considerable revenue and capital costs for the development of the Homelink program.[11]

Developing Team Dynamics

There are many formal and informal alternatives for product development.[12] For the large financial institution, current thinking suggests a growth-and-development department with a small staff, supplemented by venture teams that draw their members from operating functional areas. Major innovations using new technologies or tapping new markets are addressed by this group, whereas product-line extensions are the responsibility of product managers in the marketing department. Smaller companies usually rely on a task force or new product committee and outside agents for product development. Development is an intermittent activity and may not warrant a separate new product department.

Whatever the size of the organization, several observations are worth consideration.

1. Keep the new project team small. Extensive research by William Souder indicates that the efficiency and eventual success of the new product development process was sharply curtailed when the project team exceeded six members.[13] Keeping projects small fosters face-to-face contacts and reduces disharmony.
2. Select members of the new product team who share the institution's overall growth and innovation goals. It is a truism in new product development that "The first place a marketing person has to sell is on the inside—and that's the hardest of all." Team members must act as in-house ambassadors for the product and work hard to overcome internal resistance. When Chemical Bank was market testing its Pronto home banking system, the new product management introduced the system first to branch managers who supported the innovation. It was hoped that their enthusiasm would have a positive spillover effect on fellow employees.
3. Delineate clearly the responsibility and authority of new product team members. It can be wasteful, inefficient, and disruptive to strive repeatedly for agreement among people from different disciplines about every decision on every problem. Much more effective is to agree at the outset of the project on each party's decision authority policy. In the Homelink case, individual responsibilities were

clearly established, with the general manager assuming a leadership and coordination role. Highly qualified project managers (or product champions) are frequently able to overcome historically disharmonious relationships. But these people are rare. Bank management must develop a cadre of personnel with innovation leadership skills by instituting a long-term program of careful career pathing and coaching.

4. Be sure new product development receives genuine institutional support. Common to any system is the need for continuous (but not meddlesome) top-management involvement. Adequate human and financial resources must be committed to the development, market introduction, and management of new products. By and large, marketing is still "a tool bankers don't know quite how to pick up and use."[14] Although most of the large financial service organizations have recognized the need for the function, marketing managers are often frustrated by the paltry budgets and limited power that financially oriented managers grant to them. This bias must change as competition and the thrust for market-led innovation intensify.

IV. Conclusion

The financial services community faces a rapidly changing environment. As organizations strive to differentiate themselves in an expanding and crowded marketplace, they turn increasingly to technology in their search for a competitive edge. The widespread application of computer technology has broadened the range of financial services that can be made available. Unfortunately, this rush to technology has often preceded the identification of market needs. A recent study by Touche Ross International revealed that many banks have failed to benefit from their massive investments in technology principally because the introduction of new products and services has been driven more by technological feasibility than by demand as determined by sound market research.[15]

Financial institutions can no longer passively view product development. Bank and other personnel must learn to manage fast-paced innovation with a market orientation. In particular, skills must be developed at the marketing–technology interface to maintain competitiveness in the 1990s. This means the executive profile of innovative financial organizations will have to be markedly different from those with traditional structures. Strategic and organizational changes along the lines suggested here can help position new product management as a long-term, market-driven concern.

V. Notes

1. C. Merle Crawford, "New Product Failure Rates—Facts and Fallacies," *Research Management* (September 1979): 9–13.
2. Roger Cowe, "Technology Is the Key for Europe's Banks," *Banking Technology* (April 1986).
3. "Technology Catches On, But People Still Like People," *ABA Banking Journal* (May 1986).
4. Kenneth Thacker, "Devising a Profitable Home Banking Service," *Banking Technology* (May 1986).

5. C. Merle Crawford, *New Products Management* (Homewood, Ill.: Irwin, 1983); Glen L. Urban, John R. Hauser, and Nikhilesh Dholakia, *Essentials of New Product Management* (Englewood Cliffs, N.J.: Prentice-Hall, 1987); and Yoram J. Wind, *Product Policy: Concepts, Methods and Strategy* (Reading, Mass.: Addison-Wesley, 1982).
6. George S. Day, *Strategic Market Planning: The Pursuit of Competitive Advantage* (St. Paul, Minn.: West, 1984).
7. Urban, Hauser, and Dholakia, *Essentials of New Product Management*; and Derek F. Abell, and John S. Hammond, *Strategic Market Planning* (Englewood Cliffs, N.J.: Prentice-Hall, 1979).
8. Thacker, "Devising a Profitable Home Banking Service."
9. Urban, Hauser, and Dholakia, *Essentials of New Product Management*.
10. Carol Walcott, Robert P. Quellette, and Paul N. Cheremisinoff, *Techniques for Managing Technological Innovation* (Ann Arbor, Mich.: Ann Arbor Science, 1983).
11. Philip A. Dover, "Innovation in Banking: The In-Home Computerized Banking Example," *International Journal of Bank Marketing* (Spring 1987).
12. Crawford, *New Products Management*; and Urban, Hauser, and Dholakia, *Essentials of New Product Management*.
13. William E. Souder, "Disharmony between R&D and Marketing," *Industrial Marketing Management* (1981):67–73.
14. "The Search for Special Niches: Banking's Squeeze," *Business Week*, April 12, 1982.
15. "Banks Fail to Gain Competitive Advantage from Technology Investment," *Business International*, May 3, 1985.

Index

About the Editor

David B. Zenoff is a consultant, educator, and author specializing in the management of large companies, financial institutions, international business management, and the design of executive education programs. Since 1972, he has been president of David B. Zenoff Associates, Inc., of San Francisco and Gryon, Switzerland, which provides consultation on a variety of management challenges associated with large company management. He has authored several articles and six books, including *Corporate Finance in Multinational Companies*, *International Banking: Management and Strategies*, and *International Financial Management*. For much of the past decade, he was a part-time faculty member at the Stanford University Graduate School of Business and at IMEDE in Lausanne, Switzerland.

The Institutional Investor Series in Finance

The Institutional Investor Series in Finance has been developed specifically to bring you—the finance professional—the latest thinking and developments in investments and corporate finance. As new challenges arise in this fast-paced arena, you can count on this series to provide you with the information you need to gain the competitive edge.

Institutional Investor is the leading communications company serving the global financial community and publisher of the magazine of the same name. Institutional Investor has won 36 major awards for distinguished financial journalism—including the prestigious National Magazine Award for the best reporting of any magazine in the United States. More than 560,000 financial executives in 170 countries read Institutional Investor publications each month. Thousands more attend Institutional Investor's worldwide conferences and seminars each year.